ETHICAL THEORIES IN ISLAM

ISLAMIC PHILOSOPHY THEOLOGY AND SCIENCE

Texts and Studies

EDITED BY

H. DAIBER and D. PINGREE

VOLUME VIII

ETHICAL THEORIES IN ISLAM

BY

MAJID FAKHRY

SECOND EXPANDED EDITION

E.J. BRILL
LEIDEN · NEW YORK · KÖLN
1994

The paper in this book meets the guidelines for permanence and durability of the Committee on Production Guidelines for Book Longevity of the Council on Library Resources.

First edition: 1991
Second expanded edition: 1994

Library of Congress Cataloging-in-Publication Data

Fakhry, Majid.
Ethical theories in Islam / by Majid Fakhry
p. cm. — (Islamic philosophy and theology, ISSN 0169-8729 : v. 8)
Includes bibliographical references and index.
ISBN 9004093001 (cloth)
1. Islamic ethics. 2. Philosophy, Islamic. I. Title.
II. Series.
BJ1291.F28 1991
287'.5—dc20 90-42390
CIP

ISSN 0169-8729
ISBN 90 04 09300 1

PRINTED IN THE NETHERLANDS

TABLE OF CONTENTS

PREFACE TO THE SECOND EDITION

In attempting to give a survey of ethical theories in Islam, I concentrated, as explained in the Introduction, on the discursive aspect of Islamic ethical thought. I considered my task, therefore, to consist primarily in the philosophical analysis of ethical concepts and assumptions, without regard to sociological implications or practical applications. In fact, the whole notion of 'practical ethics', hinted at in some reviews of my book, appears to me to be self-contradictory. In ethical discourse, we aim to isolate those concepts or assumptions which have no genetic relation to practical conduct and which very often are in conflict with it. In this respect, I agree with such philosophers as Immanuel Kant, G.E. Moore and Ludwig Wittgenstein, that the realm of value which is the subject-matter of ethics, of what ought to be, is entireley distinct from the realm of fact, or what actually is.

I do not claim to have always been consistent in this undertaking, but I have at least tried to give a coherent account of theological, philosophical and religious theories of ethics in Islam. Accordingly, I believe that I was misunderstood by some of my reviewers or critics. Others, however, have expressed appreciation for my attempt to give a synoptic exposition, hitherto lacking, of principal Islamic theories of ethics. Whether such an exposition can be pushed beyond the fifteenth century, to which the last important writer on ethics, al-Dawwānī, belongs, is a legitimate question that has been raised by some reviewers; but the fact is that if we scour the literature beyond the fifteenth century, we would be hard put to produce a single ethical treatise which adds substantially to our knowledge of Islamic ethics, and this applies to modern ethical writings as well. I do not deny that it may have been fruitful to discuss the Ishrāqī philosophers' views, especially those of Mulla Ṣadra (d. 1641); but it is well known that apart from bringing Islamic Neo-Platonism and mysticism (Sufism) into some measure of harmony, the Ishrāqī philosophers have added very little to the substance of philosophical, and by implication, ethical speculation in Islam.

With respect to my relative neglect of Sufi ethics, I only wish to reiterate what I said in the Introduction, namely:

a. The discursive element in Sufi thought is, on the whole, negligible, and
b. I have given at least one outstanding example of the 'marriage' of Sufi and philosophical ethics—that of al-Ghazālī.

I leave it to other writers to probe and expound the ethical theories of other Sufis.

In light of the reviews and comments which I have received, I am satisfied that I have dealt reasonably adequately with most of the ethical writers covered in the First Edition, with the exception of Ibn Sīnā. I am, therefore, supplementing the discussion of his ethics with a translation of the chapter entited 'On Providence, Showing the Way in Which Evil Enters Into the Divine Decree', from Kitāb al-Najāt. This famous Neo-Platonist has dealt more thoroughly than any other Muslim philosopher with the problem of evil, which occupies a central position in the Neo-Platonic tradition generally, as well as the Koranic worldview proper. Muslim philosophers, and to a lesser extent Muslim theologians, did not accord that problem the imprtance it deserves in their ethical discussions. This addition and the bibliography addenda will, I hope, make this new edition of the present book even more useful to students of Islamic philosophy, ethical thought and the history of culture in general.

Washington, D.C. Majid Fakhry
April 1994

PREFACE TO THE FIRST EDITION

In attempting to expound the major aspects of ethical thought in Islam, two possible methods of presentation suggest themselves: a historical or horizontal method which simply follows the chronological line of development, and an analytical or schematic one, which deals with major ethical themes somewhat vertically. In the present work, I have preferred to adopt the second method, without altogether overlooking the first. The resultant *typology* of major ethical theories is presented within a clearly defined framework, in which the scriptural and the philosophical *types* are the two opposite poles. The first relies heavily on the text of scripture, i.e. the Koran and the Traditions of Muḥammad; the second exploits the syllogistic or discursive methods far more fully and is ultimately affiliated to Greek ethics. Between these two opposite poles move the other ethical formations: the theological, which was conditioned to some extent by philosophical categories and concepts, and the religious, which, although it does not neglect the discursive method altogether, is nevertheless far less dependent on philosophical ethics.

Accordingly, the present work has been divided into four parts dealing respectively with (a) scriptural morality, (b) theological ethics, (c) philosophical ethics, and (d) religious morality.

The question is sometimes asked whether there is such a thing as Islamic ethics. The well-meaning questioner is obviously puzzled by the legalism and ritualism of the religious and institutional life of Muslim individuals or groups, as well as the comparatively scant contribution of Muslim authors to ethical and political discussions during the classical and post-classical periods, especially when set against their massive contribution to literary, linguistic, philosophical, historical, theological and scientific subjects. The present work is a modest attempt to exhibit the ethical material in Islamic thought as objectively as possible. The task of criticism or appraisal has been kept as much in the background as possible.

Modern studies on Islamic ethics, especially in European languages, have been very limited in number or scope. One of the earliest synoptic accounts is given in de Boer's article on "Ethics and Morality (Muslim)," in: Hasting's *Encyclopaedia of Religion and Ethics*, V, 1908 – 1921 followed in 1953 by D.M. Donaldson's *Studies in Muslim Ethics*. This book contains a lot of material on Arabic and Persian ethics, but the material is presented in an ill-organized manner. More recently, G.F. Hourani has published a systematic study of ʿAbd al-Jabbār's ethics, entitled *Islamic*

Rationalism (1971), and a more recent discussion of *Ghazālī's Theory of Virtue* by Mohamed Ahmed Sherif appeared in 1974. Each is a valuable contribution to an important aspect of Islamic ethics.

Of considerable importance is the contribution of Mohammed Arkoun to philosophical ethics, especially that of Miskawayh. His French translation of *Tahdhīb al-Akhlāq* (1969) and his systematic account of that philosopher's ethics entitled *Contribution à l'étude de l'humanisme arabe au IVe/Xe siècle: Miskawayh, philosophe et historien* (1970) are particularly noteworthy. Equally important is Constantine K. Zurayk's English translation of the *Tahdhīb*, entitled *The Refinement of Character* (1968), which was preceded in 1966 by a critical edition of that important ethical treatise. Publications in periodicals, both in Arabic and European languages cannot be discussed here; many of them, however, will be referred to in our notes and given in the bibliography at the end of the book.

For the speculative contribution and the historical significance of many of the authors discussed in this book, such as al-Rāzī, al-Fārābī, Ibn Sīnā, Miskawayh and al-Ghazālī, the reader should refer to my *History of Islamic Philosophy* (1983), of which the present work is in some respects an attempt at filling the gaps in the field of ethics.

It is my pleasant duty to thank the many institutions and individuals who have contributed in one way or another to the writing of the present book. I am grateful to the Near Eastern Studies Department at Princeton University for hosting my research while on sabbatical from the American University of Beirut in 1974–75, and to the Philosophy and Classical Departments at Princeton for the opportunity to present publicly at two colloquia material embodied in this book. To Professors Gregory Vlastos and David Furley, who organized and chaired the two colloquia, I am particularly indebted for the stimulus generated by these and other private discussions. To Professor Muhsin Mahdi, I am grateful for the loan of his copy of the Arabic Ms. of the *Nicomachean Ethics* and the opportunity to present at Harvard some aspects of Islamic philosophical ethics. I am equally indebted to Professor Fauzi Najjar of Michigan State University at East Lansing, and to Professor George F. Hourani of New York University at Buffalo for arranging for me to visit these universities and speak on other aspects of philosophical ethics in Islam.

Beirut, Lebanon
November, 1985

Majid Fakhry

INTRODUCTION

An ethical theory is a reasoned account of the nature and grounds of right actions and decisions and the principles underlying the claim that they are morally commendable or reprehensible. Ethical enquiry has therefore always placed a special stress on the definition of ethical concepts and the justification or appraisal of moral judgements, as well as the discrimination between right and wrong actions or decisions. To be complete, an ethical system must deal adequately with these aspects of moral enquiry in an articulate and coherent way.

The Koran, around which the whole of Muslim moral, religious and social life revolves, contains no ethical *theories* in the strict sense, although it embodies the whole of the Islamic *ethos*. How to go about eliciting this ethos thus becomes of paramount importance to the student of Islamic ethics. There appear to be three promising directions in which the search can be fruitfully conducted, all of which lead back to the Koranic text itself: Koranic exegesis (*tafsīr*), jurisprudence (*fiqh*) and scholastic theology (*kalām*). The Ṣūfīs and the philosophers, who frequently invoked the authority of the Koran in support of their theoretical and ethical claims cannot be said to have developed a thoroughly Islamic view of the universe and of man, owing to the extraneous influences, Indian, Greek, Christian and other, which conditioned their thought. Their ethical theories therefore were marked by a high degree of complexity, which set them apart from the general class of theories rooted in the Koran and the Traditions. Those theories may be designated as 'scriptural' or 'theological', depending on the extent to which they relied on the text of Scripture or the degree to which this text was either accepted at face value or interpreted dialectically.

A *typology* of Islamic ethics of the kind that will be attempted in this study must clearly exhibit these divergences. We start from the premise that the Koran and the Traditions embody the original core of the Islamic ethical spirit, but, as already mentioned, no ethical theories in the strict sense. What sense are we to make of this original core, which each conflicting school of thought has drawn upon or appropriated? Can the twentieth-century student of Islam, or the Muslim modernist for that matter, arrogate to himself the right to advance his own interpretation as the only valid one, or must be always dutifully accept the traditional interpretation(s) as the only authoritative one(s)? Is there in the end a single and privileged interpretation of the revealed text of scripture?

These are indeed very weighty questions which meet the student of Islam at every juncture. The fact of doctrinal conflict, first among the jurisconsults (*fuqahā*ʾ) during the earliest period, and subsequently among the theologians (*mutakallimūn*) of the eighth century, clearly disproves the rival claims of infallibility, or even doctrinal pre-eminence. These rival claims are ultimately rooted in rival interpretations, which are definitely distinguishable from the original uninterpreted text of Scripture; whatever one's estimate of these interpretations, this text must to some extent be allowed to stand on its own, to speak for itself. Otherwise, the possibility of ever fresh and significant interpretations will be precluded, which must seriously endanger if not the validity of this text, then at least its relevance to every generation of searching Muslims who may wish to pattern their lives, as twentieth-century modernists and fundamentalists alike have attempted to do, on the Koranic model.

The commentators and jurists, who obviously cannot claim a monopoly of Truth, can nevertheless be said to have given the closest and most faithful interpretation of the Koranic text, grounded in traditional, grammatical, literary and linguistic usage. Such, however, is not the case of other groups of ethical and philosophical writers. The theologians, who also take their starting point from this text, have nevertheless relied in varying degrees on extra-textual evidence in their attempt to elicit the meaning of this text: Greek logic, Christian theology and the natural light of unaided reason. The philosophers, whether Neo-Platonists, like al-Fārābī (d. 950), Aristotelians, like Ibn Rushd (d. 1198), or Platonists, like al-Rāzī (d. ca. 925), fall into a different category altogether. Although they do not ignore or deliberately disavow the authority of the Koran, their primary allegiance is to the canons of philosophical evidence, as bequeathed by Greek philosophy. Their ethical discussions are sometimes *embellished* by Koranic quotations, in the manner of other pious Muslim authors, but it is primarily the dictates of syllogistic reasoning that determine the conclusions they arrive at. If the theologians are said to exploit the syllogistic process in order to elicit or defend their sense of the significance of the sacred text, the philosophers might be said to be guided primarily by this process and to recognize at best its concurrence with that text. To put it differently, for the theologians and even more so for the jurists, the sacred text is the ultimate arbiter of Truth; for the philosophers it is reason.

I

In expounding what we will term 'scriptural morality', we will attempt to examine analytically the ethical key concepts embedded in those two primary sources of Islamic religious truth, the Koran and Traditions, confining ourselves as far as possible to the *prima facie* connotation of the terms used by the writer(s) of scripture. This examination will be supported in some cases by references to some of the major commentators of the Koran, such as al-Ṭabarī (d. 923), al-Bayḍāwī (d. ca. 1291) and others. References to theological or philosophical writers will be kept to a minimum, to avoid partisanship. Most of those writers, as we have already mentioned, claim explicitly or implicitly a firm basis for their interpretations or theories in the text of scripture, the universal fountainhead of Truth.[1]

A major difficulty confronting us in this attempt is determining the type and number of ethical concepts or questions pertinent to this study. Before the ninth and tenth centuries, when systematic ethical discussion had become somewhat developed, we could only speak of pre-ethical speculation on questions, subsequently identified as the subject-matter of ethics. However, neither the commentators nor the jurists were entirely innocent of ethical culture, and their interpretations of the Koran and the Traditions inevitably reflected that culture in however elementary or primitive a manner. Accordingly, it is not altogether impossible to isolate their answers to those questions which were identified by their contemporaries or successors, philosophers and theologians alike, with the substance of ethical enquiry. These questions included the problem of free will (*qadar*) and its relation to divine omnipotence (*qudrah*); the nature of right (*birr*) and wrong; the justice of God's ways in this world (*ᶜadl*) and the reality of His judgement in the next.[2]

The discussion of theological theories of ethics is a much more complex problem. Here we must distinguish between two major currents: (a) a rationalist current initiated by the Qadarī and Muᶜtazilite theologians of the eighth and ninth centuries, and (b) a semi-rationalist and voluntarist one initiated by the ex-Muᶜtazilite Abu'l-Ḥasan al-Ashᶜarī (d. 935), who tended to defer more to the authority of scripture than to the canons of rational proof. It was this current which was ultimately identified with orthodoxy. Principal representatives of the Muᶜtazilite school are Abu'l-Hudhayl (d. 849), Bishr ibn al-Muᶜtamir (d. 825), Muᶜammar

---

[1] Toshihiko Izutsu has attempted a 'semantic' analysis of key religious and ethical terms in the Koran, but the scope of his analysis is somewhat broader than ours. See his *Ethico-Religious Concepts in the Qurʾan*, Montreal, 1966.

[2] Despite its highly controversial nature, the question of the subject-matter of ethics has received a positive answer from the leading British philosopher, G.E. Moore (1873–1959). He reduces all ethical questions to three: 1. What is *meant* by good? 2. What things are good in themselves? 3. What ought we to do to bring about the realization of this good? See *Principia Ethica*, Cambridge, 1922, 37f. H. Sidgwick, W.D. Ross and other British ethical writers tend to agree with this classification. From the standpoint of Islamic ethics, perhaps the chief omission is God's role in determining what is good and realizing it in the world. However, many other questions figure prominently in Islamic ethical discussions.

ibn ᶜAbbād (first half of ninth century), al-Naẓẓām (d. 845) and the encyclopaedic author of the eleventh century, ᶜAbd al-Jabbār (d. 1025), who has given the fullest and most systematic account of Muᶜtazilite ethics to have come down to us. Principal representatives of the Ashᶜarite school are al-Bāqillānī (d. 1013), al-Baghdādī (d. 1037), al-Juwaynī (d. 1064) and al-Shahrastānī (d. 1153). Al-Ghazālī (d. 1111) and Fakhr al-Dīn al-Rāzī (d. 1209) also belong to this school.

A third current is the anti-rationalist current championed in the eleventh century by the Ẓāhirī author Ibn Ḥazm (d. 1064) and in the thirteenth by Ibn Taymiyah (d. 1328). These authors repudiated the validity of dialectical and theological reasoning and regarded scripture, literally interpreted, as the ultimate source of religious Truth. Their contribution to ethical theory was on that account trivial, but some of them, like the above-mentioned Ibn Ḥazm, did not overlook ethics altogether.

Philosophical theories of ethics reflect, as one would expect, the influence of the diverse Greek philosophical schools to which they were drawn. The earliest moral writings, attributed to al-Kindī (d. ca. 866) and al-Rāzī (d. 925) reflect the Socratic-Platonic influence as conditioned by later Cynic and Stoic thought. In the writings of later philosophers, like al-Fārābī (d. 950), Ibn Sīnā (d. 1037), Yaḥyā ibn ᶜĀdī (d. 974) and the Brethren of Purity (tenth century), the Platonic influence receives further confirmation and its political dimension, ignored heretofore, begins to come to the fore. In the work of the principal writer on ethics in Islam, Miskawayh (d. 1030), Platonism serves as the groundwork of an elaborate ethical system in which Aristotelian, Neo-Platonic and Stoic strands are skillfully woven together, probably under the influence of Porphyry's lost commentary on Aristotle's *Nicomachean Ethics*, known exclusively from Arabic sources.[3] But here too the political dimension is lacking. It reemerges fully in the ethical writings of his Persian successor and interpretor, Naṣīr al-Dīn al-Ṭūsī (d. 1274), who recognized, far better than his illustrious predecessor, the organic unity of ethics and politics.

The influence of the *Nicomachean Ethics*, translated either by Isḥāq ibn Ḥunayn (d. 911) or his father Ḥunayn (d. 873), was decisive.[4] Important commentaries on it by al-Fārābī, Ibn Rushd and Prophyry circulated in

---

[3] Ibn al-Nadīm, *al-Fihrist*, Cairo, n.d., 366. Cf. R. Walzer, "Porphyry and the Arabic Tradition," in: H. Dörrie, *Porphyre: 8 exposes suivis de discussions*, (Entretiens sur l'antiguité classique), xii, Vandoeuvres-Genève, 1966, 294f.

[4] On the recently discovered Ms. of the *Nicomachean Ethics* in Arabic in Qarawīyīn Library in Fez. see A.J. Arberry, "The Nicomachean Ethics in Arabic," in: *Bulletin of the School of Oriental and African Studies*, XVII (1955), 1–9 and D.M. Dunlop, "The Nicomachean Ethics in Arabic, Books I–VI," in: *Oriens*, XV (1962), 18–34. Cf. Arabic edition by ᶜA.R. Badawī, Kuwait, 1979.

learned circles and influenced or conditioned the thought of philosophers of the most diverse persuasion: Neo-Platonists, like al-Fārābī and Miskawayh, Aristotelians, like Ibn Rushd, and even litterateurs like Abu'l Ḥasan al-ᶜĀmirī (d. 992) and al-Mubashshir ibn Fātik (d. 1048).

We have already referred to the Socratic-Platonic influence on the earliest writers on morality. The character of this influence was so eclectical that it emerges as a blend of Socratic, Cynic and Stoic morality. Due to their somewhat restricted knowledge of Greek and Roman Stoicism, Muslim ethical writers reflect the influence of the Stoa in a rather undefined manner. Arabic sources refer to the "People of the Stoa" (*ahl al-usṭuwānah*) as well as the Porch (*al-riwāqiyūn*), but the name of Zeno of Citium is often confused with that of the Eleatic; Chrysippus is often quoted in collections of aphorisms, such as al-Mubashshir ibn Fātik's *Mukhtār al-Ḥikam* and al-ᶜĀmirī's *K. al-Saᶜādah wa'l-Isᶜād*. However, the name of Epictetus was unknown to them, as far as I am aware, and Roman Stoic literature never found its way into Arabic. This deficiency is often made up in peculiar ways: Diogenes the Cynic, often confused with Socrates, as we mentioned earlier, is represented as a model of asceticism, as are Empedocles and Pythagoras, who emerge as outstanding 'Stoic' moralists and pious religious figures.[5]

The influence of Persian and Indian literature is exhibited in the numerous collections of moral aphorisms, which greatly enriched Arabic literature and added an exotic dimension to philosophical, political and mystical thought. To the most important ethical writer in Islam, Miskawayh, we owe a collection which embodies extensive quotations from such real or legendary Persian sages as Buzurgmihr, Anūshirwān, Hūshang and others, and al-Bīrūnī (d. 1048), the great mathematician and polymath, translated the *Patanjali* and gave in his *India* a comprehensive account of Indian religious and ethical thought in which he attempts to underscore the points of contact between Indian and Greek thought.

A more diffuse influence of Indian ethical thought on Arabic literature was exerted by the Arabic version of the Fables of Bidpai, or *Kalīlah wa-Dimnah*, allegedly translated from Pahlavi by Ibn al-Muqaffaᶜ (d. 759), a major figure in the history of Arabic literature and author of a number of books on morals (*adab*) which have enjoyed a well-deserved reputation, both on account of the nobility of their themes and the elegance of their style. On the other hand, Hindu mysticism had a decisive influence on the history of Muslim asceticism and Ṣūfism, and this influence was certainly not free of moral implications.

---

[5] See M. Fakhry, "Qudamāʾ Falāsifat al-Yūnān ᶜinda'l-ᶜArab," in: *al-Abḥāth*, X (1957), 391f.

Insofar as this 'aphoristic' literature was widely read—not only by the philosophers, but also by the learned public, who saw in it a store of moral and literary edification—it may be said to have had a much broader impact than the more specialized ethical treatises. It cannot be said, however, to belong to the category of 'ethical' literature in the strict sense, and reference to it in this study will be brief and incidental. It did nevertheless enrich Arabic ethics by providing the ethical philosophers with a certain amount of raw material for their discussions.

The types of ethical theories that emerge from this survey may now be given under four principal headings:

a. Scriptural morality, as exhibited in the moral and quasi-moral pronouncements of the Koran and the Traditions in partial abstraction from their elaboration and analysis by the philosophers and the theologians in the light of the discursive methods and categories developed in the eighth and ninth centuries.

b. Theological theories, with their ultimate grounding in the Koran and the Traditions, and a heavy reliance on these categories and methods. Their two major protagonists are the Muᶜtazilah, who formulated between the eighth and tenth centuries the rationalistic Islamic ethical system, with basic deontological presuppositions, and the Ashᶜarites, who stood for a rigorous 'voluntarist' system of morality, which did not reject the discursive methods of the philosophers altogether, but remained thoroughly committed to the Koranic concept of an omnipotent Deity, Who is the sole Creator and Lawgiver, as well as the ultimate source of Being and Goodness in the world.

c. Philosophical theories, stemming ultimately from the ethical writings of Plato and Aristotle, as they had been interpreted in late antiquity by Neo-Platonic authors. Porphyry of Tyre (d. ca. 304), who is known from the Arabic sources to have written a twelve-book commentary on Aristotle's *Nicomachean Ethics*, is the major link in this process, and the available evidence strongly suggests that it was his commentary which served as the basis of Miskawayh's attempt to fuse Platonic and Aristotelian ethical doctrines, and present them in a Neo-Platonic, and to some extent mystical, guise.[6] Galen (d. ca. 200), whose *Peri Ethon* has survived only in an Arabic version, provided the other major link in the general endeavor to fuse Stoic, Platonic, Pythagorean and Aristotelian doctrines, a basic feature of the ethical thought of Miskawayh and his successors as well.

---

[6] See R. Walzer, "Porphyry and the Arabic Tradition," 294f. Cf. H. Daiber, "Ein bisher unbekannter pseudoplatonischer Text über die Tugenden der Seele in arabischer Überlieferung, in: *Der Islam* 47 (1971), 25–42.

Two of those successors are particularly noteworthy: Naṣīr al-Dīn al-Ṭūsī (d. 1274) and Jalāl al-Dīn al-Dawwānī (d. 1501). Neither of them has added much to the substance of Miskawayh's ethics, their avowed model, but both have greatly expanded the scope of their study by incorporating into it extensive sections on the domestic science (*ᶜilm-i tadbīr-i manāzil*) and politics. Al-Ṭūsī has, in addition, expounded the psychological substructure of the ethics by incorporating into it important elements from Avicenna's psychology, whereas al-Dawwānī has underscored the Shīᶜite notion of the pre-eminence of man and his role as God's vicegerent (*khalīfah*) on earth.

A comparatively early treatise which belongs to the general class of philosophical ethics may be mentioned here. This is the *Book of Happiness and Making Happy* (*Kitāb al-Saᶜādah wa'l-Isᶜād*) written by an erudite author of the tenth century, Abu'l-Ḥasan al-ᶜĀmirī (d. 992), who draws extensively on Plato, Aristotle, Galen and Persian 'sages' in a rhapsodic manner.[7] Although this book contains a vast amount of material, it cannot be regarded as an ethical treatise in the strict sense. Miskawayh was undoubtedly acquainted with its author and has profited from it in his own writings, both in the *Orders of Happiness* and the *Essence of Justice*, but the influence of al-ᶜĀmirī on his successors is neither extensive nor explicit. His name does not occur in Miskawayh's systematic treatises, as far as can be ascertained,[8] but is quoted extensively in *Jāwīdān Khirad*, under the rubric 'Excerpts and Aphorisms of al-ᶜĀmirī'.[9]

d. RELIGIOUS THEORIES grounded ultimately in the Koranic conception of man and his position in the universe. These theories differ somewhat from those types of morality which we have termed as scriptural in that their protagonists had received the impact of Greek philosophy and Islamic theology and were accordingly anxious to come to terms with the dialectical current unleashed in the eighth century as a result of confrontation and contact with Greek philosophy and Christian theology at Damascus, Baghdad and other centers of learning in the Near East.

The major ingredients of religious ethics are the Koranic world-view, theological concepts, philosophical categories, and in some cases Ṣūfism.

---

[7] See A.A. Ghorab, "The Greek Commentators on Aristotle quoted in al-ᶜĀmirī's *As-Saᶜāda wa'l-Isᶜād*," in: *Islamic Philosophy and the Classical Tradition*, eds. S.M. Stern, A. Hourani and V. Brown, Columbia, South Carolina, 1973, 77–88.

[8] In *al-Ḥawāmil wa'l-Shawāmil*, ed. A. Amin, Cairo, 1951, 82, Miskawayh refers to a tract of Galen on justice, which appears to be excerpted by al-ᶜĀmirī. See *Al-Saᶜādah wa'l-Isᶜād*, ed. M. Minovi, Wiesbaden, 1957–58, 233–42. Cf. A.J. Arberry, "Some Plato in an Arabic Epitome," in: *Islamic Quaterly* II (1955), 86–99.

[9] See *Jāwīdān Khirad*, ed. ᶜA.R. Badawī, Cairo, 1952, 347f. These excerpts should be compared with parts of his recently published *Al-Amad ᶜala'l-Abad*, ed. E.K. Rowson, Beirut, 1979.

Accordingly, this system of ethics emerges as the most complex, as well as the most characteristically Islamic. Among its chief exponents, we will mention al-Ḥasan al-Baṣrī (d. 728), the great divine and ascetic of the eighth century; al-Māwardī (d. 1058), the Shāfiᶜī jurist and theologian, who wrote a major ethical treatise entitled *Right Conduct (adab) in Matters Worldly and Religious*, which will be discussed in due course; and al-Rāghib al-Iṣfahānī (d. 1108), author of a major ethical treatise, *Kitāb al-Dharīᶜah ilā Makārim al-Sharīᶜah*, which influenced al-Ghazālī and other religious authors. The former author came into contact with contemporary theologians, including the Muᶜtazilah, with whom he was accused of concurring. Al-Ghazālī (d. 1111), whose system of ethics is a blend of philosophical, theological and Ṣūfī morality, is undoubtedly the most representative example of the type of ethics we have termed religious; both his *Criterion of Action (Mīzān al-ᶜAmal)*, and his *Revival of the Religious Sciences* (*Iḥyāʾ ᶜUlūm al-Dīn*) are major sources of ethical and religious thought in Islam. Finally, Fakhr al-Dīn al-Rāzī (d. 1209), whose thought is thoroughly impregnated with Avicennian and al-Ghazālian elements, may be regarded as an important representative in the late classical period of ethical and philosophico-theological writing. He is concerned more than any of his predecessors with the problem of reconciling Islamic philosophy, in its Avicennian form, with theology and the religious tradition in general. His *Kitāb al-Nafs wa'l-Rūḥ* reflects the influence of Avicenna and al-Ghazālī in the fields of metaphysics and ethics, and deserves, on that account, to be discussed in this ethical study.

Although a case may be made for Ṣūfī ethics, I have not dealt with it in this study except insofar as it entered into or conditioned religious morality. In defending this course, it will be enough to mention that despite its moral significance, the Ṣūfī pathos is not amenable to systematic treatment, and except for al-Ghazālī, not much serious work has been done by scholars to draw out the ethical implications of Ṣūfism in a methodical way. Appendix C at the end of the book consists of an important selection from one of al-Ghazālī's works, *Mīzān al-ᶜAmal*, which sets out in a very clear way the climactic point in the development of Ṣūfī ethics. Moreover, the discussion of this eminent theologian's ethical theory should exhibit the positive manner in which he successfully integrated Ṣūfism into his ethical system. Appendices A and B, on the other hand, present the rival 'philosophical' ideal as expounded by Aristotle and Avicenna. They formed the two parts of an article which was first published by the author in the *Journal of the History of Philosophy*, 14 (1975), 137–145, and are reprinted at the end of the book with minor changes.

PART ONE

SCRIPTURAL MORALITY

CHAPTER ONE

THE KORANIC ETHOS

I. Text and Interpretation

Ethical thought as such presupposes an advanced stage of intellectual systematism and sophistication. Prior to the advent of theology (*kalām*) and philosophy in the eighth and ninth centuries, such an activity was virtually foreclosed. The early commentators of the Koran, the Traditionists and jurists naturally engaged in analysis and interpretation involving a large measure of intellectual activity in the broad sense, but such an activity was closely linked to the original sources of religious Truth, i.e. the Koran and the Traditions, and lacked for that reason the character of genuine dialectical or rational activity, with its double imperative of coherence and comprehensiveness. What emerged in the process was at best a series of moral insights or reflections, not an ethical theory in the strict sense.

To the extent the attempt was made by the commentators, Traditionists and jurists to expound or justify the moral *ethos* of the Koran and the Traditions, their incursions into the ethical field may be said to constitute the substance of what we have termed 'scriptural morality'. It is to be stressed that we clearly distinguish between two levels or strata in the development of Islamic ethics: (a) the ethos of the Koran and the Traditions, in their original uninterpreted form, so to speak, and (b) the ethical theories developed by the three groups of writers mentioned above. We believe this distinction between the two levels to be of vital importance, since it was the same ethos which conditioned or shaped the most conflicting ethical and theoretical interpretations by subsequent rival groups of philosophers and theologians.

The Koranic ethos is naturally a very vague and elusive concept. The most we can do to gain some insight into this ethos is to highlight and inventorize Koranic passages bearing on the three fundamental problems referred to in the introduction, namely, (a) the nature of right and wrong, (b) divine justice and power, and (c) moral freedom and responsibility. These problems, as already mentioned, formed in due course the stuff of ethical discussion in juridical, theological and philosophical circles alike, although they did not in the nature of the case exclude other subsidiary questions.

II. Goodness (*khayr*) and Righteousness (*birr*)

With regard to the first problem, we are faced from the start with intricate linguistic difficulties. The Koran uses a whole cluster of terms to denote the concept of moral or religious goodness: *al-khayr* (goodness), *al-birr* (righteousness), *al-qisṭ* and *al-iqsāṭ* (equity), *al-ᶜadl* (justice), *al-ḥaqq* (truth and right), *al-maᶜrūf* (known and approved), and finally *al-taqwā* (piety). Pious actions are normally referred to as *ṣāliḥāt*, whereas impious or sinful actions are termed *sayyiᵓāt*. The abstract moral or religious quality of the latter type of actions is generally designated as *ithm* or *wizr*, i.e. sin or wickedness, meaning originally 'a load'.

The term *maᶜrūf*, which is the passive participle of the verb to know, may best be translated as 'approved', whereas its antithesis *munkar* may be translated as 'disapproved' or 'reprehensible'. The conventional or 'common moral' implications of these two terms follow from the fact that the commonest Arabic term to denote convention is a derivative from the verb *ᶜarafa* (to know) and that they were already used in pre-Islamic poetry to express moral approval and disapproval.[1] In Koran 2:263, the term is used in conjunction with speech (*qawl*) to denote kind or approved, but in at least thirty other verses the term is contrasted with *munkar* to denote morally approved action, as in the key passages 3:104, 114 and 115, where the term occurs in the same context as *khayr*, or good. Verse 3:104 reads as follows: "Let there be among you a nation calling to goodness (*khayr*), bidding the approved (*maᶜrūf*) and forbidding the disapproved (*munkar*); these are the prosperous."[2] In 3:114, the 'People of the Book' are commended as "those who believe in God and in the Last Day" and "command what is approved, prohibit what is disapproved and speed on the good works (*khayrāt*)", and are then described as the righteous (*ṣāliḥūn*). In the following verse, a general maxim is formulated, that "whatever good is done will not be disallowed, and God knows well the pious."

The term *khayr*, which is more general and more abstract, occurs no fewer than 190 times in the Koran. In most cases, however, it is used in the morally neutral, comparative form. When it occurs in the substantive, it is often conjoined to the verb denoting 'to call to' (*yadᶜū ilā*) or 'perform' (*yafᶜal*). Hence in the previously quoted verse, 3:104, and in 41: 49, calling to the good occurs; whereas in 3:115 and 22:77, performing

---

[1] See Abū Tammām, *Kitāb al-Ḥamāsah*, III, Cairo, 1331 A.H., 24. Cf. T. Izutzu, *Ethico-Religious Concepts in the Qurᵓan*, 213f.

[2] In Palmer and Rodwell, the verb is given in the subjunctive. Arberry uses the terms 'honour' and 'dishonour' to translate the two Arabic terms. I have given as literal a translation as possible. Unless otherwise indicated, the translation of Koranic passages is mine.

the good is spoken of, and in 3:114 speeding on the good works (*khayrāt*). Verse 22:77 is particularly noteworthy, for it links doing the good to performing the ritual acts of prayer and worship. It reads as follows: "O believers, bow down and prostrate yourselves and worship your Lord, and do good that you may prosper."

Probably the term that expresses the moral and religious spirit of the Koran better than any other is *al-birr*, which I will translate as righteousness. Although it does not occur as frequently as the two above mentioned terms, it occurs nevertheless in a number of verses in which the nearest attempt is made in the Koran to formulate an Islamic creed. Thus in verse 2:177, the purely ritual aspect of righteousness, or piety, is repudiated and genuine faith and righteousness are asserted in the following terms, as in Arberry's translation: "It is not piety (*birr*), that you turn your faces to the East and to the West. True piety is this: to believe in God and the Last Day, the angels, the Book, and the Prophets, to give of one's substance, however cherished, to kinsmen and orphans, the needy, the traveller, beggars, and to ransom the slave, to perform the prayer, to pay the alms. And they who fulfill their covenant when they have engaged in a covenant, and endure with fortitude misfortune, hardship and peril; these are they who are true in their faith, these are the truly godfearing."

Although the terms denoting righteousness often occur in somewhat abstract contexts, the term denoting good works (*ṣāliḥāt*) occurs almost invariably in what may be described as eschatological contexts: the performance of these works is linked to their just reward in the world to come. A good example of this correlation of good works to their just reward is 98:7–8, which reads as follows in Arberry's translation: "But those who believe, and do righteous deeds, those are the best of creatures; their recompense is with their Lord—Gardens of Eden, underneath which rivers flow, therein dwelling for ever and ever. God is well-pleased with them, and they are well-pleased with Him; that is for him who fears his Lord."[3]

The reference to God's good pleasure (*riḍā*) in the last part of this verse brings out another important aspect of Koranic morality that was at the basis of subsequent ethical controversies, viz. the sanction of goodness is not exclusively the consequential one of punishment and reward in the hereafter, it is also God's good pleasure and love. Thus in numerous verses, such as 2:195; 3:134,148; 5:13,42,93; 49:9; 60:8, it is asserted in emphatic terms that God loves the doers of charity (*muḥsinūn*) and the doers of just actions (*muqsiṭūn*). In other passages, God is said to love the

[3] Other verses in which this correlation is asserted are 2:277; 4:122,173; 5:19; 10:4,9; 16:97; 19:76; 29:7,9,58; 48:29, etc.

penitent and the purified (2:222), the pious (*muttaqūn*) (3:76), the patient (3:146), and those who trust (3:159). The double sanction of punishment and reward on the one hand, and that of divine love or good pleasure on the other, raises the question of internal coherence. A teleological morality in which the emphasis is placed on punishment and reward is not necessarily compatible with one in which God's love or good pleasure is the ultimate test of righteousness. Of the different ethical schools that flourished in the eighth and ninth centuries, it was the Ṣūfīs, like the great Rabīᶜah (d. 801), who stressed the love of God; the jurists and the theologians, especially the Muᶜtazilah, stressed punishment and reward as inevitable logical consequences of God's irrevocable 'threats and promises' in the Koran.[4] The important point to note at this stage is that we have in the Koran an explicit textual basis for the two types of morality, around which serious controversy raged in the generations to come.

III. Divine Justice

The Koran is categorical on the second major issue destined to set the theologians at loggerheads with each other for centuries, the question of divine justice. As the verses 3:182; 8:51; 22:10 and 41:46 have put it, God is not an "unjust dealer (*ẓallām*) with His servants", He enjoins justice (7:29; 16:90), disapproves of the unjust (3:57,140; 42:40) and loves the equitable (*muqsiṭūn*) and pious, as we have already seen. A recurrent theme in this connection is the Koranic assertion that God "will not guide the unjust people" (28:50; 46:10; 61:7; 62:5). In most of these verses, this assertion is conjoined to the perpetration by the unjust of some reprehensible act or other, so that the inference is inescapable that God's refusal to guide the unjust is not the consequence, but rather the cause or ground of this perpetration. The ethical implications of this proposition can only be alluded to here, but there is no question that the rationalist theologians and philosophers were exercised by the logical bearing of divine guidance on divine justice.[5]

A noteworthy linguistic point is that the Koran affirms God's justice in almost exclusively negative terms. That God may be termed just (*ᶜādil*) on the basis of Koranic evidence, and that on that basis the term may be included, as it actually is, in the list of 99 'beautiful names' of God is not in question; it is, however, not without significance that the term *ᶜādil* in the adjectival form does not occur in the Koran at all and is never con-

---

[4] See M. Fakhry, *A History of Islamic Philosophy*, New York/London, 1983, 55f.
[5] See *infra*, 42.

joined, even in other forms, with the divine name. The most explicit predication of justice to God occurs in verse 16:90, which reads in Rodwell's translation as follows: "Verily God enjoins justice and the doing of good and gifts to kinsmen; and He forbids wickedness and wrong and oppression. He warneth you haply ye may be mindful." In almost all the other passages in which the term *ᶜadl*, *ᶜidl* and their derivatives occur, the term is used either in the sense of associating an equal (*ᶜidl*) with God, as in 6:1,150; 27:61, or that of giving in ransom or compensation, as in 2:48,123; 6:70 or in the ordinary sense of performing human acts of justice, as in 2:282; 4:58; 7:159,181; 16:76; 42:15; 49:9; 65:2. It is, however, obvious that none of those connotations of the term *ᶜadl* or its quasi-homonym *ᶜidl* is relevant to the problem of predicating justice to God.

In one verse, 6:115, the term *ᶜadl* is conjoined to the term *ṣidq* (truthfulness) in a context in which God (or His words) is clearly the subject. This verse reads in Arberry's translation: "Perfect are the words of thy Lord in truthfulness and justice; no man can change His words." This verse may be taken as added textual confirmation of the indirect predicability of justice to God, but such verses remain nevertheless very scant. One may wonder in the circumstances whether one should not seek other synonyms of justice in the Koran, such as *ḥaqq* (truth), *qisṭ* and *iqsaṭ* (equity), etc. The first term, which occurs very frequently in the Koran, is not free from ambiguity. There are three connotations of this term that are pertinent. In the first of these, the term denotes truth, but not in the abstract or philosophical sense; instead it denotes truth in the concrete, religious sense as the revelation to Muḥammad and the prophets who preceded him, from Abraham downward. Such, for instance, is the connotation of this term in verses 2:26,91,109; 21:55; 34:6; 39:2, etc. Secondly, the term appears in some passages to refer more specifically to the Koran itself, as the embodiment of the definitive and consummate revelation of the divine word, as in verses 13:1; 32:3; 60:1; 69:51. Thirdly, in other passages, the term is identified with God Himself, who "indeed is the Truth," as verses 22:6,62; 24:25; 31:30 put it.

Another generic connotation, which is also common in the Koran, is the one in which God is said to create the world *bi'l-ḥaqq*, an expression which we believe can be neutrally translated as 'in justice' or 'in truth', and which is not therefore free from moral undertones. The following passages might be cited as examples: 14:19; 16:3; 30:8; 39:5; 45:22; 46:3; 64:3, but the actual connotation of this expression is very elusive and has brought the commentators into serious difficulties.[6]

---

[6] See al-Ṭabarī, *Jāmiᶜ al-Bayān*, 2nd edition, Cairo, 1373/1954, 30 vols., *ad. loc.*

Al-Bayḍāwī, for instance, interprets the expression *bi'l-ḥaqq* to mean "in wisdom and in the manner it (i.e. the world) should have been created"[7] or "according to that measure, form, position or quality He determined and specified through His wisdom"[8] or finally "in accordance with the right, necessitating justice."[9] Sometimes, however, he interprets it in unquestionably moral terms, as in his comments on verse 46:3, where he writes: "We have not created the heavens and the earth and what lies between them, except in truth; that is except as a creation clothed in truth, which is what wisdom and justice stipulate, demonstrating the existence of the wise Creator and the truth of the resurrection."

Al-Ṭabarī (d. 923), a more rationalist commentator on Koranic texts and an outstanding historian who inclined to Muᶜtazilism, interprets the expression *bi'l-ḥaqq* to mean "single-handedly, without any assistance or help",[10] an interpretation which appears to be suggested by the context in which this expression occurs. His general tendency, however, appears to be to regard the terms *ḥaqq* and *ᶜadl* as synonymous and interchangeable, so that the moral implications of the creative act of God are for him unmistakable. Thus in his comments on verse 16:3, he writes: "Your Lord, o people, has created the heavens and the earth in justice, which is the truth. He created them single-handedly, without association with any partner assisting Him in their creation or production."[11] Commenting on verse 30:8, he reaffirms the justice of the Creator who will never deal unjustly with His creation, "since He is that justice which will never err" and "He has not created the heavens and the earth and what lies in between, except in justice (*ᶜadl*) and in order to establish the right (*ḥaqq*)."[12] Commenting on verse 45:22, he re-asserts the correlation of right or truth and justice, denouncing the view of those who regard the sinners and the disobedient as equally justified in the sight of God as the righteous and obedient. The same note is sounded in his comments on verses 46:3 and 64:3, where the justice of God is stressed in the same emphatic terms that the Muᶜtazilite theologians had made the hallmark of their theodicy, as we shall see in due course.[13]

The Shīᶜite commentator al-Ṭabarsī (d. 1157) interprets *bi'l-ḥaqq* to mean "by uttering the truth" or "for the right reason and in the right order, which is religion and worship."[14] He does state, however, in

---

[7] See *Anwār al-Tanzīl*, Leipzig, 1846, I, ad 14:18. Cf. *ibid.*, ad 64:3.
[8] *Ibid.*, I, ad 16:3.
[9] *Ibid.*, II, ad 45:22.
[10] See *Jāmiᶜ al-Bayān*, ad 14:19.
[11] *Ibid.*, ad 16:3.
[12] *Ibid.*, ad 30:8.
[13] See *infra*, 40f.
[14] See *Majmaᶜ al-Bayān*, Beirut, 1961, ad 14:22.

commenting on the word 'creation' that it consists in "making in accordance with order and harmony" or "in accordance with the dictates of wisdom." In commenting on 16:3, he adds to the above interpretation that *bi'l-ḥaqq* denotes that God created the heavens and the earth, "so that through them He will be known deductively, and by reflecting upon them the knowledge of His perfect power and wisdom will be achieved."[15] A further meaning is elicited in his commentary on 45:22, where *bi'l-ḥaqq* is interpreted to mean "for the welfare of His creation, by making them accountable for their actions and liable to ample reward." This interpretation, which is in full agreement with Muᶜtazilite theodicy, as will appear in due course, is reaffirmed in his commentary on 46:3, but the moral implications of the divine creative act are not explicitly spelt out. However, in his commentary on 64:3, *bi'l-ḥaqq* is expressly identified with *bi'l-ᶜadl*, which he explains as "in justice and perfect craftsmanship and right determination."[16] In fact, the persistent theme in his interpretation of 'in truth' is the twofold connotation, referred in one case to the tenth-century grammarian al-Zajjāj, namely (a) the demonstration of the existence of the Creator, and (b) the assertion of the creature's liability to punishment and reward.[17]

The term *qisṭ* and its derivatives occur frequently in the Koran to denote justice, either as a property of human actions approved by God, or as the transcendental norm of God's actions and decisions. Thus in 7:29, the prophet is commanded to inform mankind simply that "God commands equity" (*qisṭ*), which al-Bayḍāwī interprets as the mean between excess and defect.[18] Elsewhere (5:42), equity is conjoined to judgement as an imperative of God, "Who loves the just." In 10:4, God assures mankind that His 'promise' to initially create them and recreate the world after it is destroyed is true, and that His purpose therein is to "reward those who believe and have performed right actions, justly (*bi'l-qisṭ*)," an assertion which is graphically linked in 21:47 to the 'just scales' set up by God, on the Day of Judgement. In one verse (3:18), God's justice (*al-qisṭ*) is made an object of God's own vindication on the one hand, and that of the angels and men of learning on the other, so that its validity can never be questioned.

IV. Human Responsibility

Many of the Koranic passages reviewed in the two previous sections logically presuppose the phenomenon of human responsibility. What is

---

15 See *Majmaᶜ al-Bayān*, ad 14:19.
16 *Ibid.*, ad 16:3.
17 See comments ad 30:8.
18 See *Anwār al-Tanzīl*, ad 7:29.

needed now is textual evidence from the Koran to support this thesis.

An initial complication is that pre-philosophical Arabic has no abstract term to denote responsibility. The root-verb in the passive voice, *yusʾalu*, is derived from the active voice denoting to ask; both voices occur frequently in the Koran. In some cases, such as 2:119; 33:14 and 81:8, the term is used in the passive voice in the morally neutral sense, but in a group of other verses the moral connotation is unmistakable. The term occurs in this context almost invariably in the passive voice and should be rendered as 'liable to question', i.e. responsible or answerable for doing or believing that which, from the standpoint of the author of scripture, is clearly reprehensible. Affirming this liability to question are verses 16:56,93; 21:23; 29:13; 43:44. In some of these verses the unbelievers (*kāfirūn*) or polytheists (*mushrikūn*) (e.g. 16:56; 29:13; 37:24) are stated to be answerable to God Almighty for their misdeeds or their unbelief on the Day of Judgement, whereas in others, this 'answerability' is expressed in much broader terms, and can be construed as laying down the general imperative of moral responsibility.

Thus verse 16:93 simply states: "And you will surely be questioned about the things you wrought." (trans. Arberry). Verse 43:44, addresses the Prophet in these terms: "Surely it (i.e. the Koran) is a Reminder to thee and to thy people, and assuredly you will be questioned."

However, in a series of passages, the contrary thesis is advanced, at least as regards the impious and the infidels, either because they are past all answerability, having already been judged on the Last Day, as in 55:39, or because they are originally foredoomed, as in 28:78. This last verse states that "the criminals shall not be questioned about their sins," which al-Bayḍāwī interprets to mean that they will not be questioned in the sense of a "request for information, since God Almighty is already conversant therewith" or in the sense of punishment, since He will torture them on account of their sins at once.[19] As to the former verse, which states that "on that day none shall be questioned about his sin, neither man nor jinn" (trans. Arberry), he interprets it likewise to mean that God, Who will recognize the sinners by their looks (*bi-sīmāhum*) as soon as they emerge from their graves and are summoned before His judgement seat, each in accordance with his rank, will not need to question them about their deeds or misdeeds.[20] Neither the sinners nor the Prophet, who in a sense assumes the moral responsibility for instructing them, is answerable on the Last Day. For, as verse 2:119, has put it: "Thou (i.e. the Prophet) art not answerable, concerning the people of Hell."

---

[19] See *Anwār al-Tanzīl*, II, ad 28:78.

[20] *Ibid.*, II, ad 55:39.

It is by virtue of the irreversibility of God's decrees, then, that sinners shall not be questioned on the Last Day. Throughout their life and up to that fateful moment, mankind is asserted by the Koran to be answerable for both its beliefs and its transgressions; whether the imperative of answerability can be so generalized as to apply to angels and to God Himself is not very clear. In a classic passage which asserts that "He (i.e. God) shall not be questioned concerning what He does, but they (i.e. mankind) shall be questioned" (21:23, trans. Palmer), this divine freedom from this imperative is vindicated in dramatic terms. Not only the commentators, from the tenth century on, but the Ashᶜarite theologians understood this verse to mean that God is to be relieved of the responsibility of answering for His actions or His decisions. Commenting on this verse, al-Bayḍāwī writes: "He (i.e. God) is not liable to quetion concerning what He does, on account of His majesty and the power of His sovereignty and the fact that sovereignty and essential domination belong exclusively to Him. They (i.e. mankind), as well as the gods of the polytheists mentioned in the previous verse, are liable to question, because of their subordination and their servile status."[21]

Apart from knowledge or consciousness, the most fundamental precondition or ground of human responsibility is that of freedom. In the absence of such a precondition, the human agent is reduced to the status of an automaton, as all forms of mechanism and determinism logically presuppose, or that of a slave of the Almighty, as all forms of theistic determinism (or predestinationism) entail. The vindication of human freedom (*qadar*) or capacity (*istiṭāᶜah*), as we shall see in due course, was the first major theological issue to split the Muslim community, as early as the seventh century, into the protagonists of human freedom (the *Qadarīs*) and their opponents, generally designated as the Determinists (*al-Mujbirah* or *al-Jabriyyah*).[22] The ultimate resolution of the antithesis by al-Ashᶜarī (d. 935), which was destined to be identified with orthodoxy, recognized the inescapability of affirming freedom in some sense or other, but could not disavow the Koranic concept of God's overwhelming domination and supremacy in the world, to which we have just referred. Our aim at this stage is to elicit any *prima facie* evidence for or against human freedom in the Koran.

The abstract Arabic term for freedom *al-ḥurriyah* does not occur in the Koran in the substantive form, but derivatives from the original consonantal stem do occur, both in the adjectival and transitive forms, in the sense of freeman (*ḥurr*) as opposed to slave, or that of emancipation or

---

[21] *Anwār al-Tanzīl*, I, ad 21:23, cf. al-Ṭabarī, *Jāmiᶜal-Bayān*, ad 21:23 also.
[22] See, e.g., al-Shahrastānī, *al-Milal wa'l-Niḥal*, ed. A.-A al-Wakīl, Cairo, 1968, I, 28.

manumission (*taḥrīr*). In verse 2:178, the *lex talionis* is expressed in these terms: "O believers, prescribed for you is retaliation, touching the slain; freeman for freeman (*al-ḥurr bi'l-ḥurr*), slave for slave, female for female" (trans. Arberry). In verse 5:89, the punishment for careless oaths is stated to be the feeding of ten poor men or clothing them, or the "freeing" (*taḥrīr*) of a single slave. This latter punishment is imposed in 4:92 on whomever kills a believer inadvertently and in 58:3 on him who divorces his wife by declaring her to be to "him like the back of his mother (*yuẓāhirūna*),[23] but recants later.

In verse 3:35, the wife of ᶜImrān (identified by al-Bayḍāwī with St. Anne) vows to consecrate her child, who is born free (*muḥarrar*), to God, but it is obvious that the term here, as in the previous case, means simply a freeman. None of these terms bears the slightest relation to the problem of moral freedom or self-determination, except insofar as the social status of the freeman can be said to have a bearing on his moral decisions or actions. The term *qadar*, and its derivatives when applied to man, would appear to be the nearest equivalent to moral freedom or capacity. When applied to God, the root either denotes His preordination (*taqdīr*), as in 6:96; 36:38; 41:12, or His omnipotence (*qudra*), as in 2:20,106; 5:17; 6:17; 8:41; 41:39; 57:2; 64:1. And this indeed is the connotation of the term in the overwhelming majority of cases. Only in verses 16:75 and 76 is the term predicated of man, and in both cases in the negative. In the first case, God is stated to have given as a parable the example of an "owned slave" (*ᶜabdan mamlūkan*) able to do nothing" (Palmer), and in the second that of a "dumb person, who is a burden to his master", to illustrate the powerlessness and stupidity of the deities worshipped by the idolators. In all the other cases, in which the term occurs either in the indicative (*yaqdir*), as in 13:26; 17:30; 28:82; 29:62; 30:37; 34:36,39; 39:52; 42:12, or *naqdir*, as in 21:87, or in the active participle (*qādir, qādirūn*), as in 6:37; 10:24; 17:99; 23:18,95; 36:81; 46:33; 75:40; 86:8, or *muqtadir*, as in 18:45; 43:42; 54:42,55, the term invariably refers to God's power or preordination. One recurrent theme in these verses is God's power to quicken the dead or recreate them on the Day of Resurrection, by dint of His original creative power (36:81; 46:33; 75:40); another is His ability to grant to whomever He pleases provision (*rizq*) in accordance with His bounty and will, a theme which recurs in almost ten verses already listed, and which all read as follows: "God expands the provision to whomever He wishes and is able (*yaqdir*)" (13:26; 42:12) or determines his share of it (*yaqdir lahu*) (29:62; 34:39).[24]

---

[23] See al-Bayḍāwī, *Anwār al-Tanzīl*, II, ad 58:3.

[24T] The ambiguity of the verb in these two groups of verses is obvious. See al-Bayḍāwī, *Anwār al-Tanzīl*, II, ad 42:12.

The other Arabic term which denotes power or capacity and which, like *qadar*, became one of the chief points of controversy in theological circles is *istiṭāᶜah* and its derivatives. It occurs frequently in the Koran, but always in the verbal form. In some verses, the term clearly refers to capacity, as a precondition of moral or religious obligation, as in 3:97, which declares that the yearly pilgrimage to Mecca (or Bekkah) "is due to God from man ... whoever can find his way there (*man istaṭāᶜa*)" (trans. Palmer); or in 8:60, which calls upon the believers to prepare against the infidels "what force and companies of horse" they can for holy warfare. In 64:16, the believers are exhorted to "fear God as far as you are able, and give ear, and obey, and expend well for yourselves" (trans. Arberry). In these and other verses the capacity to perform certain actions, such as holy war (9:42) or reform (11:88), is clearly affirmed, with the consequent implication of moral freedom and responsibility. In almost all the other verses, capacity is repudiated and the infidels are challenged to call upon other deities besides God, if they can (10:38; 11:13), considering that they are unable to help or harm them (7:192,197; 16:73; 21:43; 36:75). In 55:33, the whole of mankind and jinn are challenged to "pass through" the confines of heaven and earth if they can, or produce the like of the Koranic chapters, even with the help of any other deities than God upon whom they could call (10:38; 11:13). In almost all the other cases, the term occurs in a negative context, as in the admonition to would-be polygamists that they will not be able to treat all their wives equitably, even if they tried (4:129), or to those who cannot marry freeborn women to marry their slave girls (4:25), or to those who are unable to fast for two months in atonement for putting away their wives, to feed sixty poor men instead (58:4). In one verse (5:112), the disciples of Christ challenge him, saying: "Is thy Lord able to send down to us a table from heaven?",—a probable reference to the Eucharist, and God is able to meet the challenge, as we learn from the sequel.

The only other verb in Arabic which denotes ability is the verb *mkn*, but although derivatives of this verb occur in the Koran, it is never used except in the transitive form. Therein the subject is invariably God, Who is said to "have given power (*amkana*) over them" (i.e. enemy captives (8:71), or to have "established dominion" (*makkana*) upon earth for Alexander the Great (18:84,95) or for Joseph (12:21,56), or for the unbelievers generally (6:6; 7:10; 22:41; 28:57; 46:26), who have persisted in their unbelief notwithstanding, or for the weak and downtrodden (28:6) and the pious (24:55). In none of these cases, however, is there the barest hint of power or capacity being a prerogative of man, as a free agent.

CHAPTER TWO

THE EVIDENCE OF THE TRADITIONS

The overall results of our textual investigation of *prima facie* evidence for moral self-determination or capacity in the Koran can now be summarized. The predominant moral motif of the Koran is undoubtedly the stipulation that the human agent ought to place himself in an appropriate relationship to God or His commandments if he is to satisfy the conditions of uprightness (*birr*) or piety (*taqwa*) or to earn his rightful position in Paradise. However interpreted, this stipulation is grounded in the concept of religious obligation (*taklīf*) and its inevitable prerequisite, obedience (*ṭāᶜah*). The violation of this precept results, of course, in the nullification of the right relationship between God, as Lawgiver and Lord, and man, as creature or servant, designated by the Koran as disobedience (*al-maᶜṣiyah*) or sin.

Although this God-man relationship can be defined in purely mechanical terms, so that the infringement of the divine precepts is construed as a violation of necessary laws, in very much the same way as physical objects can in accidental cases or general cataclysms violate the laws of their motion or development,[1] the Koranic concept of the soul (or the agent) earning (*kasabat* and *iktasabat*) the deserts of its actions (2:134,141,286; 3:25,161; 6:70; 14:51; 30:41; 40:17), performing (*atat*) (2:233; 29:28,29; 30:39) or doing (*ᶜamal*) certain kinds of action for which it will receive its due reward (3:30; 6:54; 16:28,97,111; 20:69; 30:44,45; 37:61; 40:40; 66:7) clearly implies that of moral responsibility, ultimately predicated on a certain measure of free will or self-determination. The concept of insinuation (*taswīl*) is particularly revealing in this context. In Surah 126, the brothers of Joseph are reprimanded for their ill-treatment of their young brother by reason of what "their souls insinuated to them" (*sawwalat*) (18,83) and in verse 20:96 the Samaritan confesses that his soul induced him to mislead the Jews into worshipping the calf. In the only other verse in which this term occurs (47:25), it is Satan himself who is accused of seducing (*sawwala*) the renegades or hypocrites to "turning back after they had seen the guidance clearly." Other terms, such as *waswasa, ṭaghā*, etc. frequently occur in the Koran to convey the idea of Satan's evil insinuations or machinations, of which mankind is often the prey.

---

[1] It is noteworthy that such a mechanical theory of obligation was indeed entertained by the Determinists of Islam, the Jabriyyah. See *infra*, 46f.

It is, however, fair to say that despite this impressive *implicit* evidence for moral responsibility and self-determination, the *explicit* textual evidence in the Koran is nevertheless rather scant, especially when set against the overwhelming power and sovereignty of God portrayed in such dramatic terms in the Koran.

The Ḥadīth, which differs from the Koran in the more circumstantial and juridical character of many of its pronouncements, is even less explicit. In fact, it provides us with an even dimmer view of the intricate correlations between the three ethical concepts with which we started: the nature of the good or the right, divine justice and human freedom. Significantly enough, the two major canonical collections of Ḥadīth, that of al-Bukhārī and Muslim, each contain a separate section (or book) on *qadar*, understood in the sense of divine power rather than human capacity,[2] but there are no separate sections either on the nature of the good or on divine justice, a problem destined to play such a decisive role in the development of moral theology from the eighth century on. Nor are there any sections or books on justice in general.

Here and there, however, there are Traditions which are of definite ethical relevance. For instance, in *Kitab al-Manāqib*, al-Bukhārī reports a Tradition with illustrates very well the preoccupation of the early Muslim community with the question of right and wrong and its bearing on religious belief. How early this Tradition should be dated, however, cannot be readily determined. Insofar as it smacks of definite sectarian bias, it appears to belong to the period of acute controversy into which the Khārijites, the Murjiʿites and the Qadarites entered at the end of the seventh and the beginning of the eighth century. In this Tradition, which I will give in full, Ḥudhayfa ibn al-Yaman is reported as saying: "People kept asking the Apostle of God (may God bless and greet him) about the good (*khayr*), whereas I kept asking him about evil, for fear it will attain me. Thus I said: O Apostle of God, we were in a period of ignorance (*jāhilīyah*) and evil, but God brought us this good.[3] Now, will there be any evil, following this good? He said: Yes. I said: But will there be, following that evil, any good? He said: Yes; and it will contain a flaw. I said: What is this flaw? He said: A people calling to a guidance other than mine; some you will recognize, others you will not. Thereupon I said: But will there be, following that evil, any good? He said: Yes, a group who call to the

---

[2] Books 82 and 46, respectively. The only other collection containing a section on *qadar* is that of al-Tirmidhī, bk. 30. See Wensinck, *A Handbook of Early Muhammadan Tradition*, Leiden, 1927, XI et. seq.

[3] The context suggests that by "this good" is meant Islam or the revelation of the Koran.

gates of Hell; whoever listens to them will be thrust into it on their account.[4] I said: O Apostle of God, describe them to us. He said: They are of our stock and they speak our language. So I said: What do you command me to do, should that [call] reach me? He said: Cling to the community (*jamā*ᶜ*ah*) of Muslims and their head (*imām*). I said: But suppose they had no community or a head? He said: Then you shun (*i*ᶜ*tazil*) all these sects, even if you have to bite the trunk of a tree until death overtake you, while you are in that state."[5]

Although this Tradition does not give us a definition of what the good and evil referred to really are, we can clearly infer from it the express identification of goodness with conformity to the dictates of Islam or the Koran, as opposed to the pre-Islamic or heathen condition of 'ignorance' (*jāhiliyyah*). But in view of the violent schisms and heresies that were to rock the Muslim community subsequent to the death of Muḥammad in 632, the goodness in question is asserted to consist simply in conformity to the will of the (orthodox) community and its head, and in dissociation from any schismatic or heretical groups.

In this view, goodness turns out to be essentially a matter of faith (*īmān*), or even of loyalty to the community. As one might expect, a more explicit statement of what goodness means occurs in the context of the Traditions' disquisition on faith and related questions. Thus both al-Bukhārī and Muslim report a number of Traditions in *Kitab al-Īmān* which make of the love of the Prophet (Bukh. II, 6,13,14; Muslim I, 69,70; XLV, 161,162), the love of God and the Prophet jointly (Bukh. II, 20: Muslim I, 67,68; XLV, 161–64, or the love of one's neighbour (or brother) (Bukh. II, 12; LXVIII, 42, Muslim I, 71,72,93; XLV, 37) the criteria of genuine faith and *eo ipso* goodness. Aḥmad b. Ḥanbal (*al-Musnad*, III, 172,174,192,200, etc.) and Mālik b. Anas (*al-Muwaṭṭa*ᵓ, XLVII, 15,16, 17; LI, 14,16) stress the importance of the love of God and of one's neighbour to genuine faith.[6]

The emphasis on love in the canonical collections should not be interpreted as precluding other concrete criteria of faith or goodness. Thus al-Bukhārī, in the opening part of *Kitab al-Īmān*, reports that the Prophet had stated that Islam has five ingredients: confessing the unity of God and the prophethood of Muḥammad, performing the ritual prayer, giving alms, pilgrimage and fasting (II, 7), and proceeds to support this statement by

---

[4] This might refer to the Khārijites and their rigid criteria of right and wrong. See, e.g., Wensinck, *The Muslim Creed*, Cambridge, 1932, 37f.

[5] *Ṣaḥīḥ al-Bukhārī*, Cairo, 1973, vol. 6, 3226.

[6] The two are sometimes combined in the oft-mentioned expression 'love in God'. See al-Bukhārī, I, 6; Muslim, XLV, 37,38; Tirmidhī, XXXIV, 53; A. b. Ḥanbal, II, 237,292, etc.

quoting the already-mentioned verse (Koran 2:177), which identifies righteousness (*birr*), as we have seen, with a series of articles of faith coupled with a series of good works. Muslim, on the other hand, identifies righteousness with good character (XLV, 14,15) and its opposite (*ithm*) with malice or, as he has put it, "what churns within your breast and you do not wish people to become privy to." Such good character is then reduced to a series of moral prescriptions and prohibitions governing one's relation to one's fellows or one's kin, foremost among which is the duty of a good Muslim not to cut off his brother, backbite him, think ill of him, eavesdrop on him (XLV, 25,28–31, etc.) beat him unjustly or belittle him (*ibid.*, 32).

To reinforce the thesis that righteousness or piety (*taqwa*) is not a matter of outward attitude or performance, a Tradition reports a statement made by the Prophet, as he pointed to his breast thrice, to the effect that piety is 'within' and adding, according to another version of this Tradition (XLV, 33): "God will not look at your bodies or forms, but at your hearts."

This Tradition should be set against one of the best known Traditions, reported very early by al-Bukhārī and Muslim (in *Kitab al-Īmān*, also) and asserting: "Verily works are a matter of intention, and upon every one shall devolve what he [originally] intended."[7] The locus of intention is then declared to be the heart (*qalb*)—a concept which has played an important part in the history of religious and mystical thought in Islam. Faith, coupled with this good-heartedness, is the only precondition of salvation, according to these Traditionists, who do not appear to fully grasp its inconsistency with a religious ethics in which works of piety (*ṣāliḥāt*) must inevitably play a decisive role, as we have seen in reviewing the evidence of the Koran. Al-Bukhārī thus reports the Tradition asserting that: "Whoever says there is no God but Allah and there is in his heart the weight of a grain of barley (variants: grain of wheat or atom) of goodness (*khayr*) shall get out of Hell."[8] Muslim's version of this Tradition is even stronger in its antinomianism: "No one in whose heart there is a mustard-seed's weight of faith shall enter Hell."[9] This faith, which consists solely, according to Muslim, of the act of professing the unity of God, will not only shield him against the torments of Hell, but will assure him of a well-deserved place in Paradise, no matter what his transgressions in this life may have been.[10]

---

[7] Bukhārī, II, 1; Muslim, I, 203f and XXVIII, 155, etc. Cf. Wensinck, *Handbook*, Intention.

[8] Bukhārī, I, 41; II, 15.

[9] Muslim, I, 148.

[10] *Ibid.*, 154, etc.

The ambivalence of the Traditions on the vexed question of the relation of faith to works is not mitigated by such conflicting pronouncements, or indeed by the spectacle of God's irreversible and eternal decree, to which we will turn. The concept of human actions or works (*aᶜmāl*), coupled with the concept of intentions (*niyyāt*), would appear to presuppose a certain measure of self-determination, as a prerogative of man. Both concepts, as we have seen, form an integral part of the textual, ethical evidence of the Traditions, and yet from the start the canonical collections inveigh in no uncertain terms against libertarianism. The very first Tradition in Muslim's *Saḥīḥ* (I, 1) informs us that a certain Yaḥya b. Yaᶜmar, beset by the problem of *qadar* (first raised by Maᶜbad al-Juhanī (d. 703) at Baṣrah) set out to seek guidance on this question from the companions of Muḥammad at Madīnah. He met ᶜAbdullah, son of ᶜUmar, the Second Caliph, who informed him that his farther had told him that when asked what faith (*īmān*) was the Prophet had replied: "To believe in God, His angels, His book, His Apostles and in the Last Day; and to believe in the divine decree (*al-qadar*), good or evil."

The circumstantial character of this Tradition and its reference to Maᶜbad al-Juhanī by name definitely weaken its authority, and it is not without some significance that another variant of this Tradition, reported on the much more reliable authority of Abū Hurayrah does not mention *qadar* in one case (I, 5), or speaks of the 'whole of *qadar*' somewhat ambiguously in another (I, 7).

It is equally significant that al-Bukhārī has not reported this particular Tradition in his Book of *Qadar*, although other Traditionists, such as Aḥmad b. Ḥanbal (III, 21,22,23,24,26,37,40, etc.) and al-Tirmidhī (XXX, 10,17; XXXVIII, 4) have done so.[11] The Traditions which identify belief in *qadar* with orthodoxy, as the Ashᶜarite theologians were to do in the tenth century, and those which denounce the Qadarite and by implication the Muᶜtazilite sect,[12] obviously cannot be taken at face value, but should be dismissed as fabrications of eighth or ninth-century doctors determined to find a textual basis in the Ḥadīth for their strictures against their scholastic opponents.

However, despite these necessary reservations, the *qadar* or predestinarian thesis is stated in such dramatic terms in the Ḥadīth that one cannot escape the conclusion that the opponents of the Qadarīs were so influential or skilled that they monopolized the Ḥadīth compilation industry, or that alternatively the vast number of Traditions vindicating *qadar* must have all been uttered by the Prophet, or at least some of them.

---

[11] See Wensinck, *Handbook*, Decree (ḳadar).

[12] E.g. Tirmidhī, XXX, 17; Ibn Ḥanbal, I, 30, 86; II, 86, 125, etc. See Wensinck, *Handbook*, Ḳadarites.

Two or three examples of these Traditions as reported by al-Bukhārī and Muslim will suffice to highlight the categorical emphasis on the divine *qadar* in the Ḥadīth.

1. "God entrusted the womb to an angel, who said: O Lord, a sperm; O Lord, a leech; O Lord, a piece of tissue! If God wishes to decree its creation, [the angel] says: O Lord, a male or a female, wretched or happy, what is its provision (*rizq*) and its term (*ajal*) to be? All of this is then written down while it is still in its mother's womb."[13]

2. "God wrote down the decrees of the Creation, before He created the heavens and the earth by fifty thousand years."[14]

3. "There is not one of you, not a single breathing soul, whose place in Heaven or Hell God has not written down, or whom He has not predestined to be either wretched or blessed. A man then asked: O Apostle of God, should we not stick to our writen decree (*kitābinā*) and leave off work? [The Prophet] replied: Whoever is destined to be blessed will be made to do the work of the blessed people, and he who is destined to be wretched will be made to do the work of the wretched people."[15]

The theme of the written decree or 'book' is a commonplace theme of both the Koran and the Ḥadīth and, as Wensinck has shown, is not specifically Islamic, but 'has a broad Semitic basis, as is proved by Babylonian and Israelitic religious tradition."[16] It is noteworthy, as Wensinck has also observed, that the notion of the eternal pre-determination of the individual fates of men is even more graphically set out in the Ḥadīth than in the Koran. A large number of Traditions stresses the irreversibility of the divine decree, already adumbrated, but perhaps one of its most emphatic affirmations occurs in this Tradition of Ibn Ḥanbal: ᶜAbdullah b. ᶜAmr b. al-ᶜĀṣ is reported as saying: "Once the Apostle of God came out to meet us with two books in his hand. He said: Do you know what these two books are? We said: No, you tell us, O Apostle of God. Whereupon he said of the book in his right hand: This is a book from the Lord of the Worlds, may He be blessed and exalted, containing the names of the people of Paradise and the names of their parents and their tribes. The last name thereof has been sealed, so that no increase or decrease can ever be made in the list. Then he said of the one in his left hand: "This is a book that contains the people of Hell, with their own names, their parents

---

[13] Muslim, XLVI, 5 and 1–4. Cf. Ibn Ḥanbal, III, 117,148,397, and al-Bukhārī, LXXXII, 1.

[14] Muslim, XLVI, 16; Ibn Ḥanbal, III, 1.

[15] Muslim, *Ibid.*, 6,7. Cf. 10,11,30; al-Bukhārī, LXXXII, 4,5; Ibn Ḥanbal, III, 27,28,29,31.

[16] *Muslim Creed*, 54.

and their tribes'; the last of which has also been sealed, so that no increase or decrease can ever be made in their number.''[17]

This cursory review of the ethical implications of the Ḥadīth may appear sketchy. However, one should not be misled into assuming that a substantive and systematic theory of justice and moral responsibility is articulately laid out in the canonical collections. In fact, as our discussion has revealed, although the three basic problems we have isolated as ethical parameters are only casually touched upon in the Ḥadīth, it would be a mistake to place profound and far-reaching moral constructions upon circumstantial utterances, legal pronouncements or reports of personal and communal expressions of opinion. Except for the problem of free will and predestination (*qadar*), dealt with at the end of this section, not much systematic material can be produced, and even this material is of questionable historical value, since it appears to reflect that theological partisanship which we associate with the major religious groups, which were actively involved in theological and legal controversy following the death of the Prophet. Within the context of that controversy and the subsequent development of moral theology in Islam, such material is of profound significance, but its historical authenticity cannot for that reason alone be vindicated. From the standpoint of ethical development, the theological trends which will be discussed in the next part are of far greater significance, and to these trends we will now turn. This part has accordingly been termed Theological Ethics.

---

[17] *Al-Musnad*, II, 167.

PART TWO

THEOLOGICAL ETHICS

CHAPTER ONE

ETHICAL RATIONALISM

I. The Deontological Grounds of Right and Wrong

As we have already mentioned, the Muᶜtazilah were the first genuine moralists of Islam. Not only did they formulate coherent answers to the three principal ethical questions we have isolated, but they laid down the groundwork for all subsequent ethical developments, especially in theological circles.

One of the notable Muᶜtazilite doctors, Abu'l-Ḥusayn al-Khayyāṭ (died end ninth century) has listed in his *Kitāb al-Intiṣār* the five fundamental principles on which the different sections of the Muᶜtazilite school were agreed. The fifth of these principles is expressed by him as 'enjoining what is [morally] approved (*maᶜrūf*) and prohibiting what is [morally] disapproved (*munkar*).'[1] The clearest and most succinct gloss on this statement is to be found in *al-Milal wa'l-Niḥal*, written in the twelfth century by the erudite and perceptive Ashᶜarite author, Muḥammad al-Shahrastānī (d. 1153). "They (i.e. the Muᶜtazilah) were agreed," he writes, "that the principles of knowledge and gratitude for benefaction (*niᶜmah*) are obligatory, prior to the advent of revelation (*samᶜ*). Similarly, that right and wrong ought to be known through reason, and the adoption of right and the avoidance of wrong is likewise obligatory. The advent of religious obligation (*taklīf*) is a grace from God Almighty which He imparted to mankind through the Prophets to test and prove them, so that 'whosoever perished might perish by a clear sign, and by a clear sign he might live who lived'." (Koran 8:42, trans. Arberry).[2]

The correlation between knowledge and right in this gloss is the keynote of this rationalist thesis of the Muᶜtazilah. These theologians were concerned to establish in the face of traditionalist protestations by Aḥmad ibn Ḥanbal (d. 855) and his followers, on the one hand, and those of Jahm ibn Ṣafwān (d. 745) and the Determinists generally,[3] on the other, that the nature of right and wrong can be determined rationally and that it is ultimately independent of the divine prescriptions as laid down in the

---

[1] See *K. al-Intiṣār*, ed. and trans. into French by A. Nader, Beirut, 1957, 53. On the Koranic background of these two terms, see *supra*. Cf. al-Ashᶜarī, *Maqālāt al-Islāmiyyīn*, ed. H. Ritter, Istanbul, 1929–30, I, 378.

[2] Al-Shahrastānī, *Al-Milal wa'l-Niḥal*, I, 29.

[3] See *infra*, 46.

Koran; in short they wished to establish that the two moral categories of right and wrong can be known by unaided reason and the ground of their validity can be rationally justified.

We find in the recently published theological *summa* of the late Muᶜtazilite author *al-qāḍī* ᶜAbd al-Jabbār, entitled *al-Mughnī fī Abwāb al-Tawḥīd wa'l-ᶜAdl*, the fullest and most systematic discussion of this problem. The author begins by considering the nature of action (*fiᶜl*) in relation to an agent who is both capable and conscious. He finds in this relation the defining ground of that type of action by which he clearly means human action. He rejects accordingly the definition of action as "an event (*kāʾin*) that comes into being after it was not", i.e. is produced in time (*muḥdath*) on the grounds that: (a) it is known to be so produced *after* it has come into being, and (b) the actual or present status of the action should not be injected into the definition. The temporal determination in other words is not essential, but accidental; the action should be defined instead by reference to the factor which 'exhibits' the purpose underlying it, as envisaged by a willing and capable agent. The relation to this agent actually determines the moral quality of the action in question. For not all actions are morally determined, only those which possess an adventitious quality (*ṣifah zāʾidah*), identified alternatively as good (*ḥasan*) and bad (*qabīḥ*), or praiseworthy and blameworthy, and stemming ultimately from the will of the agent.[4]

This correlation between good and praiseworthy and the one hand, and bad and blameworthy on the other, enables the author to subdivide good actions into three groups: (a) permissible (*mubāḥ*), or capable of being done or left undone without earning commendation or reproach: (b) admonished (*mandūb ilayh*), or exhorted to (*muraghghab fīh*), or deserving of praise if done, but not of reproach if left undone; and (c) obligatory (*wājib*), or deserving of reproach if not done, but not of praise if done. The obligatory has two subdivisions: (a) obligatory in the 'narrow sense', and (b) obligatory in the 'broad sense'. Omitting a particular action is obligatory in the first sense; omitting the action and its kind is obligatory in the second.[5]

The knowledge of the "adventitious quality' of goodness is stated by this Muᶜtazilite author, as indeed by the Muᶜtazilite school as a whole, to be a matter of intuitive certainty. Some, he argues, have claimed that

---

[4] *Al-Mughnī*, Cairo, 1962—, VI, i, 6f. and VI, ii, 65f. ᶜAbd al-Jabbār rejects in this connection the 'ontological' view advocated by Islamic Neo-Platonists like al-Fārābī and Ibn Sīnā, according to which a thing is good simply because it is. *Ibid.*, 9 and 77f.

[5] *Ibid.*, VI, i, 7f. Cf. G.F. Hourani, *Islamic Rationalism. The Ethics of 'Abd al-Jabbār*, Oxford, 1971, 39.

the goodness and badness of certain actions is known esthetically, i.e. in the same way in which a picture is known to be beautiful or ugly.[6] However, the analogy between the two classes of objects involved will not do; a picture is ugly in the sense that some are 'repelled' by it, but not others, and this repulsion, which is entirely subjective, is not an object of commendation or reproach, two of the criteria of goodness and badness, as we have seen. Others, like the Determinists (Mujbirah) and the Ash^c arites, as will appear from the next chapter, claimed that goodness and badness are determined by, respectively, the divine command (*amr*) and prohibition. This claim, however, is rejected on the grounds that, were the commanding or prohibiting the essential basis of the goodness or badness of the action, any action prohibited or commanded would *ipso facto*, be, respectively, good or bad, regardless of the status of the author of the prohibition or command, be it God or any one else; this is absurd, however, since it renders goodness and badness entirely arbitrary. In fact, it is only by virtue of the intrinsic goodness or badness of the action that it becomes a fitting object of God's command or prohibition.[7]

Now this intrinsic goodness or badness is known to us, the author argues, 'by necessity'. Whoever questions this knowledge "repudiates necessity" and his repudiation is not worth attending to. Should he, however, grant the substance of the distinction between good and bad, and yet insist that allegedly good actions, such as equity and gratitude, are not obligatory or praiseworthy, and contrariwise bad actions, such as falsehood and injustice, are neither prohibited nor blameworthy, his contention would turn on purely semantic points which could be settled by reference to linguistic usage.[8]

An important characteristic of this intuitive ethical knowledge is that it is autonomous and self-validating: it requires neither 'acquired' nor 'deductive' evidence to support it, not even the warrant of divine revelation (*sam^c*). Rather the contrary, for unless the grounds of religious or revealed Truth, such as the wisdom of God and the truthfulness of the Prophet who bears His message to mankind, are rationally known, the Truth of revelation, identified by ^cAbd al-Jabbār with the Koran and Traditions, would remain forever questionable.[9]

In view of this autonomy of rational knowledge, one might ask what function, if any, can revelation discharge in the ethical field, and what

---

6 Al-Mughnī, VI, i, 19f. It is noteworthy that identical terms are used to denote good and beautiful (*ḥasan*) and bad and ugly (*qabīḥ*).

7 *Ibid.*, VI, i, 102f. Cf. XIV, 153 *et passim*.

8 *Ibid.*, VI, i, 18f. and 43.

9 *Ibid.*, XIV, 151.

bearing can it have on the problem of moral and religious obligation and responsibility (*taklīf*). For neither ᶜAbd al-Jabbār nor his Muᶜtazilite colleagues made so bold as to declare revelation to be entirely superfluous, as did some naturalist philosophers of the ninth and tenth centuries, such as al-Rāzī (d. 925).[10] It can, according to ᶜAbd al-Jabbār, 'exhibit' the principles already established by reason, but does not confirm or validate them. For, (a) having been established by reason as necessary, they obviously are not in need of confirmation of any kind, (b) the validity of revelation, as already mentioned, being dependent on reason, cannot without *petition of principle*, depend on revelation, and, finally, (c) were revelation to confirm these principles, it would require another revelation to confirm it, and so on *ad infinitum*.[11]

Another function which devolves upon revelation is the arbitration between conflicting revelations or parts of revelation. Whenever error or disagreement arises, revelation is required in order to correct this error or 'abrogate' (*nasakha*) an outdated revelation. In cases in which the responsible agent is known to have fulfilled all his obligations, or to have discovered rationally all the principles of morality, revelation is entirely superfluous.[12]

A third function is that of specifying those particular acts which are morally commendable and whose goodness is determined by reason, but only in general terms. The prophets are sent by God, argues ᶜAbd al-Jabbār, in order to instruct us concerning those actions that He had already instilled in our intellects, with a view to confirming (*taqrīr*) and specifying them in detail.[13]

To illustrate the type of 'rational obligation' incumbent on the agent, ᶜAbd al-Jabbār lists three categories of action: (a) those that are obligatory by virtue of an intrinsic property, (b) those that are obligatory by virtue of a divine grace (*luṭf*), which presumably specifies or confirms the goodness of the action, and (c) those that are obligatory by virtue of the advantage accruing to the agent from performing them or avoiding their opposites. (a) is then subdivided into actions which define our obligations: (1) towards our fellowmen, such as returning what is entrusted to us, (2) towards ourselves, such as guarding against injury, and (3) towards God,

---

[10] See M. Fakhry, *A History of Islamic Philosophy*, 94f. The thesis that revelation (or prophethood) is superfluous is attributed in the Arabic sources to the Brahmins (*al-Barāhimah*), cf. *al-Mughnī*, XIV, 160 *et passim*, and ᶜAbd al-Jabbār's other important treatise, *Sharḥ al-Uṣūl al-Khamsah*, Cairo, 1965, 564f. and Hourani, *op.cit.*, 134f. Cf. Barāhima in *Encyclopaedia of Islam*².

[11] *Al-Mughnī*, XIV, 151f. and VI, i, 64. Cf. Hourani, *op.cit.*

[12] *Ibid.*, XIV, 151f.

[13] See *Sharḥ al-Uṣūl al-Khamsah*, 564f. Cf. Hourani, *op.cit.*, 135.

such as gratitude (*shukr*) for His benevolence and forgiveness.[14] (b), on the other hand, includes all those obligations which are revealed to man as a divine grace and cannot be known rationally, such as the duty of reflecting on God and conforming to the precepts of the Holy Law.[15] Finally, (c) includes a large class of actions whose goodness is a feature of the advantage, pleasure or interest that the agent can derive from them. The 'utilitarian' maxim that man ought to ward off injury to himself and seek his own advantage in matters spiritual and temporal is regarded by this Muᶜtazilite theologian as incontrovertible; revelation, as already mentioned, simply exhibits the mischievous quality of certain actions, but does not validate or affect the maxim itself. A corollary of this maxim is the right to self-defense, even if it involves the killing of an aggressor who threatens one's life or property, and provided the killing is not sought for its own sake.[16]

However, the line of demarcation between rational and religious obligation is not always clearly drawn by ᶜAbd al-Jabbār. Apart from 'specifying' the general moral maxim, or reaffirming it, revelation defines the kinds of sanctions attached to them in the life-to-come. In that respect, revelation (or scripture) does no more than restate the obligation in the general theological or eschatological context: bad thus becomes equivalent to the prohibited (*maḥẓūr*), unlawful (*muḥarram*), or sinful (*maᶜṣiyah*),[17] all of which describe the action in terms of violating the precepts laid down by God. Contrariwise, good becomes equivalent to the permitted (*mubāḥ*), lawful (*ḥalāl*), allowed (*jāʾiz*), or the act of obedience (*ṭāᶜah*).[18] If we abstract this theological ground of compliance or violation, as well as the sanctions attached to each, the difference between the two sets of terms becomes purely semantic.

II. Human Capacity and Responsibility

A moral action is defined, as we have just seen, in terms of its relation to an agent who is both conscious (*ᶜālim*) and capable (*qādir*). The consciousness in question, as we have also seen, bears on the general moral

---

[14] *Al-Mughnī*, XIV, 161f.

[15] *Al-Mughnī* ᶜAbd al-Jabbār's thinking on the relation of reason and revelation is not free from inconsistency. Like other Muᶜtazilite doctors, he believed that God can be known rationally. The two obligations in question appear to refer to the sanctions attaching to this knowledge, and the advantage of seeking it, as well as the obligation to *start* the deductive process (*istidlāl*) leading to the knowledge of God. See *al-Mughnī*, XII, 230f. and 325f.

[16] *Ibid.*, 168f. Cf. pp. 33f. ᶜAbd al-Jabbār, however, regards the distinction between right (*ḥasan, ṣalāḥ*) and useful (*nafᶜ*) to be purely semantic. *Ibid.*, 35f.

[17] Other synonyms are *dhanb*, *khaṭīyah*, *sayyiʾah*.

[18] *Al-Mughnī*, XVII, 95f.

quality of an action as rationally or religiously determined. Power (*qudrah*) or capacity (*istiṭāᶜah*) bears on its production either directly (*mubāsharah*) or indirectly (*bi'l-tawallud*). The theological problems which this production raised were legion. Starting from the Koranic premise that God was Omnipotent, the Determinists (*al-Mujbirah*) asserted that man is incapable of any activity, since he is fully determined (*majbūr*) in his actions, which are wholly created by God. In fact, actions are predicated of man purely metaphorically (*majāzan*), in exactly the same way as they are predicated of inanimate objects. Even reward and punishment are a matter of compulsion (*jabr*).[19] The Traditionists, like Ibn Ḥanbal and his school, tended to agree with this thesis, but in their deference to the sacredness of the Koranic text, they refused to even debate these questions, and so did the Ashᶜarites in the tenth century, who virtually inherited all the basic presuppositions of the *Mujbirah*.

Against this gloomy background heightened by the explicitness of the Traditions on the question of predestination, as well as the ambiguity of the Koran, the Muᶜtazilite school as a whole affirmed capacity as a precondition of morality. As adumbrated by al-Shahrastānī, their moral theory consisted in the view "that the servant is the creator of his deeds, good or bad, and is deserving of reward and punishment in the life-to-come for whatever he does."[20] God, it followed from this view, was to be exonerated from the responsibility for human actions, whether good or bad, since such responsibility belonged exclusively to man. In speaking of man, or the 'servant', as the creator of his deeds, the later Muᶜtazilites simply intended to underscore this responsibility, rather than posit a second creator alongside God, as their Ashᶜarite opponents actually charged.[21]

It is perhaps not the assertion of human capacity, but rather the sophisticated way in which the Muᶜtazilah rationalized it that gave their moral doctrine its particular significance. Power, which was predicated of man, his spirit or soul, depending on the anthropology adopted by the theologian in question, was stated by some to be an accident and by others to be a more general condition of physical fitness. It was unanimously asserted, however, to precede the action. Some theologians, like Abu'l-

---

[19] See al-Shahrastānī, *al-Milal wa'l-Niḥal*, I, 87. Cf. *al-Ashᶜarī, Maqālāt*, I, 279f. and *infra*.

[20] *Al-Milal*, I, 45.

[21] Al-Juwaynī attributes to 'later Muᶜtazilites' the predication of the term creator (*khāliq*) of man. See *al-Irshād*, ed. J.D. Luciani, Paris, 1938, 106. The charge of positing man as co-creator recurs in almost all Ashᶜarite treatises and is even supported by a Tradition: "The Qadarīyah (i.e. Muᶜtazilah) are the Magians of this community." See, for instance, al-Ashᶜarī, *al-Ibānah ᶜan Uṣūl al-Diyāna*, Hyderabad, 1948, 6f. and *Maqālāt*, I, 223.

Hudhayl, maintained that it endured for a certain period of time; others, like al-Balkhī, that it did not.[22] Its impact on the object gave rise to elaborate theories of direct and indirect causation. The distinction between these two modes is crucial to understanding Mu^c^tazilite ethics. As has become abundantly clear in recent years, the Mu^c^tazilah, like the vast majority of the Mutakallimūn, subscribed to a metaphysics of atoms and accidents intended to account for observable physical processes in a manner which accorded with the Koranic world view.[23] To account for the moral efficacy of the agent and to ensure a real connection between the will and the action, they were compelled to accord to the atoms and accidents making up physical objects a certain measure of durability and continuity, and safeguard thereby the causal dependence of physical processes on the will. This is precisely what their theory of 'generation' (*tawallud* or *tawlīd*) actually did; the action stemming from the will of the agent causes it to take a certain form corresponding to this will, or else his responsibility for the action cannot be vindicated.

Bishr ibn al-Mu^c^tamir (d. 825), head of the Mu^c^tazilite school of Baghdad who apparently initiated the theory of 'generation', argued that 'generated actions,' like the pain caused by a blow of the hand, the pleasure caused by eating, the flight of the arrow when released from the bow or the perception ensuing upon use of a sense organ,—all these are of 'our own doing' and are "produced by the causes emanating from us." We are accordingly responsible for them.[24] Abu'l-Hudhayl (d. 849), head of the rival school of Baṣrah, confined the responsibility of the agent to "whatever is generated by him in such a way that he knows its modality." Everything else, he argued, is the product of God's action, such as the accidents of color, humidity, dryness and the like. In fact, this doctor appears to have restricted 'generated actions' to the motion and rest produced in the agent or in other entities, as well as their consequences, however remote.[25] Al-Naẓẓām (d. 845) was even more rigorous in restricting all actions, such as love and hate, prayer and fasting, knowledge and ignorance, to the one accident of motion; even rest was to him nothing but the act of moving in the same place twice. Anything which occurs out-

---

[22] See al-Ash^c^arī, *Maqālāt*, I, 229f. On the question of the essence of man, some, like al-Naẓẓām and Mu^c^ammar, identified it with spirit; others, like ^c^Abbād ibn Sulaymān, said that it is body; others still, like Bishr ibn al-Mu^c^tamir, that it is the union of both. See *Maqālāt*, II, 329f., and ^c^Abd al-Jabbār, *al-Mughnī*, XI, 310f.

[23] See M. Fakhry, *Islamic Occasionalism and its Critique by Averroës and Aquinas*, London, 1958, Ch. I, and *Maqālāt*, II, 301ff. Cf. H. Daiber, *Das theologisch-philosophische System des Mu^c^ammar Ibn ^c^Abbād as-Sulamī (gest. 830 n. Chr.)*, Beirut-Wiesbaden 1975.

[24] See al-Ash^c^arī, *Maqālāt*, II, 401f.

[25] *Ibid.*, 402f.

side the 'locus of man', on the other hand, is the product of God's action "through a creative necessity", such as the falling of the stone or the flight of the arrow. By this creative necessity, al-Naẓẓām, a qualified naturalist, apparently meant, as al-Ashʿarī observes, that God had endowed the object upon its creation with a specific nature (*ṭabʿ*), which determines its subsequent operations in a necessary manner, all physical entities and properties having been created initially and at once.[26]

Other Muʿtazilite doctors, such as Muʿammar (first half of ninth century), denied that motion and rest are generated acts, confining this property to the will and related psychic phenomena, like knowledge, hatred and perception. Still others, such as Thumāmah (d. 828), confined it exclusively to motion. Everything other than will is "produced without a producer", such as the falling of the stone when catapulted by man, to whom the action is attributed purely metaphorically.[27]

As already mentioned, actions were either directly (*mubāshar*) or indirectly produced (*mutawallid*). Accordingly, late Muʿtazilite authors, like ʿAbd al-Jabbār (d. 1025), al-Jubbāʾī (d. 915) and Abū Hāshim (d. 933), dwelt at length on these two divisions which amounted in fact to primary and secondary operations. Sounds, pains and composition were asserted to be generated or secondary effects; others, like will and similar psychic phenomena, as primary. Still others, such as the modes (*akwān*) of motion, rest, composition and location, were sometimes regarded as primary, sometimes as secondary. As to the external accidents of colors, tastes, sounds and smells, as well as life, power and body, they were produced neither directly nor indirectly by man, but only by God, either throught a cause (*sabab*) or without a cause.[28]

This highly sophisticated disquisition on the types of action and their relation to the agent, who was asserted to be responsible for them, led the Muʿtazilah to speculate on the will and the way in which its object (*murād*) emanated from it and affected the external objects coming within its purview. The act of willing is known intuitively to us, according to ʿAbd-al-Jabbār, in exactly the same way as the act of believing, desiring or thinking is, and accordingly requires no proof. For, as he writes, "no rational person can deny that he is able to intend the action, will or choose it, as well as discriminate between this specific condition (of choice) and

---

26 *Maqālāt*, II, 403f, Cf. *al-Mughnī*, IX, 11, and M. Fakhry, *History of Islamic Philosophy*, 49f.

27 *Ibid.*, II, 407. Cf. *al-Mughnī*, IX, 11. ʿAbd al-Jabbār reports the vaccilation of this scholar on the author of this kind of action, whom he identified sometimes with God, sometimes with physical objects. Cf. also *al-Milal*, I, 71; al-Baghdādī, *al-Farq bayn al-Firaq*, Beirut, 1973, 319 and 328.

28 *Ibid.*, IX, 13f. Cf. 125f.

that of aversion, or between what he wills (or wants) from himself and from another.''[29]

A fundamental characteristic of the willed action is its correspondence with what the will originally intended. For it is logically impossible that the action should occur in a determinate way, unless the will has deliberately determined this occurrence, and brought it about through the organs of the body.[30] In this and other respects, the will differs from both wish and desire in the following ways: (a) will determines the occurrence of the action, as just mentioned, but desire does not, (b) will may be directed towards a repugnant object, but desire may not, (c) enjoyment is a by-product of desire, but not of will, (d) desire may grow or wane, whereas the will remains constant, and (e) will is within our power, but desire is not. Likewise, wish differs from will in a number of ways: (a) it can have a bearing on the past, as when we wish that what is done be undone, (b) it does not affect the object of wishing in any way, whereas will certainly does, as the theory of 'generation' incidentally assumes, (c) will can become its own object, as when we will to will, but wish cannot, and (d) will has an opposite, but wish does not.[31].

The object of willing is simply defined by ᶜAbd al-Jabbār and his masters as that which is known to be possible, excluding thereby the impossible, in the sense of (a) what can never come to be in the absolute sense or (b) what can never come to be in a particular way.[32] As to what ought to be willed, the author denies that it depends on the willed object and argues instead that it depends on the motive (*dāᶜī*) which impels the agent to choose, as long as his will is not shackled. As to the act of willing itself, it is not an object of willing for him, despite the assertion to the contrary. That is why, as he states, that which is generated by reasoning cannot be willed, until one comes to know that it belongs to the category of belief or certain knowledge. In other words, one must understand first that it is an object of knowledge, either in the weak or the strong sense.

The key concept in this argumentation is the consciousness of the connection of the will to its object; when the motive has determined the will of the agent, he cannot but will it, as a matter of necessity. For, as his master Abū Hāshim apparently held, it is impossible that the agent should know what he is doing without willing it; this would entail that he could 'hate' what he is doing or will its opposite.[33] Nevertheless, the will does not determine the action necessarily; it would otherwise have to determine

---

[29] *Al-Mughnī*, VI, ii, 8.
[30] *Ibid.*, VI, ii, 22.
[31] *Al-Mughnī*, VI, ii, 35f.
[32] *Ibid.*, VI, ii, 78.
[33] *Al-Mughnī*, VI, ii, 80. The Arabic for hate, *yakrah*, is the antonym of will, *yurīd*; hence the plausibility of this argument.

all the consequences of this action, including the actions of others, insofar as they are caught up in the network of conditions stemming from it. This, however, is impossible, because the will of the agent can, by definition, affect his own action only. The illusion that the will determines the willed object necessarily arises from the observation that they always occur in conjunction; such conjunction does not entail causal determination, however, only temporal contiguity. This contiguity itself is not necessary, since the will can either precede the object or occur together with it. It follows that it is neither the will nor the object, but rather the 'motive' (*dāᶜī*), that determines both.[34]

The moral implications of this view are not far to seek. If the will determined the object in every way, it would have to determine its goodness or badness as well, but as we have seen, the Muᶜtazilah regarded these two moral categories as intrinsic or objective properties of the action which depended neither on the will of man nor that of God. The will simply determines that the action should occur in a certain way, which is subsequently characterized as objectively good or bad. Some actions, it is true, are morally determined by the will of God, such as the performance of the ritual prayer and other religious observances; thereupon they become acts of worship through the will. Such actions, however, belong to the category of religious, rather than moral obligation.[35]

Should the agent will what he knows with certainty to be evil, his will would be unquestionably evil and the corresponding action unquestionably blameworthy. However, to will what is only deductively known to be evil cannot be as readily determined from a moral standpoint. Its moral quality should first be deductively determined. Once it is established that it is morally evil, such as commanding what is intolerable, then it will be unquestionably proved that willing it is evil. The same is true of willing the good to no avail or in vain (*ᶜabathan*), for the futility of the action is evil, and to will such futility is equally evil. God's actions could not therefore be spoken of as entirely without purpose, without derogating from His wisdom and justice.[36] The two propositions, that God can command the intolerable (*mā lā yuṭāq*) and will the creation of the universe for no reason, were, as will appear from the next section, two major aspects of the polemic between the Muᶜtazilah and their opponents.

III. Divine Wisdom and Justice

If human capacity is regarded as the first cornerstone of Muᶜtazilite

---

[34] *Al-Mughnī*, VI, ii, 88.
[35] *Ibid.*, VI, ii, 94 and 99.
[36] *Al-Mughnī*, VI, ii, 99.

ethics, the justice and wisdom of God are the two other cornerstones of this distinctly theological ethics. The former tended to be interpreted in autonomous terms, but could obviously not be entirely divorced from their theodicy or their conception of God's role in the world, and in particular His relation to man.

As we have seen, the intrinsic goodness or badness of actions can be established on purely rational grounds; theological arguments can, however, be advanced in support of this quasi-deontological theory of right and wrong and reinforce it thereby in no small measure against the attacks of theological adversaries, such as the Ashᶜarite Voluntarists and the Jahmite and Ḥanbalite Determinists.

The Muᶜtazilah argued that the claim that God can will evil, apart from being rationally repugnant, can be rebutted on the ground that it entails frivolity (*safah*) or futility (*ᶜabath*) on the part of God. In addition, to induce man to desire evil and be repelled by the good contradicts the very essence of desire, as the urge to will the good, and of revulsion, as the urge to avoid evil. It would also rob man of the opportunity to earn the reward meted out by God to those who choose the right.[37]

Moreover, to will evil is evil. Accordingly, God can neither will the evil done by others nor initiate it Himself. If one were to object, in the manner of Voluntarists and Determinists, that the divine act of willing determines the goodness of the action, just as the divine prohibition determines its badness, one would be reminded that this claim is irreconcilable with the intrinsic morality of action, which we have already established.[38] The act of commanding or prohibition, as indeed the status or condition of its author, is entirely irrelevant to the goodness or badness of the action; otherwise any command, regardless of its author or its merit, would be right, and any prohibition would be wrong, but this would obviously make a mockery of the very distinction between good and evil, and render these two irreducible concepts purely arbitrary.

The theological complement of this argument is skillfully presented by ᶜAbd al-Jabbār. Prior to revelation (*al-samᶜ*), man cannot be expected to recognize certain actions as obligatory except through natural reason, as shown by the case of atheists and naturalists, such as the already-mentioned Brahmins (*al-Barāhi mah*), who deny revelation altogether.[39] It follows that he cannot be bound by any (moral) obligations whatsoever, since he cannot be expected to rationally anticipate the revealed commands upon which obligation turns.[40]

---

[37] *Al-Mughnī*, VI, ii, 218f.
[38] See *supra*, 33, and *al-Mughnī*, VI, i, 102f.
[39] See *supra*, 34, note 10.
[40] *Al-Mughnī*, VI, ii, 232.

It is, moreover, incompatible with God's justice, affirmed repeatedly in the Koran.[41] God could not without self-contradiction will injustice and command it. Nor could He dispense His graces, such as the grace of guidance (*al-hady*) or provision (*rizq*), freely to some and deny them to others. Indeed, the very conception of such graces, especially guidance, implies that they are dispensed universally, rather than selectively. Those who persist in their error and refuse to be guided obviously have only themselves to blame.[42]

Whether God could be described as capable (*qādir*) of doing wrong and refraining from right was apparently a highly debatable question in theological circles, both Mujbirite and Muᶜtazilite, and it is not without interest to note that, in consonance with their vindication of divine justice, the Muᶜtazilites, including al-Naẓẓām, al-Aswārī (d. middle ninth century) and al-Jāḥiẓ (d. 868), denied this thesis, despite the protestations of their opponents that this would entail the limitation of God's power. Other Muᶜtazilites, like Abu'l-Hudhayl, Abū Hāshim and ᶜAbd al-Jabbār, however, qualified this thesis in a subtle way. God, they argued, is capable of wrongdoing, but does not actually do wrong, by virtue of His wisdom and mercy, thereby satisfying the double requirement of omnipotence and justice.[43]

ᶜAbd al-Jabbār inveighs in particular against the Mujbirite view that the denial of God's capability of wrong-doing involves a limitation of His power, on the grounds that it rests on a misconception of the relation between His actions and His will. The divine will bears either on what is an object of God's power or that of His creatures, including man. That which is an object of divine power is inexorable and irreversible; that which is an object of the creature's power is either compulsory or voluntary. The fact that voluntary actions do not always accord with the divine will does not entail any deficiency or weakness in God, since it was His intent initially that the agent should choose the action freely and earn thereby the reward attached to the deed. Should the agent nonetheless fail to act rightly, the responsibility should be imputed to his 'evil choice' rather than to God's.[44]

A major corollary of divine justice, as conceived by the Muᶜtazilah, was the duty incumbent on God to act in accordance with the universal precepts of wisdom. The three test cases of this thesis that were actively debated in theological circles were: (a) whether God had created mankind

---

[41] ᶜAbd al-Jabbār quotes the following Koranic verses: 3:108; 40:31.

[42] *Al-Mughnī*, VI, ii, 238f.

[43] *Al-Mughnī*, VI, i, 127f. Cf. al-Ashᶜarī, *Maqālāt*, I, 200f. and II, 555f.

[44] *Al-Mughnī*, VI, ii, 256f. and 274.

for a reason (ᶜ*illah*), (b) whether God could demand what is intolerable (*mā lā yuṭāq*), and (c) whether God could torture the innocent, without any reward (*bilā* ᶜ*iwaḍ*).

Some of the Muᶜtazilah, such as ᶜAbbād ibn Sulaymān (d. 864), denied that God's creation had a reason, or, such as Muᶜammar,[45] that the infinite series of reasons could be exhausted, every reason according to them having a reason *ad infinitum*, but the majority asserted in response to the first question that God had created mankind for a positive reason, which they identified with their own advantage (*manfa*ᶜ*ah*).

ᶜAbd al-Jabbār regards the first thesis as an instance of the more general maxim that God can only act for the sake of the good (*al-ḥasan*). To prove his point, he impales the opponent on the horns of a dilemma: whether God created mankind (a) to benefit, (b) to harm, or (c) neither to benefit nor to harm it. (b) and (c) are incompatible with God's justice and wisdom—in the first case, because God's intent would be definitely evil, and this is contrary to His justice, and in the second, because a knowing agent (ᶜ*ālim*) must act for the sake of a definite purpose, and this we know from (b) to be the good. It follows that God can only create mankind in order to benefit it.[46] The subsidiary alternative that God has created the world accidentally (*bi'l-ittifāq*) is discounted on the ground that the creation of every entity in its specific location clearly proves that it was created for a purpose.[47]

What befits God to create in the first instance, according to this theologian, is a living, perceiving (*mudrik*) and desiring entity. Such an entity need not direct its perception or desire, and consequently the satisfaction of desire, towards anything external to it; in other words, its activity of perception or desire could be entirely self-centered. The other attributes we associate with the living, such as power, knowledge and will, are not necessary; God is not compelled therefore to create them. Even the creation of space and time, as well as the vault of heaven and the orb of the world, is not necessary for vindicating God's goodness, since it is possible for the living, perceiving and desiring entity to achieve its goal, which is pleasure, without any of these external conditions.[48] From this it appears that by the 'advantage' stipulated by this theologian and his school should be understood as pleasure, or the satisfaction of desire. This pleasure is of two kinds: (a) direct or conducive to this satisfaction instantly, and (b)

---

[45] Al-Ashᶜarī, *Maqālāt*, I, 253. Cf. al-Khayyāṭ. *K. al-Intiṣār*, 26. Cf. Daiber, *Mu*ᶜ*ammar*, 236f.

[46] *Al-Mughnī*, XI, 58f.

[47] *Ibid.*, 66.

[48] *Ibid.*, 72.

indirect or attended by temporary pain, but resulting in eventual satisfaction. The hedonistic theory, which defines pleasure as relief from pain, adopted as we shall see by contemporary philosophers such as Miskawayh, is rejected by ᶜAbd al-Jabbār on the grounds that certain positive pleasures, on the one hand, and certain positive pains, on the other, are intuitively known to be generically different; we could not without circularity define one in terms of the other.[49]

More pertinent to his theological purposes, perhaps is ᶜAbd al-Jabbār's division of advantages into deserved and undeserved. The former is subdivided into (a) what is earned by the agent as a reward for his actions, and (b) what is dispensed by someone else as restitution or payment of what is due. Undeserved reward, on the other hand, is a matter of gracious benevolence (*tafaḍḍul*) on the part of the benefactor. It follows that God's actions are good in four different respects: (a) insofar as they benefit man directly, such as the creation of life or reason, (b) insofar as they benefit him indirectly, such as the creation of animals and inanimate objects to serve him, (c) insofar as they are conducive to his being rewarded for his good deeds, such as the creation of obligation and pains, and (d) insofar as they are conducive to the creation of the world at large in a specific way.[50]

God, however, is not compelled, by reason of His essential goodness, as the Neo-Platonists have argued, to create this world or any other at the specific time He has created it. For "the knowledge of the goodness of the object by the agent does not entail its production necessarily, but simply the possibility of choosing it for that reason, and the fact that, accordingly, His choice would be good for that reason (. . .) For motives do not necessitate the action, but only that its choice is more justifiable than any other."[51] In short, God is at liberty to create or not to create the world at any time or in any manner He pleases, through an act of gratuitous benevolence (*tafaḍḍul*). This was obviously ᶜAbd al-Jabbār's answer to those Ashᶜarites and Determinists who accused the Muᶜtazilah and the Neo-Platonists of subjecting God to a creative imperative which He could not violate. And it is noteworthy that Muslim Neo-Platonists, like al-Fārābī and Ibn Sīnā, were in fact driven by the inexorable logic of divine goodness to describe the emanation of the world from God in necessary or quasi-necessary terms.[52]

With this rigorous conception of the justice and wisdom of God went

---

[49] *Ibid.*, XI, 80, cf. *infra*, 72.
[50] *Ibid.*, XI, 84f.
[51] *Ibid.*, 98. Cf. p. 125.
[52] See M. Fakhry, *History of Islamic Philosophy*, 118 and 156f.

the Muᶜtazilite thesis that God could not demand the intolerable from His creation. The very concept of obligation (*taklīf*), as well as the already mentioned imperative of grace or benevolence, logically entailed that God's demands be rationally tolerable. In their desire to magnify God's power, the Determinists and Ashᶜarites who went so far as to ascribe to God the capacity to demand the intolerable tended in fact to derogate from His wisdom and justice, according to the Muᶜtazilah.[53]

The concrete instance of demanding the intolerable or perpetrating it was the capacity, ascribed to God by the Determinists and the Ashᶜarites, to inflict unrequited pain on His creatures. Accordingly, the discussion of suffering figured prominently in theological treatises. Its reality, like that of other psychic affections, is for ᶜAbd al-Jabbār unquestionable.[54] Its divisions are two: (a) some pains are praiseworthy, such as putting up with hardship for the sake of a noble cause, or bearing a small pain for the sake of a greater advantage, and (b) other pains are entirely evil, because they result in unqualified injury (*ḍarar*). An agent is not justified in inflicting the latter type of pain on others, for such infliction is entirely unjust (*ẓulm*), injustice being defined as "every action not attended by an advantage exceeding it, or aimed at warding off an undeserved or inordinate injury."[55] So long as the action is a cause of unqualified injury (*ḍarar*), and so long as it is pointless or futile (*ᶜabath*), it is an unqualified evil, regardless of whether it is perpetrated by God or man. It follows therefore that the claim of the Mujbirah and their followers that God can torture children and brutes and inflict other forms of sickness or suffering on mankind, is entirely false. It was predicated on the thesis, universally rejected by the Muᶜtazilah, as will appear more clearly in the next chapter, that actions of this kind are perfectly justified since they are performed by God. The goodness or badness of actions was for them entirely independent of the status of the agent or his relationship to the action, being intrinsic qualities intuitively known by reason as self-evident.[56] We should not, however, in determining the moral quality of a painful action, overlook the many aspects of the action, which, though *prima facie* evil, may in reality be good. Thus pain or injury should only be regarded as unqualified evil once the following conditions are fulfilled: (a) it is not counterbalanced by a greater advantage, (b) it is not counterbalanced by the repulsion of a greater pain or injury, (c) it is not requited altogether, and (d) it is not an object of belief (*ẓann*) rather than of certainty.[57]

---

53 *Al-Mughnī*, XIV, 156f.
54 *Ibid.*, XIII, 229f.
55 *Ibid.*, 298f.
56 *Ibid.*, 303f. Cf. al-Baghdādī, *Uṣūl al-Dīn*, Istanbul, 1928, 240f. and al-Baqillānī, *al-Tamhīd*, ed. R.J. McCarthy, Beirut, 1957, 254 and 341f.
57 *Ibid.*, 316f.

CHAPTER TWO

ETHICAL VOLUNTARISM: THE EARLY DETERMINISTS AND THE ASHᶜARITES

I. The Divine will as the Ground of Right and Wrong

The Muᶜtazilite theologians, who, as we have seen, had developed in the ninth century a quasi-deontological theory of right and wrong fit into a peculiar theological framework, were arguing against an established theory, attributed by ᶜAbd al-Jabbār and other heresiographers to the Mujbirah, or early Determinists.

Three major representatives of this school are mentioned by al-Ashᶜarī, our earliest authority, and his successors: Jahm ibn Ṣafwān (d. 746), Ḍirār ibn ᶜAmr (d. middle of eighth century) who is sometimes regarded as a Muᶜtazilite, and al-Ḥusayn ibn Muḥammad al-Najjār (d. middle of the ninth century). Other less important figures are Muḥammad ibn ᶜĪsā, nick-named Burghūth (the Flea) and Bishr ibn Ghiyāth al-Marīsī (d. ca 33).[1] From the scant information that has come down to us, it appears that these Determinists were unanimous that God is the real author of every action or occurrence in the world, and that accordingly voluntary actions are imputed to man purely metaphorically. In fact, as one authority has put it, "actions are imputed to him, just as they are imputed to inanimate objects, and just as we say (for instance) that the tree bore fruit, water flowed, the stone moved, the sun rose and set (...)"[2]

Apart from this Determinist maxim, their teaching revealed considerable divergence, but it is significant that they did not devote as much attention to the distinction between right and wrong as their Muᶜtazilite rivals had done. However, it is a fair inference from their general theological and moral presuppositions that they identified right with what God wills or commands and wrong with what He prohibits. Jahm, the most illustrious Determinist we are told by al-Ashᶜarī, surprisingly accepted (*intaḥala*) the Muᶜtazilite theory of right and wrong, or approved (*maᶜrūf*) and disapproved (*munkar*), as he had accepted their view of the created Koran and the identity of attribute and essence in God.[3]

---

[1] See al-Ashᶜarī, *Maqālāt*, I, 279–85; al-Shahrastānī, *al-Milal*, I, 85–91 and al-Baghdādī, *al-Farq*, 195–202.

[2] *Al-Milal*, I, 87.

[3] See al-Ashᶜarī, *Maqālāt*, I, 279 and al-Khayyāṭ, *K. al-Intiṣār*, 92.

More sophisticated, however, was the speculation of al-Najjār, a vehement rival of al-Naẓẓām, on the question of right and wrong. He is reported to have argued that actions, whether right or wrong, are of the creation (*khalq*) of God, and the doing (*fiᶜl*) of man—an obvious rebuttal of the Muᶜtazilite thesis that man is the 'creator' of his deeds. His conception of the divine will, however, was so encompassing that it left nothing out, whether in the domain of acting or willing, so that both good and evil, justice and injustice were comprehended within it. It followed therefore that the very determination of right and wrong was, according to him, an object of this will. When empowered to act, through the capacity (*istiṭāᶜah*) which God creates in him at the time of action, as the Ashᶜarites were to hold a generation later, it was still possible for 'an act of obedience' to exist apart from the act of disobedience, or sin, corresponding to it simply through the divine determination.[4] He also allowed that God could punish innocent children in the life to come or withhold punishment from them, as He pleased. His many writings on such subjects as justice and injustice, the 'necessitating', capacity, the divine decree and predestination (*qaḍāᵓ wa-qadar*), although lost, strongly suggest that al-Najjār was exercised by many of the problems which exercised the Muᶜtazilite theologians as well, and that he had in fact reacted against their ethical rationalism by seeking the ground of good and evil in the divine will.[5]

However, these early Determinists were superseded in the tenth century by the Ashᶜarites, who virtually took over all their major tenets, to refine and develop them. Almost simultaneously, Abū Manṣūr al-Māturīdī of Samarqand (d. 944) developed, in his *Kitāb al-Tawḥīd*, a voluntarist ethical theory which was analogous to that of al-Ashᶜarī. Thus on the questions of divine justice and wisdom, creation and acquisition and the nature of right and wrong, their positions are almost identical. Accordingly, the dependence of both the Ashᶜarite and Māturīdī schools on their Mujbirite predecessors is confirmed; the identity of their views on such fundamental issues could not have been purely fortuitous.[6]

The impact of the Ashᶜarite school has been so decisive in the subsequent history of Islamic theology and ethics that al-Māturīdī's contribution to the ethical controversy can be accorded no more than a casual mention; besides, it lacked the subtlety and sophistication of parallel contributions by Ashᶜarite doctors, whose thought is far more prototypical.

---

4 Al-Ashᶜarī, *Maqālāt*, I, 283.

5 For a list of his writings,, see Ibn al-Nadīm, *al-Fihrist*, Cairo, 269.

6 For al-Māturīdī's views, see *Kitāb al-Tawḥīd*, ed. F. Kholeif, Beirut, 1970, 215f., 221f., 225f. *et passim*.

Abu'l-Ḥasan al-Ashᶜarī (d. 935), the founder of the school which was named after him, took an almost diametrically opposed stand on all the major ethical questions adumbrated by the Muᶜtazilah. Thus on the question of the obligation, he denied that reason stipulates anything as morally or religiously necessary. The knowledge of God, for instance, may be attained (*taḥṣul*) through reason, but it becomes obligatory (*tajib*) only through revelation. Similarly, gratitude, rewarding the pious and punishing the sinner are 'necessitated' through revelation, rather than through reason. For, as al-Shahrastānī (d. 1153), a subtle and erudite Ashᶜarite author, has put it: "Upon God nothing is rationally incumbent, neither the good nor the better, not even grace (*luṭf*). For whatsoever is stipulated by reason as a matter of necessitating wisdom, can be countered by its contrary from a different standpoint."[7] The very concept of obligation is not incumbent upon God insofar as it entails no advantage to Him or wards off any injury. Not that God is incapable of imparting every grace or advantage to mankind, but the ground of imparting it is not any abstract moral precept, such as the Muᶜtazilite concept of divine justice and wisdom, but rather the unfettered and gratuitous benevolence (*ifḍāl, tafaḍḍul*) of the Benefactor Who, as the Koran has put it, "shall not be questioned as to what He does, but they shall be questioned."[8]

We have in this account of obligation the complete reversal of the position of the Muᶜtazilah to which al-Ashᶜarī had until his fortieth year actually subscribed. That this was the consensus of the Ashᶜarite school in the tenth and eleventh centuries may be inferred from the list of fundamental principles (*uṣūl*) accepted by the mass of Ashᶜarite theologians and set forth by an eminent Ashᶜarite authority of the eleventh century, ᶜAbd al-Qāhir al-Baghdādī (d. 1037), in *al-Farq bayn al-Firaq*.

The actions of responsible agents are divided by al-Baghdādī into: (a) obligatory (*wājib*), (b) prohibited (*maḥẓūr*), (c) promulgated (*masnūn*), (d) bad (*makrūh*), and (e) permissible (*mubāḥ*).[9] By obligatory we are to understand what God has commanded as a matter of necessity in such a way that its omission is a sin deserving of punishment. By prohibited, on the other hand, we are to understand what God has countermanded in such a way that its perpetration is likewise deserving of punishment. The promulgated action is in an intermediate position: whoever performs it will be rewarded, but whoever omits it will not be punished. The bad, on the other hand, is that action whose omission is rewarded whereas its per-

---

7 *Al-Milal*, I, 102.
8 Koran, 21:23 (trans. Arberry).
9 Cf. ᶜAbd al-Jabbār's list, *supra*, 32.

petration is left unpunished. Finally, the permissible is not an object of reward or punishment at all.[10]

The grounds for such an obligation, whether in the domain of speaking or acting, is God's command and prohibition. Had no command (*amr*) or prohibition (*nahy*) emanated from God, the human agent would have been liable to no obligation whatsoever, contrary to the contention of the Muᶜtazilah and the Barāhimah, who alleged that obligation is a matter of reasoning or deduction, accessible to man prior to the advent of revelation.[11]

Al-Juwaynī (d. 1085), illustrious teacher of al-Ghazālī, confirms this account of al-Baghdādī. The only grounds of moral goodness or badness is, for him, revelation (*samᶜ*) and the religious law (*sharᶜ*). For nothing is good in itself or bad in itself, because goodness and badness are neither generic nor essential qualities of the action. The good is what is commanded by the religious law, whereas the bad is what is proscribed.[12]

The claim of the Muᶜtazilah that goodness and badness, being essential characteristics of the action, can be rationally known is rejected by this Ashᶜarite author, on the grounds that the presumption of intuitive certainty in the apprehension of good and evil is contradicted by the disagreement of vast numbers of people on the allegedly certain maxims of morality. Moreover, many actions deemed necessarily bad by the Muᶜtazilah, such as unrequited suffering, are attributed to God and consequently regarded as positively good; accordingly, the goodness of such actions cannot be an intrinsic quality intuitively and indubitably known through reason.[13]

The other Muᶜtazilite argument already discussed in the previous chapter,[14] that the goodness and badness of certain actions is rationally known even to those who, like the Brahmins and the atheists, deny revelation altogether, is discounted by al-Juwaynī on the grounds that it rests on an equivocation. Those irreligious groups do not have a certain knowledge (*ᶜilm*) of right and wrong, but only belief (*iᶜtiqād*). Moreover, many actions regarded by them as evil, such as slaughtering animals and inflicting pain and hardship on them, are regarded as perfectly permissible by the majority of mankind.[15]

A related Muᶜtazilite argument, which has also been broached ear-

---

10 See al-Baghdādī, *al-Farq*, 337. Cf. *Uṣūl al Dīn*, 207f.
11 *Al-Farq*, 338.
12 Al-Juwaynī, *al-Irshād*, 148f.
13 *Ibid.*, 150.
14 See *supra*, 34.
15 *Al-Irshād*, 151.

lier, is that reasonable men everywhere regard charity (*iḥsān*), rescuing the drowning and coming to the aid of the dying as good, injustice and aggression as evil, regardless of whether they have been stipulated by revelation or not. The goodness or badness of such actions is rooted in customary usage (*ᶜādah*). It is refuted by al-Juwaynī on the grounds that many actions, such as allowing slaves to engage in debauchery, are reprehensible, whereas the lawgiver has permitted them.[16]

The second major line of reasoning adopted by al-Juwaynī in refuting the deontological position of the Muᶜtazilah is the consideration of the connotation of the term obligatory (*wājib*). Obligatory, according to him, may mean what devolves as a duty either upon man or upon God. In the first instance, obligatory is synonymous with the rationally good, and the Ashᶜarite strictures against the Muᶜtazilite position on this score have already been examined. In the second, obligation, insofar as it involves the notion of constraint (*ījāb, ilzām*), is not applicable at all, since God is not liable to any constraint whatsoever. In addition, it involves a relationship of subordination between commander and subject, which does not apply to God, the 'Supreme Commander', either. Finally, insofar as it refers to actions whose omission may result in injury, obligation does not apply to God, the Being who is neither liable to injury or advantage, nor to pleasure or pain.[17]

In his major scholastic treatise, *Nihāyat al-Iqdām*, which marks in may ways the culmination of the scholastic Islamic tradition, al-Shahrastānī, a generation later, marshalls an array of even more sophisticated arguments to support the Ashᶜarite position on the grounds of goodness and badness. Like al-Juwaynī, he denies that these two categories are intrinsic properties of acting, entailing *per se* reward or punishment, praise or reproach, respectively. The alleged certainty of these two moral concepts is to be distinguished from theoretical certainty. If we imagine a person born fully competent to understand and reason, but one who has not received any moral education of any kind, he will recognize at once the truth of the proposition that two is larger than one, but will suspend judgement on the proposition that lying is bad, or that it entails reproach from God. This clearly shows, according to al-Shahrastānī, that there is no analogy between theoretical and moral propositions.[18] The definition of truth is conformity between the statement and the fact, whereas falsehood is their divergence. He who apprehends this conformity or divergence will recognize the truth or falsity of a statement, without apprehending its

[16] *Ibid.*, 153.
[17] *Ibid.*, 156ff.
[18] See *Nihāyat al-Iqdām*, ed. A. Guillaume, London, 1934, 391f.

goodness or badness. It follows that these two moral concepts do not form part of the essential attributes of the statement and are not necessarily conjoined to it. Hence some true assertions are blameworthy, such as informing on the movements of a fugitive prophet, and very often good and bad are predicated of actions, in accordance with conventions prevalent at a certain time or place, whereby people designate as bad what is harmful to them, and good what is profitable.[19]

An interesting variation on this "intuitionist" theory is attributed to the philosophers, by whom al-Shahrastānī obviously means the Neo-Platonists of the type of Ibn Sīnā. Those philosophers, he argues, divide being into absolute good, absolute evil and a mixture of both. The absolute good is identified by them with the desirable in itself, whereas the absolute evil is identified with the undesirable in itself, and the mixed type with the partly desirable, partly undesirable in itself. Now it is indubitable, according to them, that the desirable is morally good (*mustaḥsan*) and the undesirable is bad, 'sound human nature' calling us to choose the first and shun the second, regardless of whether it is prescribed by a lawgiver (*shāriᶜ*) or not. Examples of the first type of actions are the virtues of temperance, generosity, courage and succor; examples of the second one, the corresponding vices.

Moreover, the perfection of man consists in fulfilling his intellectual and practical capabilities, by emulating God and the spiritual beings, according to the measure of human capacity. Religions have simply confirmed what reason has already discovered, rather than modify or alter it; these would have been unnecessary but for the deficiencies of individual reasons and their liability to error. Accordingly, divine wisdom has stipulated that religious ordinances and beliefs be laid down, so as to guide mankind to the modes of right living and inform them of the rewards and punishments meted out to them in the life-to-come, to insure thereby the preservation of their species and of the universal order of the world.[20]

In his rebuttal, al-Shahrastānī observes that the philosophers' threefold division of being is contradicted by their well-known equation of being with goodness and non-being with evil. This twofold division, however, leaves undetermined the moral status of actions, which varies with varying relations and circumstances and cannot be known speculatively. Accordingly, the nature of obligation and the reward and punishment attached to it cannot be known either.

---

[19] *Ibid.*, 373. Cf. al-Juwaynī, *al-Irshād*, 143.

[20] *Ibid.*, 375. Cf. al-Shahrastānī's account of Ibn Sīnā's theory of good and evil and their moral implications, in *al-Milal wa'l-Niḥal*, II, 39f. and Ibn Sīnā, *Aḥwāl al-Nafs*, ed. A.F. al-Aḥwānī, Cairo, 1952, 127f.

Al-Shahrastānī further observes that the philosophers' theory of happiness and misery, predicated on the actualization of man's intellectual aptitudes, is shot through with difficulties. According to them, this actualization depends ultimately on the Necessary Being, who through the intermediary of the active intellect, fulfills the intellectual and moral nature of man and otherwise operates in the world. Individual intellects, argues al-Shahrastānī in rebuttal of this view, may elicit intuitively the first principles depending on them, but may not elicit the mode of their necessity or whether they are universally obligatory or not. Only the prophet assisted and inspired by God can. That is why we hold, he concludes, that the principles of knowledge are known through reason, but become obligatory through revelation only.[21]

What determines the validity of obligations in the Muᶜtazilite view, as we have seen, is ultimately divine wisdom. The Muᶜtazilah, according to this Ashᶜarite doctor, simply misunderstood the connotation of wisdom. By wisdom we should understand, he argues, "the occurrence of the action in accordance with the foreknowledge [of the agent], regardless of whether any interest or purpose is involved or not."[22] God's actions are by definition wise, insofar as they invariably occur in accordance with His foreknowledge, and are conditioned by no other factor than His will. In fact, the whole concept of an obligation incumbent on God, or of a necessary desert (*istiḥqāq*) due to the creature, is entirely irrational; God, who has dispensed to mankind His infinite blessings is under no obligation to reward them, or even to create them in the first place.

Another argument may be advanced against the concept of an obligation rationally incumbent on God. Prior to revelation, reason could not discover the truth of the proposition that God is the author of those commands or prohibitions which constitute the substance of obligation (*taklīf*), since the attribute of commanding and prohibiting is not an essential attribute of God.[23] By this subtle argument, al-Shahrastānī appears to mean that, being relational attributes, commanding and prohibiting cannot be rationally predicated of God prior to the act of His commanding, through the intermediary of the Prophet, certain actions as lawful and prohibiting others as unlawful. Reason can establish at best the possibility (*jawāz*) of these attributes prior to the revelation of God's commands and prohibitions, but not their necessity.

---

[21] *Nihāyat*, 391f.
[22] *Ibid.*, 385.
[23] *Ibid.*, 385.

II. Capacity and Acquisition (*kasb*)

The early Determinists (*Mujbirah*), as we have already mentioned, tended to rule out the role of the agent in human activity and to refer, probably in agreement with the general predestinarian sentiments of the public and the learned Traditionists, all activity to God. The Ashᶜarite doctors were in sympathy with the substance of this Determinist view, but tried, on the one hand, to offer dialectical justification for it and, on the other hand, to reconcile it to the phenomenon of human responsibility. Accordingly, they rejected, as we are also told by al-Baghdādī, the two extreme theses of the Mujbirah and the Muᶜtazilah. By describing man as the 'creator' (*khāliq*) of his deeds, in the manner of late Muᶜtazilite authors,[24] the former had repudiated the uniqueness of God as sole Creator; the latter had repudiated His justice.[25] The Ashᶜarites substituted for the determinism (*jabr*) of the first group and the libertarianism (*qadar*) of the second, the concept of acquisition (*kasb* or *iktisāb*), which became from the tenth century on the touchstone of orthodoxy in religious circles.

This elusive concept was given a certain measure of articulation by the Ashᶜarite doctor al-Bāqillānī (d. 1013), probably for the first time. In his best-known work, *al-Tamhīd*, he brings out vividly the relation between the three foregoing cognate concepts. Is man capable (*mustaṭīᶜ*) of earning (*kasb*) the credit for his action, he asks in the opening part of the chapter dealing with capacity (*istiṭāᶜah*), and answers this question in the affirmative. He adds by way of amplification that man knows instinctively (*min nafsih*) the difference between voluntary actions, such as standing up or sitting, and involuntary actions, such as trembling or convulsion. He knows likewise that the two types of action do not differ in point of genus, place or will, but rather in point of the power created in him by God at the very moment of performing the voluntary action.[26]

Although it may appear at first sight that acquisition (*kasb*) of the action is not really different from creating (*khalq*) it, and that accordingly the Ashᶜarite position on the subject of free will or self-determination (*qadar*) is identical with that of their predecessors, the Determinists, further reflection reveals a commendable preoccupation on the part of the Ashᶜarites with the problem of finding some ground for distinguishing between them, on the one hand, and restoring a measure of responsibility to the human agent, from which he had been completely robbed by the Determinists, on the other.

---

[24] See al-Juwaynī, *al-Irshād*, 106.
[25] Al-Baghdādī, *al-Farq*, 328.
[26] *Al-Tamhīd*, 286f.

In seeking to determine this ground, al-Shahrastānī, expounding and defending the methods of al-Ashᶜari and al-Bāqillānī on the subject of acquisition, reduces it to: (a) the mode or scope of the knowledge of the object by the Creator or agent, and (b) the type of relationship of the object to the agent. The Creator has an all-comprehending knowledge of His object, whereas the human agent has a determinate and circumscribed one; the former knows the object in every detail, the latter has no more than a general and potential knowledge of it only. In addition, the 'created power' by which man acts can bear on the object (*al-maqdūr*) in a particular way also. A power which can bear on the object in a universal way is competent to produce every kind of being. For in point of being or existence (*wujūd*), all accidents or substances are alike in depending on the Creator from whom their being is derived.[27]

As to the mode of relationship of the action to the agent, al-Ashᶜarī, we are told, had denied that the 'created power' has any effect on its object, either in point of being or its many determinations. Al-Bāqillānī, on the other hand, observing the already mentioned difference between voluntary and involuntary motions, attributed it to a condition extraneous to their being, which he designated as contingency (*ḥudūth*) or possibility (*imkān*). The action, he argued, admits of a variety of conceptual aspects, whether general, such as being or contingency, on the one hand, or particular, such as colour, motion or rest, on the other. In itself, the action possesses none of these attributes; they are all entirely derived from God, with the exception of contingency. Now as a particular and contingent event, such as writing or speaking, the action is in relation to a particular agent, who is the writer, speaker, etc. This particular agent is the acquirer (*al-muktasib*), as distinguished from the creator (*al-khāliq*). The power of the former can only have a specific relation to a certain type of object or accident, whereas the latter has a universal relationship to a single object, which is being (*al-wujūd*). That is why it can bear on the production of everything at all times, unlike the 'created power', which is thoroughly circumscribed by the conditions of space and time.[28]

If we ask now whereto does the responsibility for the acquired action attach, the answer can only be to those aspects which depend on the 'created power' of the agent and are liable to change through his action, rather than to the original being, which depends, as we have seen, exclusively on the creative or 'eternal power'. Indeed, the 'created power' of the agent can never be independent of God, Who creates in him at every moment such power or capacity (*istiṭāᶜah*) as is proportionate to the

---

[27] *Nihāyat*, 70f.

[28] *Nihāyat*, 72–6. Cf. al-Bāqillānī, *al-Tamhīd*, 303ff.

production of the intended action. The human agent is by himself entirely incapable of carrying out any of his own designs, for he lacks the properties of self-sufficiency and independence, which are the genuine marks of efficacy. He knows instinctively (*min nafsih*) the measure of his dependence and his need for assistance in whatever he does; that is why he calls constantly on God to accord him such assistance and succor.[29]

III. Justice and Injustice as Applied to God

Despite their dramatic insistence on the supremacy of divine power, the Ashᶜarites were unanimous, as al-Baghdādī has put it, that "even had God Almighty not imposed any obligation (*taklīf*) on His servants, that would be perfectly just (. . .) They (i.e. the Ashᶜarites) also claimed that had He added to or subtracted from what He has imposed, that would be permissible, contrary to those Muᶜtazilites who denied this. Likewise, had He refrained from creating the world, He would not thereby violate the precepts of wisdom (. . .) and had the Almighty created inanimate objects without creating the animate, that would be permissible too (. . .) To Him belongs the power to command and to prohibit, and the judgement; He does what He pleases and judges as He wills."[30] The scope of God's power and will was so all-embracing that any limitation of this scope, in the name of His wisdom, would be a completely unwarranted repression (*hajr*). God's activities and decisions are not subject to any transcendental norms or precepts, other than the dictates of His will.

As one might expect, the major line of attack on the Muᶜtazilite concept of a transcendental and objective system of duties and obligation, to which even the Almighty was subject by virtue of His wisdom and benevolence, was the linguistic line. One primary connotation of justice, argues this eminent Ashᶜarite, is that type of action one is empowered to do; the second connotation is that type of action which is in conformity with the divine command (*amr*). Contrariwise, injustice (*jawr, ẓulm*) denotes actions improperly done, or done in violation of God's command.[31] It follows at once from this double definition that justice and injustice should be determined in terms of the relationship of the agent or his action to God, as Supreme Commander or Ruler, and that accordingly those two terms have no application to God whatsoever. In fact, what God does or decrees is by definition just; what he refrains from doing or prohibits is unjust. If accordingly it is asked whether it is permisible (*yajūz*) for God

---

29 *Ibid.*, 87f.
30 *Al-Farq*, 331f. Cf. *Uṣūl al-Dīn*, 145f.
31 See *Uṣūl al-Dīn*, 131f.

to torture children, order the beasts to be slaughtered and made to suffer, and to demand from His servants the intolerable (*mā lā yuṭāq*), without any reward or advantage accruing to them, we would answer, writes al-Bāqillānī: "Yes, for this would be just, if done by Him, and permissible (*jāʾiz*) and praiseworthy (*mustaḥsan*) as far as His wisdom goes."[32]

To justify this rigid voluntarism, it is enough, according to this Ashʿarite doctor, to recognize the fundamentally different grounds of right and wrong, as applied to our actions and those of God. The above-mentioned actions are regarded as evil or unjust, simply by virtue of their being prohibited by God; had He not prohibited them, they would not, if done by us, be evil. The grounds of goodness and badness are not rationally determined, otherwise all reasonable men would concur in recognizing those grounds, and particular actions would be good or bad to the extent they partake of the particular property of the reprehensible action.[33] God, being the "ruler and conqueror (*al-qāhir*) to Whom all things belong (. . .) and over Whom no commander (*āmir*), who permits or prohibits, has any say," it follows that His actions can never be decried as evil, by analogy to our actions.[34]

Moreover, were the badness of the inflicting of suffering (*īlām*), without advantage or reward, evident *per se* (*li-nafsih*), its evil would be apprehended necessarily (*iḍṭirāran*), but this is far from being the case. In the second place, the action in question would be universally bad, regardless of the agent, or the place in which the action occurs. Consider, however, the case of motion *per se* (*li-nafsihā*); it is motion wherever it occurs, and that (although this proviso is left out by al-Bāqillānī) regardless of the cause initiating it. The inflicting of unrequited pain would by analogy be evil even if committed by a beast, and this beast would be deserving of reprisal and would be designated a sinner (*fāsiq*). However, the general consensus of mankind (*al-ittifāq*) shows this to be false.[35]

Significantly enough, al-Bāqillānī does not rule out rational deduction in substantiating this voluntarist thesis. If it is asked whether God, who is at liberty to act so ruthlessly in the world, can commit a falsehood (*kādhib*), the answer would be no. However, it is not because such commission is morally reprehensible (*yustaqbaḥ minh*); but rather because the attribute truthful (*ṣādiq*) is one of the essential attributes of God and He cannot therefore without contradiction be said to lie. The case of commanding falsehood or sin is entirely different; were He to command them, they

---

[32] *Al-Tamhīd*, 341.
[33] See *al-Tamhīd*, 341f. and 293f.
[34] *Ibid.*, 342.
[35] *Ibid.*, *loc.cit.*

would no longer be sins, but would become instead acts of piety (*ṭāᶜah*) deserving of praise, since it is not by virtue of its genus that, as has been repeatedly mentioned, an action is sinful, but rather of the divine prohibition. "In fact, God has commanded us to lie on certain occasions; a person who is in fear for his life in the country of the infidels (*dār al-ḥarb*) has been allowed to lie."[36]

It is noteworthy, however, that the thesis that God could command (*yaʾmur*) or will (*yurīd*) evil or sinful actions was not affirmed without qualification by all Ashᶜarite doctors. To mollify the impact of the predication of the power to command evil of God, some Ashᶜarite theologians, we are told by al-Juwaynī, resorted to various linguistic expedients. When asked whether God wills the evil of infidelity or sin, some of them refused to give a specific answer, confining themselves to the general proposition that God's will bears on all contingent events (*ḥawādith*) whether good or evil, useful or harmful, and avoiding thereby the presumption that whatever God wills. He actually commands or exhorts to.[37]

Much more skillful is al-Shahrastānī's attempts to rationalize the voluntarist position of his school. It is necessary in speaking of the object in its relation to the will, he argues, to distinguish between what we might call its ontological status, on the one hand, and its moral or axiological status, on the other. All actions, insofar as they are contingent particular occurrences in the world, fall within the purview of God's all-comprehending will, and are ordered towards the universal good and order of the world, which is the 'pure good'. When God is spoken of as willing evil and disobedience, on the one hand, or goodness and righteousness, on the other, it should be clearly understood that He does not will all these things insofar as they are evil or good respectively, but rather insofar as they are events occurring in the world at specific times and according to certain specific determinations (*aqdār*). Only in relation to the acquisition (*kasb*) and capacity (*istiṭāᶜah*) of the human agent, as we have seen in the previous section, are they designated as acts of obedience or disobedience, depending on whether they conform to the divine command or not. The divine will does not bear (*tataᶜallaq*), therefore, on sins insofar as they are sins, nor does the divine power bear on the actions of the agents insofar as they are his acquisitions, but only insofar as they are morally neutral occurrences in the world, so to speak.[38]

In this subtle distinction between the action as a determinate occur-

---

36 *Ibid.*, 344.
37 See *al-Irshād*, 135f.
38 See *Nihāyat al-Iqdām*, 255f. and 258f.

rence in the world, directly referable to God's will and power, on the one hand, and as a deed performed or acquired by the human agent, on the other, al-Shahrastānī succeeds in removing the linguistic sting from the crude assertion that God is the willer (*murīd*) of sins (*al-maᶜāṣī*), without removing its moral sting. God, Who creates the action as a physical occurrence, and determines the relation of the human acquirer (*kāsib*) to it, as well as the obligation incumbent on him to conform to the command by virtue of which it becomes morally binding, cannot surely be relieved of the ultimate responsibility for bringing it about in a particular way at the hand of a particular agent at a particular time or place.

PART THREE

PHILOSOPHICAL ETHICS

CHAPTER ONE

GREEK SOURCES OF PHILOSOPHICAL ETHICS

I. Channels of Transmission

Greek ethical material found its way fairly carly into Islamic intellectual circles in one of two ways: (a) diffuse literary infiltration, and (b) textual translation or transmission.

From the ninth century on gnomological collections containing a lot of Greek ethical material were in circulation; the literary quality, as well as the moral appeal of these collections of aphorisms, recommended them to a fairly large reading public. One of the earliest collections of this type is *Nawādir al-Falāsifah* (Anecdotes of the Philosophers), translated and compiled by Ḥunayn Ibn Isḥāq (d. 873); it contains a vast amount of ethical dicta by the Greek philosophers and has influenced almost all subsequent writers.[1] Contemporaneous with Ḥunayn is the first major Arab philosopher al-Kindī (d. ca. 866), who made a compilation of Socratic excerpts (*Alfāẓ Suqrāṭ*) which parallels a similar compilation by Ḥunayn, but differs from it in some essential respects: the personality of Socrates is confused with that of Diogenes the Cynic in al-Kindī's, but not in Ḥunayn's compilation.[2]

One of the less known writers on Greek philosophy, Abu'l-Ḥasan al-ᶜĀmirī (d. 991), has written a compilation entitled *al-Saᶜādah wa'l-Isᶜād* (On Happiness and Making Happy), which contains a lot of ethical material derived from the earlier translations,[3] in addition to a historical excursus on the rise and development of wisdom from the time of Luqmān to al-ᶜĀmirī's own day, entitled *al-Amad ᶜala'l-Abad* (Time and Eternity).[4]

More substantial both in its historical scope and the erudition of its author is *Ṣiwān al-Ḥikmah* (The Closet of Wisdom) by Abū Sulaymān al-Sijistānī (d. ca. 988), which contains a large amount of ethical material

---

1 See K. Merkle, *Die Sittensprüche der Philosophen*, Leipzig, 1921. Cf. Istanbul MS. (Köprülü, I), 1608.

2 See M. Fakhry, "Al-Kindī wa-Suqrāṭ", in: *Al-Abḥāth*, 16 (1963), 23–34. Cf. Köprülü MS. 1608, fols. 22r–25r and 48r–512. Cf. D. Gutas, *Greek Wisdom Literature in Arabic Translation*, New Haven, 1975, 38f.

3 See Minovi's facsimile edition, Wiesbaden, 1957–58.

4 See E.K. Rowson's edition, Beirut, 1979. A new edition, with commented English translation, appeared in Rowson, *A Muslim Philosophy on the Soul and its Fate*, New Haven, Conn., 1988.

attributed to Pythagoras, Socrates, Plato, Aristotle, Alexander the Great, Hippocrates and Galen.[5]

Another comparatively early collection is *Al-Kalim al-Rūḥāniyyah fi'l-Ḥikam al-Yunāniyyah* (Spiritual Elements of Greek Maxims) by Abu'l-Faraj Ibn Hindū (d. 1019 or 1029), which contains numerous sayings from Greek authors, including the philosophers and poets. Its author was a contemporary of Miskawayh (d. 1030), who wrote one of the most extensive gnomological collections in Arabic. This collection purports to consist of the testament of the Persian King Hūshang to his son and the kings who succeeded him, coupled with what the author "had compiled of the testaments and moral aphorisms (*ādāb*) of the four nations, I mean the Persians, the Indians, the Arabs and the Greeks."[6] Entitled *Jāwīdān Khirad* (Eternal Wisdom), this collection embodies a series of Socratic maxims derived from Ḥunayn's already mentioned collection, a group of Hermetica, Plato's "testament to his disciple Aristotle", a testament of Aristotle to Alexander, Pythagoras' 'Golden testament', and, finally, the 'Myth of Cebes, the Platonist'. Much of this gnomological material recurs in other Arabic collections and its Greek source(s) cannot be ascertained.

By far the most extensive compilation in Arabic is a later gnomological collection entitled *Mukhtār al-Ḥikam* (Selected Maxims) written in 1048 by al-Mubashshir Ibn Fātik (d. ca. 1087), an Egyptian scholar and patrician of Syrian origin. This collection achieved great notoriety in Europe and was translated into Spanish, Latin, French, English and other languages.[7] From the start, the author states that his purpose in making his 'selection' is moral or didactic and supports his claim by quotations from the Koran and the Traditions of the Prophet. In the Preface, he writes: "I selected the statements of the divinely inspired among the sages, including the monotheists (...) and coupled them with their successors who were famous for their wisdom and good deeds." He left out everything which is incompatible with religion (*sharᶜ*), or reason, however, comparing his activity to that of the bee, which picks from every flower its sweetest parts and leaves out its vilest.[8] Al-Mubashshir's collection starts with the sermons of Hermes, identified in the Arabic tradition with the prophet Idrīs and the Biblical Enoch, and his moral maxims, followed by the maxims of Homer, Solon, Zeno, Hippocrates, Pythagoras, Diogenes, Socrates, Plato, Aristotle, Alexander the Great, Galen and many other less illustrious Greek writers. The Greek origins of many of the maxims

---

[5] See ᶜA.R. Badawī's edition, Tehran, 1974. New edition by D.M. Dunlop, The Hague-Paris-New York, 1979.

[6] Miskawayh, *Jāwīdān Khirad*, ed. ᶜA.R. Badawī, Cairo, 1952, 5f.

[7] See introduction to ᶜA.R. Badawī edition of *Mukhtār al-Ḥikam*, Madrid, 1958.

[8] *Mukhtār al-Ḥikam*, 3.

contained in this collection can be identified as Ḥunayn's *Nawādir*, Diogenes Laertius' *Lives of Eminent Philosophers*, Plato's *Phaedo* and Aristotle's *Nicomachean Ethics*, whereas the origins of many others cannot be identified. However, al-Mubashshir's collection illustrates very well the Arab fascination with Greek gnomological material, both as belles-lettres (*adab*) and as ethical or moral literature.

II. Greek Ethical Texts

More important for the development of philosophical ethics in Islam is the considerable number of writings attributed to Galen, Porphyry, Aristotle, and others, translated into Arabic as early as the middle of the ninth century. These writings had a direct impact on the moral philosophers and conditioned their views on the nature of moral activity, right and wrong, virtue, happiness, deliberation and choice, and related ethical questions. In many cases, this impact was not limited to the philosophers, but extended to the theologians, especially the rationalists among them, such as the Muᶜtazilah, as we have seen in a previous part.

One of the most important texts to be translated by Ḥunayn Ibn Isḥāq is Galen's *Peri Ethon*, whose Greek original is lost. However, the Arabic version to have reached us is an abridgement (*mukhtaṣar*), probably made by a later scholar, Abūᶜ Uthmān al-Dimashqī (d. 900).[9]

Claudius Galenus (d. c. 200) is an outstanding figure in the history of Islamic medicine, logic and ethics. His 16 medical treatises were translated into Arabic by Ḥunayn and his associates and served for centuries as the basis of medical research and instruction in Arabic. As a philosopher, his influence was equally great in the fields of logic and ethics, and we owe to him the epitomes of Plato's *Republic, Timaeus*, the *Laws* and other Dialogues which were also translated by Ḥunayn and his school. In the field of ethics, not only the *Peri Ethon*, but two other tracts, on *Man's Recognition of His Own Faults* as well as *The Advantage the Virtuous Derive from Their Enemies*, are attributed to Galen in the Arabic bibliographical tradition and are frequently referred to or quoted by the ethical philosophers, including al-Kindī, al-Rāzī and Miskawayh.[10]

As one would expect, Galen attempts in the *Peri Ethon* to bring into har-

---

[9] P. Kraus, "Kitāb al-Akhlāq li-Jālīnūs," in: *Bulletin of the Faculty of Arts* (Egyptian University), V, I (1937), 1–51. Cf. Ibn Abī Uṣaybiᶜah, *ᶜUyūn al-Anbāᵓ fī Ṭabaqāt al-Aṭibbāᵓ*, ed. N. Riḍā, Beirut, 1965, 316. Engl. trans. by J.N. Mattock, in *Islamic Philosophy and the Classical Tradition*, edited by S.M. Stern and others, Columbia, South Carolina, 1973, 235–260.

[10] See Ibn al-Nadīm, *Kitāb al-Fihrist*, Cairo, 419; Miskawayh, *Tahdhīb al-Akhlāq*, ed. C.K. Zurayk, Beirut, 1966, 189, 190; al-Rāzī, "Al-Ṭibb al-Rūhānī," in: *Rasāᵓil al-Rāzī al-Falsafiyyah*, ed. P. Kraus, Beirut, 1977, 33f.

mony the psychological and ethical teachings of Plato and Aristotle. He begins by asserting that in his book on the *Opinions of Plato and Hippocrates*, he had shown that man possesses three parts: the rational, the irascible and the concupiscent; whether these three aspects should be called parts (following Plato) or faculties (following Aristotle), or even souls, does not trouble him. He finally settles for calling them respectively the rational soul, the irascible and the concupiscent and identifies them with the human, the animal and vegetative souls. This tripartite division, as well as the terminology, became the basis of Arabic psychological taxonomy from the time of al-Kindī to Ibn Sīnā and beyond.

Equally important for the development of Islamic ethics is Galen's adoption of the Platonic table of the virtues of wisdom, courage and temperance, which correspond to each of the three parts of the soul, and of which justice is the harmony (*ittifāq*) or equilibrium (*iᶜtidāl*).[11] A parallel is then drawn between soul and body. To the extent the functions and movements of the body are in equilibrium, it is healthy and beautiful. The beauty of the soul likewise consists in knowledge and its ugliness in ignorance, and the measure of such knowledge or ignorance is determined by the nobility of the objects it seeks. Such a soul is healthy and beautiful and is able to preserve its own health and beauty, as well as those of the body on which it depends in carrying out its external operations.[12]

Another ethical treatise, which was probably translated as early as the *Nicomachean Ethics*, has been preserved as an appendix to that Ethics.[13] It was first studied and commented on by M.C. Lyons in 1960. The scribe calls it: "An introduction to the science of ethics, not attributed to an author, but I attributed it to Nicolaus." M.C. Lyons has argued that this author cannot be Nicolaus of Damascus, the well-known first-century commentator of Aristotle, but could be Nicolaus of Laodicea, who lived during the reign of Julian the Apostate (361–63), and was 'preeminent in the study of philosophy', according to Bar Hebraeus.[14] This treatise embodies material derived from Plotinus' *Enneads*, in addition to Platonic Peripatetic and Stoic material, which played a decisive role in conditioning Islamic philosophical ethics. Apart from adopting, like Galen, the tripartite theory of the soul, and the fourfold table of the cardinal virtues, it proceeds to give a detailed account of the 'specific' virtues, or subdivisions of the four 'generic' virtues, as the author calls them. This procedure became the standard practice in philosophical circles, as the elaborate tables given by Miskawayh, al-Ghazālī and others will show.

---

[11] P. Kraus, "Kitāb al-Akhlāq," 33 and 39. Cf. Mattock, *op. cit.*, 243.

[12] *Ibid.*, 43. (Mattock, 243).

[13] See ᶜA.R. Badawī's edition of Aristotle's *Kitāb al-Akhlāq*, Kuwait, 1979, 389–431.

[14] See Bar Hebraeus, *Taʾrīkh Mukhtaṣar al-Duwal*, ed. A. Ṣālḥānī, Beirut, 1958, 82. Cf. M.C. Lyons, "A Greek Ethical Treatise," in: *Oriens* 13–14 (1960–61), 48.

Another Greek text which influenced medieval Arabic and Latin ethical discussions is a summary known in Latin as the *Summa Alexandrinorum*. The extant Arabic version of this summary, whose author is unknown, contains fragments of Books I, VII and VIII of the *Nicomachean Ethics*, but the Latin version made in 1243 or 1244 by Hermann the German is more complete and is entitled: 'Translatio Alexandrina in X Libros Ethicorum'. This version was later translated into Italian and French during the thirteenth century.[15]

III. The Nicomachean Ethics

By far the most important Greek ethical text to influence Islamic ethics is Aristotle's *Nicomachean Ethics*, which was translated by Isḥāq Ibn Ḥunayn (d. 911) and commented on by al-Fārābī (d. 950), Ibn Rushd (d. 1298) and others. Although the Arabic translation has survived and was published in 1979, a puzzling feature of the Arabic *Nicomachia* is that reference is made in the original Fez manuscript as well as other sources to eleven books instead of the traditional ten, whereas the recently published edition contains only ten books, the eleventh book interposed between Books Six and Seven of the original having disappeared. In addition, Ibn al-Nadīm (d. 997), our earliest source for the translation of Greek texts, states with reference to the *Nicomachean Ethics*: "The Ethics, commented on (*fassarahu*) by Porphyry in 12 books, and translated by Isḥāq Ibn Ḥunayn."[16]

Porphyry's commentary, mentioned only in the Arabic sources is unfortunately lost, but that it was in existence during the early part of the eleventh century is confirmed by references in Miskawayh's *Tahdhīb al-Akhlāq* to 'Porphyry and others', in connection with the types of good according to Aristotle.[17] The role of Porphyry in the development of Arabic logic is well known, but there is no question that he was a major link in the transmission of Neo-Platonism into the Arab world. The summary of the last three books of the *Enneads*, translated into Arabic by ᶜAbd al-Masīḥ Ibn Nāᶜimah al-Ḥimṣī (d. 835) under the rubric of *Uthūlūjīya Arisṭūṭālīs* (The Theology of Aristotle), bears the subtitle: "A discourse on divinity commented on (*tafsīr*) by Porphyry of Tyre."[18] In addition,

---

[15] See Concetto Marchesi, *L'Etica Nicomachea nella tradizione latina medievale*, Messina, 1904. For the Arabic fragments, see D.M. Dunlop, "The Manuscript Taimur Pasha (290 aḫlāq) and the Summa Alexandrinorum," in: *Arabica*, XXI (1974), 252–63.

[16] *Kitāb al-Fihrist*, ed. Cairo, 366.

[17] *Tahdhīb al-Akhlāq*, 73 and 76. Cf. also al-Fārābī, *Al-Jamᶜ bayn Raʾyay al-Ḥakīmayn*, ed. A. Nader, Beirut, 1960, 80.

[18] ᶜA.R. Badawī, *Plotinus apud Arabes*, Cairo, 1955, 3. Cf. M. Fakhry, *History of Islamic Philosophy*, 19f.

despite the role of Aristotle, both in ethics and metaphysics, as the ground upon which Arab philosophers constructed their ethical and metaphysical systems, the cornerstone of most of these systems remains Neo-Platonic. This is particularly true of the great ethical systems, such as that of Miskawayh and al-Ghazālī, and thus the conclusion is inescapable that those philosophers continue the Neo-Platonizing interpretation of Aristotelian ethics already begun and legitimized by the great disciple of Plotinus. The teacher had remained unknown in the Arabic sources, but his disciple's name was very familiar in the rosters of logicians, commentators and ethical writers.[19]

---

[19] See R. Walzer, "Porphyry and the Arabic Tradition," 294f.

CHAPTER TWO

SOCRATIC AND STOIC PRELUDES

I. Al-Kindī (d. ca. 866) and the Ideal of *Apatheia*

The Muᶜtazilah, as we have seen, were the first genuine ethical thinkers of Islam, but although their system of ethics was grounded in the Koran and the Traditions, their debt to Greek philosophy was considerable. Thus their preoccupation with internal coherence, as shown by their attempt to bring the data of revelation (*samᶜ*) into harmony with the postulates of natural reason (*ᶜaql*), their vindication of the rationality of God's ways, and their profound sense of the inseparability of obligation (*taklīf*) from human responsibility, grounded in turn in human freedom; and, finally, their concern with the determination of the nature and grounds of right and wrong are unmistakable bequests of Greek rationalism.

Philosophical, ethical writers start likewise from the imperative of internal coherence, but, as our analysis will show, their fundamental presuppositions are essentially Greek, i.e. Platonic, Aristotelian or Stoic. The Koran and Traditions are not altogether ignored, but to the extent they are brought into the discussion at all, it is often for the purpose of literary embellishment or dialectical reinforcement only. The impression one gains from reading ethical, philosophical literature in Islam is that ethics, according to its exponents, is an autonomous enquiry which revelation can confirm, but whose principles and precepts are valid in their own right and independently of such confirmation.

It is not without significance that the first philosophical writer in Islam, Abū Yaᶜqūb al-Kindī (d. ca. 866) was in sympathy with Muᶜtazilite theology.[1] An encyclopedic writer, he did not neglect the subject of ethics altogether, although like so many Islamic philosophers, his contribution to ethics was comparatively meager. He is reported by the classical bibliographers to have written a number of ethical treatises reflecting a profound interest in Socratic thought. Thus in addition to a treatise on *Ethics*, and more than one treatise on politics, he is credited with a work on *Paving*

---

[1] See M. Fakhry, *A History of Islamic Philosophy*, 68f. Cf. A.L. Ivry, *Al-Kindi's Metaphysics*, Albany, 1974, especially Chapters One and Three. These two chapters give a resumé of the information now available on al-Kindī's life and his Muᶜtazilite sympathies, or lack of them.

the Way to Virtue, and another one on *Exhortation to Virtue*, as well as an extant tract on the *Art of Dispelling Sorrows*. Of his Socratic writings, a tract on the *Excellence of Socrates*, a *Dialogue between Socrates and Aeschines* and another between Socrates and the Harraneans are given.[2] The only extant Socratic work is a short collection of *Socratic Utterances* (*Alfāẓ Suqrāṭ*), in which the moral personalities of Socrates and Diogenes the Cynic are inadvertently fused, and the resultant hybrid is represented as a model of asceticism and other worldliness.[3]

In the *Art of Dispelling Sorrows*, which became a recurrent theme in the writings of his successors, including al-Rāzī (d. ca. 925), Miskawayh (d. 1030) and Ibn Sīnā (d. 1037), the same Stoic, Cynic ideal of moral fortitude and *apatheia* is set out in eloquent terms. This tract starts with an account of the causes of sorrow, defined by al-Kindī as "a disease of the soul resulting from the loss of what is cherished, or the failure to attain what is sought after."[4] Now in this world of generation and corruption in which nothing endures, argues this author, no one can escape his share of sorrow or tribulation; the wish to cling permanently to the material possessions that one happens to own temporarily is a vain one, since it amounts to wishing that the perishable goods of this world shoud become imperishable or the temporary permanent. Accordingly, we should strive to avoid unnecessary sorrow by cultivating the habit of contentment (*qanāᶜah*) and recognize, as observation clearly shows, that the "sensuous objects of desire or aversion are not something necessary by nature, but rather by habit and frequent use."[5] The reasonable person will accustom himself to enjoy those temporary possessions that come his way and not pine over the loss of those which he has missed.

The antidote of "the disease of sorrow" then does not consist in drugs, potions or branding by iron, but rather in moral fortitude and resignation, whose cultivation should proceed gradually and methodically, until the habit has become fully ingrained in the soul.

Of the simple 'remedies' that may be prescribed in this connection is the consideration of the nature of sorrow as something brought about either by our actions or those of others. In the first case, our duty is to refrain from doing what is the occasion of grief; in the second, to consider whether it is in our power to avert it or not. If in our power, then our duty

---

2 See Ibn al-Nadīm, *Al-Fihrist*, Cairo, N.D., 377.

3 See M. Fakhry, "Al-Kindī wa-Suqrāṭ," in: *Al-Abḥāth*, XVI (1963), 23–34.

4 See *R. al-Ḥīlah li-Dafᶜ al-Aḥzān*, ed. H. Ritter and R. Walzer (Uno scritto morale inedito di al-Kindī) in: *Atti della Reale Accademia Nazionale dei Lincei*, VI, 8, Rome, 1938, 31. The theme was later taken over by Avicenna; cf. Helmut Gätje, "Avicenna als Seelenarzt," in: *Avicenna Commemoration Volume*, Calcutta, 1956, 225–228.

5 *Ibid.*, 34.

is clearly to do so; if not, it is foolish to grieve at the prospect of the calamity we dread before it has hit us. Instead we should continue to hope that it might be averted somehow, and to recognize that in any case its advent is not within our control. Should it nonetheless come to pass, we should do our utmost to bear the calamity with fortitude.[6]

A 'subtle device' to which we may resort in this regard is to recall how the occasions of our past sorrows and those of others have all disappeared and were gradually forgotten.

Another device is to recall that everything we have missed or lost has been missed or lost by many others before us, and that they have all in the end resigned themselves to its loss.

A third device is to recall that "to wish not to be visited by calamity is to wish that we did not exist at all." For calamities are the concomitants of the corruptibility of all existing entities, so that were there no corruption there would be no existing entities. To wish that there be no calamities then is to wish that there be no generation or corruption. However, generation and corruption exist by nature, and to "wish that what exists by nature did not exist is to wish the impossible." Now whoever wishes the impossible must surely be denied his wish and thereby be reduced to a condition of wretchedness. But, for this wretchedness brought about by his own ignorance of the nature of the possible and the impossible, he is entirely to blame.[7]

As to material possessions, whose loss is the occasion of so much sorrow, we should recall that no one of us has an exclusive title to their ownership, insofar as they are the common lot of all mankind. He who grieves at their loss is either envious or niggardly, since he resents giving them up. They are, moreover, given to us on loan by God, their real owner, to whom the right belongs to withdraw them whenever He wishes. To grieve at their loss, then, is a sign of thanklessness for the privilege of having been accorded their use for a while.[8] It follows that on no account should we grieve at the loss of material possessions, for to grieve without cause is the essence of ignorance or folly. When Socrates was asked: How was it he never grieved? He replied, "Because I have never owned anything the loss of which could cause me to grieve."[9]

Considering the transience of human existence and the vanity of material possessions, grief at the change of our estate or the loss of our

---

[6] *Ibid.*, 35f. Cf. Epictetus, *The Encheiridion*, I.

[7] *Ibid.*, 38.

[8] *Ibid.*, 39. Cf. Epictetus, *The Encheiridion*, XI.

[9] *Ibid.*, 40. Two slight variations on this alleged Socratic maxim are given in al-Kindī's 'selections' from the statements of Socrates. See "al-Kindī wa-Suqrāṭ," in: *Al-Abḥāth*, XVI (1963), 23–34.

possessions is the height of folly. Such change or loss is part of the constant permutations of existence in this world of generation and corruption, in which nothing is worthy of our attachment or our sorrow. The only genuine cause of grief is estrangement from our "true abode" in the intelligible world, in which no calamity, privation or loss is ever visited upon us.[10]

A major cause of sorrow that continually preys on our mind is the fear of death, but this fear is entirely irrational. For man, being the "living, rational, dying being," it follows that, far from being a grievous evil, death is "the fulfillment of our nature." To wish then that there be no death is to wish that there be no man, or that our nature be entirely transmuted, which is irrational.[11] To fear the natural and inevitable is equally irrational. The fear of death, which is grounded in the ignorance of the nature of things in this world of generation and corruption, is indeed an evil, from which reason alone can rid us.

The same ideal of *apatheia* and renunciation of the world is reflected in al-Kindī's 'selections' from *Alfāẓ Sugrāṭ*, which have been preserved in a solitary MS. and in which, as we have already noted, the personality of Socrates merges with that of Diogenes the Cynic. The theme of death and the irrational fear thereof is underscored, and Socrates is reported as admonishing his disciples in these words: "Take no heed of death, for its bitterness lies in the fear thereof." Or again: "Take no heed of death, or else you will perish, but let your souls die and then you will live." For "he who lets his soul die a voluntary death, will find in natural death his true life."[12] The captive of death can only be released through philosophy (*ḥikmah*). This obvious allusion to the Socratic definition of philosophy in Plato's *Phaedo* as the art of pursuing death and dying has played an important role in the history of Islamic ethics and mysticism.

II. Al-Rāzī (d. ca. 925) and the 'Philosophical Way'

The most eloquent statement of the Socratic ideal of the 'philosophical' life (*sīrah*) is to be found in the writings of the great physician and author,

---

10 *Ibid.*, 44.

11 *Ibid.*, 45.

12 See my article in *Al-Abḥāth*, 16 (1963), 33. In his treatise *On Definitions*, al-Kindī gives the following definition of philosophy, without mentioning Socrates by name: "They defined it (i.e. philosophy) as preoccupation (ᶜ*ināyah*) with death, death being for them of two types: natural, which is the renunciation by the soul of the use of the body, the second is the extirpation of the passions. This is the death which they intended, since the extirpation of the passions is the road to virtue." See [al] *Rasāʾil al-Falsafiyya*, ed. M. ᶜA.H. Abū Rīda, Cairo, 1950–'53, I, 172. For the history of this Socratic-Platonic concept, see F. Rosenthal, "On the Knowledge of Plato's Philosophy in the Islamic World," in: *Islamic Culture*, XIV (1940), 409.

Abū Bakr al-Rāzī (d. ca. 925). That al-Rāzī should be regarded as the outstanding Platonist of Islam, in the fields of metaphysics and cosmology, should be considered as established.[13] I wish to reinforce this thesis here by underscoring the chief features of his ethical Platonism, illustrated by his unqualified admiration for Plato, "the chief of the philosophers and their master", as well as his deference for Socrates' mode of life set out in a tract entitled the 'philosophical way' and elsewhere.[14] In this treatise, al-Rāzī distinguishes between an earlier and a later phase in the development of the Socratic mode of life, characterized respectively by an otherworldly and a this-worldly spirit—, a distinction reminiscent in some respects of the Socratic portraits drawn respectively by Plato and Xenophon, and adding a further dimension to the already very complex 'Socratic problem' of present-day scholarship.

The substance of al-Rāzī's ethics, however, is embodied in one of his best known treatises, the *Spiritual Physic* (*al-Ṭibb al-Rūḥānī*), one of the few philosophical works of al-Rāzī to survive in full. This treatise opens with the discussion of a theme which not only the philosophers, but even the theologians, Traditionists and Ṣūfīs, have placed at the center of their ethical concerns, *viz.* the pre-eminence of reason, God's greatest gift to man, which is not only the faculty that distinguishes man from the beasts, or the power which has enabled him to understand the world around and harness its natural forces, but also the ruling principle in the soul, whose supremacy ensures the suppression of desire and the reformation of character.[15]

The psychological framework of the '*spiritual physic*' is undoubtedly Platonic: the trichotomy of the soul and the onslaught on hedonism are expressed in emphatic Platonic terms. Plato, according to al-Rāzī, has distinguished between three souls: the rational or divine, the irascible or animal and the appetitive or vegetative.[16] The last two have been fashioned, according to him, for the sake of the rational: the vegetative in

---

[13] See my article, "A Tenth-Century Arabic Interpretation of Plato's Cosmology," in *Journal of the History of Philosophy*, VI (1968), 15–22. No modern life of al-Rāzī exists, but P. Kraus has edited al-Birūnī's inventory of his works. See P. Kraus, *Epître de Beruni*, Paris, 1936, and G.S.A. Ranking, "The Life and Works of Rhazes," in: *Proceedings of XVII International Congress of Medicine*, London, 1914, Sect. 23. A new edition of al-Bīrūnī's inventory of al-Rāzī's works is by Mehdi Mohaghegh, Teheran 1366 A.H.

[14] See al-Rāzī, *Rasāʾil Falsafiyyah*, ed. P. Kraus, Cairo, 1939, 99ff.

[15] See *Rasāʾil Falsafiyyah*, 174.

[16] *Ibid.*, 28. For the identification of the Aristotelian trichotomy of human, animal and vegetative with the Platonic, see the article by P. Kraus, "K. al-Akhlāq li-Jālīnūs," in: *Bulletin of the Faculty of Arts* (Egyptian University), V (1937), 22, 26 and 35. Cf. Engl. trans. by J.N. Mattock in: *Islamic Philosophy and the Classical Tradition*, ed. S.M. Stern et al., 235–260.

order to enable the body, which is the instrument of the soul, to grow; the irascible in order to assist the rational in repressing the appetitive and prevent it from dominating that divine part, with which the ultimate emancipation of the soul from the body is bound up.[17]

According to al-Rāzī, Plato has taught that the more specific purpose of "spiritual therapy" or the art of "persuasion through arguments and demonstration", as distinguished from "bodily therapy", is the moderation (*ta*ᶜ*dīl*) of the three parts of the soul, whereby they are guarded against excess or defect. The defect of the vegetative soul is to refrain from nutrition, growth or reproduction, even to the extent required for the survival of the body; the excess is to indulge in pleasure inordinately. The defect of the irascible is to fail to curb the appetitive soul, whereas its excess is to be puffed up by pride and the lust for conquest, as illustrated by the case of Alexander the Great.[18] The defect of the rational soul is to forego reflection on the marvels of this world, with a view to comprehending everything in it, especially the make-up of the body in which the soul is incarcerated and the destiny reserved for it after death. Its excess is to become so engrossed in reflection as to neglect altogether the body and its needs, resulting ultimately in melancholy and the disturbance of the humors. Plato believed, according to al-Rāzī, that the period assigned for the duration of the corruptible body is determined by the desire of the rational soul to prepare itself for life after death, by engaging in the contemplation of those intelligibles proper to it, and dissociating itself from the body and its pleasures. For it is only through this dissociation that the soul will be able to rejoin its abode in the intelligible world, and be restored to its original condition as a living and thinking entity, which is entirely free from corruption and pain.[19]

Only the ignorant and the unenlightened will dispute the wisdom of this Platonic-Socratic doctrine of the soul and its genuine vocation in this world, because of the firm hold that pleasure has taken upon their minds.

A good deal of al-Rāzī's 'spiritual physic' is taken up with the analysis and repudiation of hedonism. He defines pleasure as the return of the agent to the original condition from which he has been barred by the cause of pain, or very simply as "return to nature".[20] This definition which recurs in his writings and appears to have formed the subject of a separate treatise is presented as the "view of the physical philosophers", although it clearly corresponds to the view of Plato as adumbrated in *Philebus*, 31D

---

[17] See *Rasā*ᵓ*il*, 28. Cf. *Phaedo*, 76C.
[18] *Ibid.*, 29.
[19] *Ibid.*, 30.
[20] *Ibid.*, 37.

and 42C and *Timaeus*, 64D, and is reported by Galen in his compendium of the last-mentioned dialogue extant only in Arabic.[21]

It is because of their ignorance of the genuine nature of pleasure that the incontinent yearn for never-ending enjoyment, little suspecting that the duration of the pleasureable condition is impossible, since it can only come in the wake of the condition preceding it, i.e. pain. Such people are thus obsessed with the futile wish for the unattainable, i.e. a pure and uninterrupted condition of constant pleasure, entirely free from pain.

Moreover, the hedonists should be castigated, not merely because they are ignorant of the true nature of pleasure, but also because they are slaves of their passion (*ᶜishq*), to a degree which exceeds the condition of beasts in its infamy. Take sexual pleasure as an instance; unlike beasts, who are content to secure this pleasure only to the extent of relieving the pain of physical lust, incontinent lovers have turned the satisfaction of that pleasure into a fine art. Not only will they refuse to seek gratification from whatever quarter, they have compounded their slavishness by insisting on securing it from a single source. Moreover, in order to refine upon the amorous art, they have put their own reason, which is God's greatest gift, to the service of their lust, but without avail. For the more they yearn for satisfaction, the greater will they be afflicted with anxiety and frustration in the sequel.[22] This satisfaction is attended by so much hardship, anguish and deprivation that it can never be proportionate to the effort expended in achieving it. The union which lovers yearn for is in the nature of things so short-lived that its pursuit can only be the cause of untold anguish. Even when lovers are spared the trials of separation as long as they live, they cannot ultimately be spared the agony of parting consequent upon death. If this is the way of all passion, then the reasonable man (*ᶜāqil*), rather than live in anxious apprehension of this painful outcome, will not allow himself to be ensnared by it in the first place.[23]

As to those "ignorant people" who dispute this view of the philosophers, contending that love is one of the noble pursuits of which poets and even prophets, noblemen and kings have partaken, they should be deterred from their folly and reminded that genuine nobility does not consist in romantic adventures, but rather in "pursuing obscure and distant matters, rarefied and subtle sciences, the eliciting of complex and recondite subjects, and the production of useful and profitable arts." In

---

21 See Walzer and Kraus, *Galeni Compendium Timaei Platonis*, London, 1951, 19. The same view of pleasure is attributed to Galen himself in al-ᶜĀmirī's *Kitāb al-Saᶜādah wa'l-Isᶜād*, 49.

22 *Rasāʾil*, 39.

23 *Ibid.* 41.

short, true nobility consists in the "perfection of reason and wisdom," as illustrated by the case of the Greeks, the most refined and sagacious of mankind, "who gave less attention to romantic love than any other people in the world."[24]

Moreover, those misguided advocates of romanticism err in other ways. They identify intellectual refinement with grammatical, poetic and rhetorical accomplishments, and these have nothing to do with genuine wisdom. The true sage (*ḥakīm*), according to the philosophers, is "one who has mastered the conditions and rules of demonstration (*burhān*) and attained the highest degree of mathematical, physical and metaphysical knowledge attainable by man."[25]

Among the other vices which afflict the soul and turn it away from its genuine goal, al-Rāzī lists arrogance, envy, anger, falsehood, miserliness, gluttony, drunkenness, erotic passion, frivolity, avarice, worldly ambition and the fear of death. All these vices which prey upon the mind and disturb it are "affections of passion", and result from the failure of the concupiscent and irascible powers to be dominated and regulated by reason, which is man's genuine master and the source of his eventual liberation from the body.

Passion (*hawā*) conduces to anguish (*ghamm*) whenever reason is allowed to represent to itself as grievous or painful the loss of the suitable or desirable, and is therefore a "rational affection" that can cause the soul untold suffering and perturbation. It should therefore be combated in whatever way possible. Two ways are recommended by al-Rāzī, one preventive and the other palliative. Passion should be resisted before it afflicts the soul, but once it has afflicted it, it can be countered or repressed in three ways:

a. By considering that those who are most susceptible to the onset of anxiety are those whose cares are numerous and varied. The fewer our cares then, the more impervious we are to anxiety.
b. By resigning ourselves to the loss of what we cherish as unavoidable. He who has trained himself to accept loss or bereavement, will have steeled himself in advance against disaster.
c. If, however, we are unable to follow either course because of our weakness or passionate nature, the only recourse open to us is to avoid being enthralled by a single care or a single object of love, and to seek several such objects, so that the loss of one object will be offset by the retention of the rest.[26]

---

[24] *Ibid.*, 42f.
[25] *Ibid.*, 43.
[26] *Ibid.*, 67.

The most effective antidote to anxiety, as al-Kindī has also argued, is the realization that nothing in this world of generation and corruption is ever permanent, and that loss and bereavement are inevitable consequences of the endless cycle of coming to be and passing away. Rather than grieve at the loss of what he can only possess for a while, the reasonable man will regard its temporary possession as a welcome boon for which he should be thankful. "Were he to wish that it endure forever, he would be yearning for what cannot be attained, and he who yearns for what cannot be attained brings upon himself his own grief and allows his passion to get the better of his reason."[27]

Sometimes, the loss of what is not essential, instead of being attended by grief, is compensated for by the acquisition of an alternative which restores to the soul its original condition of contendedness. The reasonable man will always remind himself of that constant alternation of disaster and relief, pleasure and pain, which ensures that no one condition will ever remain unchanged. He will also keep constantly in mind the fact that none of his fellowmen is ever immune to hardship, but so many of them are "partners in adversity" from whom he should learn the art of consolation.

Above all, he should reflect carefully upon the causes of his grief. If they are such as can be averted, then it is his duty to concentrate on eliminating them, instead of wasting away in grief at their consequences. If not, then he should simply banish the object of grief from his mind altogether, and refrain from allowing it to take a firm hold on him. Indeed, it is passion rather than reason which induces us to succumb to the unprofitable emotion of grief. However, "the truly reasonable man will not be induced by anything other than the dictates of his reason, and will not dwell on any subject which he is not at liberty to dwell upon, for a clear reason or justification. He will not follow his passion, be led by it or approach it in any other [than a rational] manner."[28] For it is the mark of reason not to dwell on anything which is futile or profitless.

Of the major affections which prey upon the mind and cause it undue anxiety is the fear of death. To combat it, the soul should be persuaded to believe that, upon death, it is destined to enter upon a higher and better estate than its present one. Although al-Rāzī regards this proposition as indubitable, it cannot be accepted without a long-drawn discourse and may, at any rate, remain unconvincing. It is necessary therefore to set it aside, and demonstrate the folly of the fear of death on the alternative 'naturalistic' assumption that the soul shall perish with the body.[29]

---

[27] *Ibid.*, 68. Cf. A.J. Arberry, *The Spiritual Physick*, London, 1950, 72.
[28] *Ibid.*, 69. Cf. Arberry, *op. cit.*, 74, and Epictetus, *Encheiridion*, 1.
[29] *Ibid.*, 93.

From this standpoint, argues al-Rāzī in the manner of Epicurus in his famous letter to his disciple Menoeceus, man will not be touched or injured by death in the least. For injury or pain (*adha*) is a mode of sensation, and sensation belongs to the living so long as they live and are liable to injury. Therefore, the condition of death which is free from sensations of pain or injury is superior to the condition of life.[30]

If it is objected that the living partake of certain pleasures of which they are deprived at death, it could be retorted that the dead will surely not be injured or otherwise affected by such privation. Moreover, pleasure which is regarded as an enviable object of desire or competition is not for reason anything other than "relief from pain"[31] and only the ignorant will continue to covet it as a worthy object of desire. The dead, having been relieved from pain, are not therefore "in need of that relief, which, ensuing upon pain, is called pleasure."[32]

Furthermore, grief over what is inevitable is a form of folly. Now death is inevitable, and the feeling of grief which is attendant upon its fear is a form of folly too, whereas diverting the mind and turning it away from dwelling on it is a boon. Beasts in fact have an advantage in this respect over those who are afflicted with this fear, for they do not dwell in preconception on the prospect of death, as they do. Such dwelling increases our pain manifold. For "he who preconceives death and fears it dies with every act of preconception once, so that over a long period of time, he would have partaken of death many times."[33]

An argument is finally advanced to sway those who believe that death is a prelude to another life. For these, death will have no terror, so long as they comply with the dictates of the 'true law', which has promised the pious eternal bliss in the life-to-come. Should they be in doubt, their sole duty is to search for the Truth, and their efforts will probably be crowned with discovery. If not, as is rather unlikely, God is too merciful to demand what is intolerable.[34]

Thus al-Rāzī lays upon the believer and the agnostic alike the same duty, to search for the Truth, embodied either in the sound religious law (*al-sharīᶜah*) which guarantees his survival after death, or in a 'law of reason' which asserts that his fear of annihilation is entirely baseless. The believer is further comforted by the Muᶜtazilite maxim that surely the Almighty will not demand the intolerable from His servants. The same

---

30 *Ibid.*, 93. Cf. Arberry, *Spiritual Physick*, 103 and Epicurus' letter to Menoeceus, in Diogenes Laertius, *Lives*, X, 122f. Cf. al-Shahrastānī, *al-Milal wa'l-Niḥal*, II, 162.

31 See *supra*, 2f.

32 *Ibid.*, 95. Cf. Arberry, *Spiritual Physick*, 105.

33 *Ibid.*, 95. Cf. Arberry, *op. cit.*, 106.

34 *Ibid.*, 96.

thesis is reaffirmed in an already mentioned work entitled the *Philosophical Way* (*al-Sīrah al-Falsafiyyah*). Here he explicitly vindicates the reality of life after death, the superiority of the philosophical life and the absurdity of hedonism. "For the better estate for which we have been created (...) is not to indulge in bodily pleasures, but rather to acquire knowledge and practice justice, which are the two pathways of our transition from this world to a world beyond, in which there is no death and no suffering. Indeed, nature and passion frequently call us to prefer the present pleasure, whereas reason urges us to give up the present pleasures for the sake of those things which are far preferable to them."[35]

---

[35] See *Rasāʾil*, 101.

CHAPTER THREE

ARISTOTELIAN AND NEO-PLATONIC TENDENCIES: AL-FĀRĀBĪ (d. 950), IBN SĪNĀ (d. 1037), AND IBN RUSHD (d. 1198)

I. Al-Fārābī and the Impact of the *Nicomachean Ethics*

The predominance of the Socratic-Platonic ethical motif during the ninth century is illustrated by the writings of the two philosophers already discussed, as well as the extensive collections of moral aphorisms of al-Āmirī (d. 993) and al-Sijistānī (d. 1000), reproduced and amplified by later authors.[1] The translation of the *Nicomachean Ethics* by Isḥāq Ibn Ḥunayn (d. 911) marked a turning point in the history of philosophical ethics in Islam: it brought the Arabic philosophers into contact with the greatest, systematic treatise of Greek ethics, as interpreted in particular by Porphyry, who is known exclusively from the Arabic sources to have written a 12-book commentary on that treatise.[2] This remarkable commentary, although no longer extant, appears to have conditioned the ethical thinking of many a Muslim writer, the most notable of them Miskawayh (d. 1030), as we will see in due course.

The first Arabic philosopher to comment on parts of the *Nicomachean Ethics* is al-Fārābī (d. 950), the great Muslim logician and founder of Arabic Neo-Platonism. This commentary is no longer extant,[3] but the classical bibliographers,[4] al-Fārābī himself,[5] Ibn Bājjah[6] (d. 1139) and

---

1 Of these authors, we should mention Miskawayh, author of *Jāwīdān Khirad*, al-Mubashshir ibn Fātik, author of *Mukhtār al-Ḥikam*, and others. See M. Fakhry, "The Platonism of Miskawayh and its Implications for His Ethics," in: *Studia Islamica*, XLII (1975), 39–57.

2 See Ibn al-Nadīm, *K. al-Fihrist*, Cairo, N.D., 366. On the rediscovery of the Arabic version of the *N. Ethics*, see A.J. Arberry, "The Nicomachean Ethics in Arabic," in: *Bulletin of the School of Oriental and African Studies*, XVII (1955), 1–9; D.M. Dunlop, "The Nicomachean Ethics in Arabic, Books I–VI" in: *Oriens*, XV (1962), 18–34. See *infra*. Now published by ᶜA.R. Badawī. See Bibliography.

3 See Ahmed Ates, "Fârâbînin Eselerinin Bibliografyasi," in: Türk Tarih Kurumu, Belleten, XV (1951), 175–192.

4 See Ibn al-Nadīm, *K. al-Fihrist*, 382, where al-Fārābī is credited with a commentary (*tafsīr*) on "a piece" of the *N.E.* Cf. Ibn Abī ᶜUṣaybiᶜah, ᶜ*Uyūn al-Anbā*ᵓ, where a commentary (*sharḥ*) on the "opening part" (*ṣadr*) of the *N.E.* is mentioned.

5 See *al-Jam*ᶜ *Bayna Ra*ᵓ*yay al-Ḥakīmayn*, 95.

6 See Ibn Bājjah (Avempace), *Opera Metaphysics*. ed. M. Fakhry, Beirut, 1968, 116 *et passim*.

Ibn Rushd (d. 1198)[7] have all referred to it or discussed some aspects of it. Fortunately, however, the recently published *Excerpts from the Writings of the Ancients*[8] contains disquisitions on the subject of virtue, friendship, political association and happiness, which give the reader a fair idea of that lost commentary; they could in fact be excerpts from it in direct quotations. Additional ethical information is contained in other sources, such as the *Attainment of Happiness, Direction to the Way of Happiness* and the *Enumeration of the Sciences*.

Al-Fārābī's conception of ethics in the last-named work is conditioned by a broad political viewpoint, which is partly Aristotelian, partly Platonic. 'Political Science' (*al-ᶜīlm al-madanī*) is defined as the science "which investigates types of voluntary actions and regimes,[9] as well as the habits, states of character (*akhlāq*), traits and aptitudes from which these actions and regimes arise." It is also concerned with the ends for which they are done and the manner in which they ought to exist in man. Some of the ends are forms of genuine, others of apparent happiness, the former being attainable in the other life only. The two 'parts' of this science, identified in the Aristotelian tradition as ethics and politics, are not named by him. The first is described as aiming at the 'definition' of happiness, and the enumeration (*iḥṣāʾ*) of those actions and traits which are prevalent in states and nations, as well as distinguishing the virtuous from the non-virtuous varieties of such actions; the second is described as aiming at the "mode of orderng virtuous traits and regimes in cities and nations, and defining the 'royal' actions which make the existence of virtuous action and regimes possible."[10]

The important collection of *Excerpts*, already mentioned, opens with general psychological observations, stressing the analogy of soul and body, with respect to health and disease. More significantly, however, the author proceeds in Excerpt 7 to the discussion of the powers of the soul which Aristotle had regarded in *Nicomachean Ethics*, I, 13, as a necessary prelude to the study of ethics. The major powers (or parts) of the soul are given as five: the nutritive, the sensitive, the imaginative, the concupiscent, and the rational. The last power is then shown to have a distinctive ethical function, being the power "through which man reasons and deliberates, acquires the sciences and the arts, and distinguishes between

---

[7] See *Averrois Cordubensis Commentarium Magnum in Aristotelis De Anima Libris*, ed. F. Stuart Crawford, Cambridge, Mass., 1953, 433.

[8] Al-Fārābī, *Fuṣūl Muntazaᶜah*, ed. F. Najjār, Beirut, 1971.

[9] I read *al-Siyar*, as in variant readings. See *Iḥṣāʾ al-ᶜUlūm*, ed. ᶜUthmann Amīn, Cairo, 1948, 102f.

[10] *Ibid.*, 104. Cf. *Taḥṣīl al-Saᶜādah*, Hyderabad, 1345 A.H. 2f.

right and wrong actions.''[11] Its subdivisions are then given as theoretical and practical, and the practical is further subdivided into technical (*mihnī* or *ṣināᶜī*) and reflective or deliberative (*fikrī*). Only the last of these is said to be ethically relevant, since it is the power through which ''one considers, with respect to what one wishes to do, whenever he wishes to do it, whether it can be done or not, and if it can, how that action should be done.''[12]

In the *Attainment of Happiness*, the role of this reflective or deliberative power is developed. First, it is exclusively concerned with the discovery of the means which conduce to the specific end set for it. This end may be truly good, bad, or apparently good, and accordingly the means determined by the reflective power are either truly good, bad or apparently good. The determination of this end is said by al-Fārābī to be the business of a 'natural' aptitude of the soul to apprehend the good and strive for it, and is for that reason doubly theoretical and practical, Aristotle calls this virtue in *Nicomachean Ethics*, VI, 1144^{e}–25 'cleverness' and argues that, although it is inseparable from 'practical wisdom', it is different from it; al-Fārābī simply calls it the 'human' virtue of deliberation.[13]

Secondly, unlike the theoretical or intellectual virtues, which aim at the knowledge of the ultimate principles of reality with certainty, the subject-matter of this reflective faculty are voluntary actions insofar as they become objects of choice or actual realization. These voluntary actions are so variable that the accidents accompanying them change from day to day, even from hour to hour. It belongs to whomever wishes to bring them into actual existence to know these variable accidents at the particular time and in the particular place he intends to achieve his end. This he cannot do through the theoretical sciences, which are only concerned with the invariable principles of mathematical, physical and metaphysical knowledge. He needs instead a special skill enabling him to discern the 'voluntary intelligibles', not in themselves, but insofar as they can be brought into existence by the will at a determined time and place. This special skill is the reflective or deliberative factulty, which is a species of practical wisdom, but cannot be identified with it. Its highest manifestation is 'political deliberative virtue', which enables one to excel in the discovery of what is most useful for a virtuous end common to many nations or a single one.[14]

---

[11] See *Fuṣūl Muntazaᶜah*, 29. Cf. Engl. trans. by D.M. Dunlop, *Aphorisms of the Statesman*, Cambridge, 1961, 30. Hereafter *Aphorisms*.

[12] *Ibid.*, 30 (*Aphorisms*, 31). Cf. *N.E.*, VI, 1139^{b}–4f., and *Taḥṣīl*, 20f.

[13] *Taḥṣīl*, 27f. Cf. also *N.E.* III, 3, 4.

[14] *Taḥṣīl*, 20f.

From these preliminary, psychological observations, al-Fārābī proceeds to consider the nature and divisions of virtue and whether, as Aristotle had enquired in the *Nichomachean Ethics*, II, i, virtue arises in us by habituation or by nature. The divisions of virtue are given as moral (*khuluqī*) and intellectual (*nuṭqī*).[15] It is not possible, he argues, for man to be endowed at birth with virtuous or vicious traits, although he may be endowed with the natural disposition (*isti*ᶜ*dād*) for virtuous or vicious conduct, and this disposition can through practice develop into a habitus (*hay*ᵓ*ah*), which once ingrained in the soul is designated as virtue.[16]

However, the disposition to acquire all the virtues, like the disposition to learn all the crafts, is very hard, though not impossible. In general, a person is disposed by nature to acquire a small number of virtues, or a single one, just as he is disposed to master a small number of trades, or a single one. Once a trait, whether moral or immoral, has become ingrained through habit, it becomes difficult to eradicate. The man in whom all the virtues have become thus ingrained by the force of habit will exceed all his fellows in rank, and may be said to have risen to a superhuman level. The ancients called such a man the 'divine' (*ilāhī*), and his opposite the 'beastly' (*sab*ᶜ*ī*). These two extreme cases are very rare; the former is not intended to serve any single state, but deserves to rule them all, while the latter is not worthy to serve or rule any state either, but should be excluded from them all.[17]

The dominion of habit is so potent that some evil traits cannot be easily changed. However, they could be held in check through continence or self-control. There is, nevertheless, a subtle difference between the virtuous and the continent: the former finds the practice of virtue pleasant and enjoyable, the latter is torn between his passions and the dictates of virtue or the religious way (*sunnah*), and accordingly finds this practice onerous. In many cases, however, the continent is equivalent to the virtuous.[18]

In general, argues al-Fārābī along well-known Aristotelian lines, virtuous actions are to be identified as those which are intermediate between two extremes, each of which is a vice. Adopting again a well-known Aristotelian distinction, he insists that by the intermediate we are to understand either the intermediate *per se*, or the intermediate in relation to something else. The former, like the number six in relation to ten and two,

---

15 *Ibid.*, 30 (*Aphorisms*, 31). Cf. *N.E.* II, 1103ᵇ–25f. and *Taḥṣīl*, 20.

16 *Ibid.*, 31. Cf. *N.E.*, II, 1103ᵃ–15f. Cf. *al-Tanbīh* ᶜ*alā Sabīl al-Sa*ᶜ*ādah*, Hyderabad, 1377 A.H., 7f.

17 *Ibid.*, 33 (*Aphorisms*, 32). Cf. *N.E.*, VII, 1145ᵃ–20f. Aristotle does not mention the beastly man, but it follows from his statement in *Politics*, I, 1253ᵃ–29, that one who is unable to live in society is "either a beast or a god." Cf. also *al-Tanbīh*, 18.

18 *Ibid.*, 34f. Cf. *N.E.*, VII, 1145ᵇ–7f.

is invariable, whereas the latter, such as a food in relation to a child or an adult, varies according to the circumstances of each.[19] The art of determining the intermediate or mean consists in the consideration of the agent, his circumstances and his capabilities. In bodily matters, this is the business of the art of medicine, concerned as it is with prescribing the right foods and medicines for the right patient; in matters of action, this is the business of politics or the "royal art".[20]

The analogy between the body and the state, as well as that between the doctor and the ruler of the city (*mudabbir al-madīnah*) is pursued with relentlessness in this work, and its basic moral and political implications are drawn. Both the doctor and the ruler, according to al-Fārābī, are concerned with determining the intermediate actions or precepts conducing to the health of the body, or the well-being of the state, as we mentioned. This well-being or happiness, mistakenly identified by some with honor, conquest, wealth or pleasure, is declared by him to consist in the actualization of man's intellectual potentialities, whereby he is able to rise by degrees to a condition of immateriality or incorporeality analogous to that of the separate substances of the intelligible world.[21] This condition is designated by al-Fārābī as conjunction (*ittiṣāl*), approximation (*qurb*), likeness (*shabah*), or union (*ittiḥād*) with the lowest of these immaterial substances, i.e. the active intellect.[22]

The two divisions of the virtues are given, as we have seen, along familiar Aristotelian lines, as moral and intellectual, but a noteworthy feature of this division is the already mentioned subdivision of the intellectual virtues into two groups, theoretical and reflective, and the elaboration of the function of the reflective or deliberative virtue. The former includes intuition (*al-^{c}aql al-fiṭrī*), scientific knowledge (*^{c}ilm*) and wisdom (*ḥikmah*); the latter includes practical reason, prudence (*ta^{c}aqqul*), keenness (*al-dhihn*), sound judgement, and sound opinion.[23] Only the second group or that of 'reflective' virtues, as we have seen, is pertinent to the

---

19 *Ibid.*, 37. Cf. *N.E.*, II, 1106^{a}–25f.

20 *Ibid.*, 39. Cf. *al-Tanbih*, 13.

21 See *Fuṣūl Muntaza^{c}ah*, 97; *al-Madīnah al-Fāḍilah*, ed. A. Nader, Beirut, 1959, 85; and *al-Siyāsah al-Madaniyyah*, ed. F. Najjār, Beirut, 1964, 42, 73 *et passim*.

22 See *al-Siyāsah*, 32, 36, 79 and *al-Madīnah*, 104. According to Ibn Rushd, al-Fārābī abandoned the concept of 'conjunction with abstract intelligences' in his commentary on the *Nicomachean Ethics*, but Ibn Rushd's remarks are not free from ambiguity. See *Averrois Cordubensis Commentarium Magnum in Aristotelis De Anima Libris*, ed. F. Stuart Crawford, Cambridge, Mass., 1953, 433, 483 and 485.

23 *Fuṣūl*, 50f. Cf. *N.E.*, VI. 1139^{b}–15f. The corresponding Aristotelian list consists of art (τέχνη), scientific knowledge (ἐπιστήμη), prudence (φρόνησις), philosophic wisdom (σοφὶα), intuitive reason (νοῦς), good deliberation (εὐβουλία), correctness of opinion (εὐστοχία), and judgement (γνώμη). See Miskawayh's table in *Tahdhīb al-Akhlāq*, 19 and *infra*, 112.

study of ethics, or the determination of the right kind of action. Thus practical reason enables us to grasp, as a result of the prolonged experience and observation of sensible entities, the premises, whether universal or particular, of right action; prudence, on the other hand, enables us to grasp or elicit the right means to our ultimate goals. This virtue in turn admits of a subdivision into 'domestic' (i.e. pertaining to the management of the household), and 'political' (i.e. pertaining to the city), either with respect to good counsel (*mashūrah*) or defense (*khuṣūmī*). This is the trait by virtue of which the public designates an individual person as reasonable.[24]

The two moral virtues which figure most prominently in al-Fārābī's discussion are friendship (*maḥabbah*, φιλία) and justice. Friendship is divided along Aristotelian lines into natural, such as the love of child, or voluntary, such as the love binding partners in virtue, utility or pleasure. The friendship binding virtuous partners requires, according to al-Fārābī a certain community of beliefs or actions, which appear to be suggested by his religious preoccupations, rather than Aristotle's casual remarks that "with friends men are more able both to think and to act."[25] The beliefs which the virtuous share in common revolve round three principles: the beginning, the end, and what is intermediate. Beliefs regarding the beginning (*mabdaʾ*) include common opinions regarding God, the spiritual entities (*rūḥāniyūn*) and the saints, the origination of the world, the order of its parts to each other, on the one hand, and to God and the spiritual entities, on the other, and, finally, the relation of man to God and to these spiritual entities.

Beliefs regarding the end revolve around happiness, whereas those regarding what is intermediate revolve around the means to attaining happiness. Once the inhabitants of the city (or state) have all concurred in these beliefs, and these beliefs in turn have been consecrated by actions conducive to happiness, they will love each other necessarily; insofar as they live together in the same household or city, they will need each other, and will be useful to one another. Finally, in view of all these elements of community of virtue and advantage, they will be able to derive pleasure from their association with each other.[26]

This program of common beliefs and practices conducing to true happiness is the cornerstone of al-Fārābī's political philosophy and has been worked out in great detail in his best-known work, significantly entitled

---

24 *Fuṣūl*, 57f. Cf. *R. fi'l-ʿAql*, ed. M. Bouyges, Beirut, 1938, 4.
25 *N.E.*, VIII, 1155a–15.
26 *Fuṣūl*, 70f.

the *Opinions of the Inhabitants of the Virtuous City*. Its Greek basis cannot be easily determined, but apart from the *Republic*, the *Politicus* of Plato may be mentioned, as a possible source, in view of the profound similarity of outlook in this dialogue and al-Fārābī's political treatises.[27] Although the translation of this dialogue into Arabic is not reported in the bibliographical sources, al-Fārābī may have derived his knowledge of its fundamental themes from Neo-Platonic commentaries, notable among which is the already-mentioned commentary on the *Nicomachean Ethics* by Porphyry.

The discussion of the other major virtue, i.e. justice, is rather succinct, but it is sufficient to give us an idea of the degree of his dependence on the *Nicomachean Ethics*. Thus this virtue is divided into (a) general justice, defined as the "performing of virtuous actions by man, in his dealings with others", or (b) particular justices involving either: (1) the distribution of goods or (2) their preservation. These goods are given as security, property, honor and social station. Every member of the state is entitled to his just share of these goods, so that deficiency or excess in their distribution is unjust, either in relation to himself or to the state as a whole. Once this equitable distribution has been achieved, justice requires that it not be disturbed. Should the citizen lose his right share of the abovementioned goods, either voluntarily or by force, he is entitled to be equitably compensated for that loss.[28]

In the *Opinions of the Virtuous City*, however, a more detailed genetic account of this virtue is given. The goods which various individuals or groups are engaged in striving to acquire are listed as security, honor, wealth and pleasure, as well as the means to their acquisition. In what appears to be simply his account of prevalent theories, natural 'justice' is identified with conquest, and the duty of the just man is said to consist, as Thrasymachos has put it in *Republic I*, 337D, in "doing what is most advantageous to the conqueror" so that the subjugation (*istiᶜbād*) of the conquered by the conqueror is regarded as eminently just.[29] As to equity in commercial transactions and returning of trusts as well as avoiding acts of usurpation and repressoin, which are all simply dictated by fear or constraint from outside, it is in fact tantamount to 'conventional' justice, according to this view. For intermittent strife or conquest will sooner or later force the contestants to reach an agreement whereby principles regulating commercial transactions and social position on the basis of equality are

---

[27] Politics is described in the *Politicus* as a 'royal' or "commanding" science. Its function is declared to consist in drawing the citizens' "minds into communion with one another by unanimity and friendship" (*Politicus*, 311 BC).

[28] See *Fuṣūl*, 71f. Cf. *N.E.*, V, 1129^{b}–20.

[29] See *al-Madīnah al-Fāḍilah*, 132.

laid down and complied with, as long as the balance of power is preserved.

A third form of justice which may be termed national, although al-Fārābī has no name for it, arises when the contestants are threatened by external aggresion, and feel compelled in consequence to band together to ward off this aggression. The security assured over a long period of time and resulting in social harmony is interpreted by the people as justice, whereas in fact it is nothing but submissiveness generated by the fear of external aggression.[30]

Another ethical theme which is conspicuously absent from the *Nicomachean Ethics* but figures prominently in al-Fārābī's *Fuṣūl* is that of evil. Its discussion, however, follows familiar Neo-Platonic lines and may be said to have set the tone for similar discussions by his successors, from Ibn Sīnā (d. 1037) to Miskawayh (d. 1030), al-Ṭūsī (d. 1247), al-Suhrawardī (d. 1191), and others. According to al-Fārābī, then, evil, as a 'cosmic' entity, is entirely non-existent. Whatever exists in the universe and is independent of human willing is wholly good. For once we posit the First Cause and the series of entities which results from it in the order and disposition meted out to them, every part of the series would exist "in accordance with that order and justice of merit (*istiʾhāl*)" pertaining to it, and this is the essence of goodness. The only kind of evil which exists in the world is 'voluntary evil', which consists either in the privation of happiness or the ultimate good, designated as wretchedness (*al-shaqāʾ*), or in the performance of those voluntary actions leading to this wretchedness. For "everything natural, whose principle is a voluntary action, may be either good or bad."[31] Whenever the will is excluded, evil is excluded too.

II. Ibn Sīnā

Ibn Sīnā, the successor of al-Fārābī and most illustrious representative of Arabic Neo-Platonism in the tenth and eleventh centuries, has written a total of 276 treatises on the whole range of linguistic, scientific, philosophical, theological, and medical subjects current in his day. Despite this voluminous output, his incursions into the field of systematic ethics are almost trivial. He has written a very short tract on the science of ethics entitled *Fī ʿIlm al-Akhlāq*, another one in one and a half folios entitled *Ethics and Psychological Affections*, and finally a tract of less than one page on 'Piety and Sin' (*Fi'l-Birr wa'l-Ithm*).[32]

---

30 *Ibid.*, 133.

31 *Fuṣūl*, 81 (*Aphorisms*, 60). Cf. *Enneads*, I, 8, 3.

32 See Nos. 245, 247 and 249 respectively, in G.C. Anawati, *Essai de bibliographie Avicennienne*, Cairo, 1950.

Equally remarkable in this regard is the fact that Ibn Sīnā encyclopedic *al-Shifā*ʾ, which constitutes a detailed exposition of logical, mathematical, meteorological, astronomical and metaphysical subjects, contains no methodical discussion of ethics at all.

The short tract *Fī ʿIlm al-Akhlāq* opens with an account of the obligation incumbent on him who cares to attend to his soul: firstly to fulfill (*takmīl*) his "theoretical" nature, by mastering the sciences which are listed in books enumerating them (*iḥṣāʾ al-ʿulūm*), and secondly, to fulfill his "practical" nature, by acquiring the virtues which lead to cleansing his soul, and the knowledge of the vices, as well as the means of avoiding them, so that he "may have achieved for his humanity the perfection leading to worldly and otherworldly happiness."[33]

The principal virtues are then given as temperance, courage and wisdom, corresponding to the three powers of the soul, the concupiscent, the irascible and the rational respectively. Once each of these virtues has attained its perfection or excellence, the fourth, justice, arises. Each of the first three virtues admits, according to Ibn Sīnā, of a series of subdivisions, which are to it what the species is to the genus, or the compound to its simple elements.

The subdivisions of temperance, or the virtue of the concupiscent power, are munificence and contentment; those of courage, the virtue of the irascible, are steadfastness, patience, generosity, forgiveness, pardon, broad-mindedness, moral stamina, and keeping confidences; those of wisdom, the virtue of the rational, are eloquence, keenness, sagacity, firmness, truthfulness, loyalty, friendliness, mercifulness, modesty, magnanimity, promise-keeping and humility.[34]

Ibn Sīnā then proceeds to define the main virtues listed above. Temperance consists in curbing the passions by subordinating the concupiscent power to the rational; contentment in refusing to occupy oneself with the unnecessary or superfluous, in matters of provision, or to take any notice of the possessions of others; fortitude consists in training the irascible power to put up with pain or hardship. A key virtue is that of moral stamina (*raḥb al-bāʿ*), which, although somewhat elusive, is affiliated to the virtue of fortitude. Ibn Sīnā defines it as imperturbability in face of passion or anger, whereby man's "pure essence" is not allowed to be swayed or his mind diverted from the thought of the intelligible (*jabarūt*) and divine (*malakūt*) worlds. Through it, the soul is made to dwell on the thought of the Holy One, quit useless or vain pursuits, and avoid falsehood, whether in word and or deed; thereupon the 'conception' of the right and the true becomes ingrained habits in the soul.

---

[33] See "Fī ʿIlm al-Akhlāq" in: *Tisʿ Rasāʾil*, Consṭanṭiniyah, 1298 A.H., 107.
[34] *Ibid.*, 107f. Cf. M.A. Sherif, *Ghazālī's Theory of Virtue*, Albany, N.Y., 1974, 180.

A logical consequence of this virtue is benevolence, manifested in concern for the welfare of others, affection for those who are virtuous, and a sincere desire to deter and reform the wicked. It is moreover attended by the constant thought of immortality and an unruffled attitude towards death.[35]

Pleasure-seeking is justified, according to Ibn Sīnā, in three cases only: (a) restoring the body to health, (b) preserving the individual or the species, and (c) managing the affairs of the state. It is essential, however, that the rational power should constantly superintend pleasurable pursuits and the agent be fully conscious of the end in view, otherwise these pursuits will turn into occasions for self-gratification. Two instances are given of the right pursuit of pleasure with the right motive: "wine-drinking, which is justified for medicinal or hygienic purposes, but not for merry-making," and music or song (*samāᶜ*), which may be enjoyed for the purpose of "strengthening the essence of the soul" and reinforcing its internal powers only.

In dealing with his fellowmen, the virtuous man will approach another according to the latter's personal mood, i.e. the serious in a spirit of serious-mindedness, the frivolous in a spirit of frivolity, while guarding his own inner state (*bāṭin*) concealed from his fellows. He will assist the needy with discretion, honor his pledges and refuse to resort to oath-making.

Finally, the virtuous man will not be delinquent in performing his religious duties, or honoring the divine laws or observances. When he turns inwards, his mind will be occupied exclusively with the thought of the First King and His Kingdom, and his soul will be swept of the "dust of mankind", without his fellowmen's knowledge. Whoever has pledged himself to lead this mode of life and to adopt this religious code, will be assisted by God to achieve success in whatever he undertakes.[36]

To underscore the social dimension of justice, Ibn Sīnā lays down, in the metaphysical part of *al-Shifāᵓ*, as a precondition of realizing this virtue within the state, the existence of the Caliph, upon whom the enforcement of moral discipline devolves. With this enforcement are bound up the three cardinal virtues of temperance, courage and wisdom, of which justice is the summation (*majmūᶜ*). Coupled with "theoretical wisdom", this last virtue is the key to genuine happiness. When 'prophetic characteristics' are added to it, the man in whom it is embodied "will almost be a human lord (*rabb*), and his worship next to God Almighty will be almost

[35] *Ibid.*, 109.
[36] *Ibid.*, 110.

lawful. Such a man is the sovereign of the world and God's vicegerent (*khalīfah*) thereon."[37]

III. Ibn Rushd (d. 1198)

Ibn Rushd, the great Arab-Spanish Aristotelian, is known from the Arabic bibliographical sources to have written a summary (*talkhīṣ*) of the *Nicomachean Ethics* of Aristotle. These sources do not specify the type of summary involved, but judging from his other extant works, the term can only denote a paraphrase, not a full-fledged commentary (*sharḥ*). This paraphrase has not survived in Arabic, but a Hebrew version of it is extant in manuscript form.[38] He has in addition written a 'middle commentary' extant exclusively in Latin in two translations, one by Hermann the German (1575) and the other by Bernard Feliciano (1562),[39] and a 'paraphrase' of Plato's *Republic*, which exists only in Hebrew and English.[40] Considering the close correlation of the two parts of 'practical' philosophy in the Arabic tradition, as illustrated by al-Fārābī's classification of the sciences, the two works may be looked upon as complementary. In fact, Ibn Rushd begins his paraphrase of Plato's *Republic* by methodological observations on the relationship between the practical and theoretical sciences. The subject-matter of the practical sciences is voluntary actions, whose principle is will and choice, whereas that of the theoretical is physical entities, as in the case of the science of physics, or the 'divine things', as in the case of metaphysics, the 'divine science'. The principle of the former is nature, that of the latter is God.[41]

The first part of this practical science, ethics, deals with voluntary actions and habits, and corresponds to that part of medicine which deals with achieving good health and avoiding disease (i.e. hygiene); the second

---

37 See *al-Shifāʾ* (*Ilāhiyāt*), ed. G. Anawati a.o., Cairo, 1960, II, 455. The caliph is identified by Ibn Sīnā with the Imām, and although he is not explicit, some of his remarks about the designation of the caliph, which he calls "designation by specific nomination" (*al-istikhlāf bi'l-naṣṣ*), and his functions, including independent judgement, or *ijtihād*, betray definite Shīʿite sympathies.

38 See Cambridge MS. Add. 496. Cf. E.I.J. Rosenthal, *Political Thought in Medieval Islam*, Cambridge, 1958, 177 and 294, note 27. Cf. H.A. Wolfson, "Revised Plan for the Publication of a Corpus Commentariorum Averrois in Aristotelem," in: *Speculum*, XXXVII (1963), 94 [reprinted in: Wolfson, *Studies in the History of Philosophy and Religion*, I, Cambridge, Mass., 1973, 430–454].

39 See *Aristotelis opera cum Averrois commentariis*, Venice, 1562–74 and Venice, 1575.

40 See E.I.J. Rosenthal, ed., *Averroes' Commentary on Plato's Republic*, Cambridge, 1956, and R. Lerner, *Averroes on Plato's Republic*, Ithaca and London, 1974. The two best European studies of Ibn Rushd's life and thought continue to be E. Renan, *Averroes et l'Averroïsme*, Paris, 1882, and more recently, L. Gauthier, *Ibn Rochd* (Averroès), Paris, 1948.

41 See Lerner, *Averroes*, 3f. Cf. *In Moralia Nicomachia Expositione*, Venice, 1562, fols. 2[a] and 160[b].

part, on the other hand, deals with the manner in which these habits are established in the soul, and it corresponds to that part of medicine dealing with the preservation of health and the healing of disease, i.e. therapy.

Ethics, according to Ibn Rushd, is inseparable from politics; it is in fact the first part of the practical art, of which politics is the second, and has accordingly a certain logical precedence over it. The modes of human perfection (or virtue) as laid down in this science are four: theoretical, deliberative, moral and technical.[42] All the other perfections are subservient to the theoretical and serve simply as preparations thereto.[43] However, as a rule, it is not possible for a single individual to attain all these perfections without the assistance of his fellowmen; hence the need for political association. This is linked by Ibn Rushd to the diversity of individual aptitudes or dispositions. For it is impossible that an individual be capable of every perfection, or else nature will have done something in vain.[44]

The particular virtues of wisdom, courage and temperance are identified along Platonic lines, with the perfection of each of the three 'parts' of the soul corresponding to the three parts of the city or state. Hence, a person is wise to the extent his rational part rules the passionate and concupiscent parts, courageous to the extent his passionate part is subordinated to the rational and is exercised in the right measure and at the right time. Ibn Rushd vacillates, however, in his discussions of temperance, which, like justice, is attributed to all the parts of the soul rather than to a single one, although he recognizes that it too consists in the subordination of the concupiscent power to the rational.[45] As to justice, it is, as Plato has explained in the fourth book of the *Republic*, "nothing more than that every human in the city does the work that is his by nature in the best way that he possibly can," just as justice in the soul of each individual consists in "every one of its parts doing only what it has to do in the appropriate measure and at the appropriate time."[46] This is possible only if reason is allowed to rule over the two other powers of the soul, or the corresponding parts of the state.

This Platonic account of justice, as an 'inward' virtue of the soul or state, is modified in the commentary on *Nicomachean Ethics* V, 1129^{b} 25f. to correspond to the Aristotelian notion of universal, 'common justice' as a 'perfect virtue', not confined to oneself, but extending to our dealings

---

[42] Lerner, *Averroes*, 5. Cf. al-Fārābī's *Taḥṣīl al-Saᶜādah*, 2, *Fuṣūl*, 29, and *N.E.*, VI, 1139^{a} 4f.
[43] Lerner, *Averroes*, 5f. and 92.
[44] *Ibid.*, 6. Cf. *In Moralia*, fols. 17a and b.
[45] *Ibid.*, 7 and 8. Cf. *Republic*, IV, 431A.
[46] *Ibid.*, 7f. Cf. *Republic* IV, 432^{c}f.

with our neighbor, since it is the mark of "the perfectly just man to exercise his virtue in himself as well as in (his dealings with) others."[47] This virtue is not a part of virtue, as Aristotle has also argued, but the whole of virtue.

As to 'particular justice', its two major subdivisions are distributive and rectificatory. The former consists in distributing honors or money equitably, the latter in restoring the 'proportion' disturbed by giving to equals unequally and to unequals equally, which is the essence of injustice.[48]

To complete the ethical enquiry, three questions are then discussed:

(a) What are the conditions needed for actualizing each of the virtues? Courage, for instance, is defined as a habit within the soul, intermediate between rashness and timidity; this definition, however, is not sufficient for realizing virtue, unless the conditions under which it can be realized are clearly defined. For, as Aristotle has said, the aim of ethical knowledge is not just to know, but rather to act.[49]

(b) How are these virtues to be instilled in the youth, and once they have become ingrained in them, how are they to be preserved? Likewise, how are the vices to be eradicated? This part of the enquiry is analogous to medicine with its two divisions: hygiene, concerned with the preservation of health, and therapy, concerned with the removal of disease.

(c) What habits or virtues will strengthen or hinder other habits and virtues? For the preservation of moral character, like that of health, is best achieved if the interrelations of the parts are properly understood.

In general, Ibn Rushd believes, following Aristotle, that there are two ways of achieving the practical aims of ethics and politics, which is the inculcation of the virtues in the citizens: one is argument, the other is coercion.[50] The most interesting part of his reasoning in this connection is the determination of the type of argument appropriate to each class of citizens. To the multitude, rhetorical and poetical arguments are appropriate, to the select few, the demonstrative. Each of these classes achieves the kind of perfection which their nature admits of.[51]

The same social implications of this classification of the different types of argument are developed in *Faṣl al-Maqāl* (Decisive Treatise), with one fundamental change, namely, the introduction of an intermediate class, the people of dialectic (*jadal*), between the rhetorical and the demonstra-

---

[47] *In Moralia Nicomachia*, fol. 65^b. Cf. M. Fakhry, "Justice in Islamic Philosophical Ethics," in: *Journal of Religious Ethics*, III (1975), 248f.

[48] *In Moralia*, fols. 69f.

[49] Lerner, *Averroes*, 8. Cf. *N.E.*, II, 1103^b 26f. and X, 1179^b 1f.

[50] Lerner, *Averroes*, 10f. Cf. *N.E.*, X, 9.

[51] *Ibid.*, 10. Cf. al-Fārābī, *Taḥṣīl al-Saʿādah*, 31. Cf. Aristotle, *Rhetorica*, I, 1354^a and *Sophistica*, 165 b, for these types of argument.

tive. By this intermediate class, Ibn Rushd appears to mean the theologians (*mutakallimūn*), especially the Ashᶜarites, whose arguments fall short of the demonstrative, on account of the uncertain character of their premises, which are at best probable, or generally accepted (*mashhūrah*).[52]

The religio-ethical significance for Ibn Rushd of this threefold classification of mankind and the corresponding classification of the types of argument is that it makes it possible for religion (*sharᶜ*) to impart to the whole of mankind the knowledge of these theoretical and practical truths upon which their eternal felicity depends. The former include the knowledge of God and the rest of existing things, as they are in themselves, as well as their eternal felicity and wretchedness; the latter include the performance of those actions conducive to felicity, and the avoidance of those actions which conduce to wretchedness. These actions, in turn, include outer or bodily actions, i.e. external observances, dealt with in the science of jurisprudence (*fiqh*), and inner actions, pertaining to the soul, dealt with in the "sciences of the hereafter".[53]

This threefold classification has a further significance, namely, the vindication of the unquestioned pre-eminence of the 'people of demonstration' (or philosophers) over everybody else. To them belongs, in the state, the royal art of guardianship, and in the congregations of the learned, the art of interpreting (*taʾwīl*) the ambiguous (*mutashābihāt*) passages of scripture.[54] Their ultimate felicity does not consist, as one would expect from the dichotomy of theoretical and practical knowledge, in a balanced cultivation of the moral and intellectual virtues, which we have mentioned and which form in a sense the backbone of Aristotle's theory of virtue in the *Nicomachean Ethics*.[55] It consists instead in the Plotinian ideal of 'conjunction' with the active intellect, with which, as al-Fārābī, Ibn Sīnā and Ibn Bājjah (d. 1138) had argued, the fulfillment of man's essential nature is realized. Like his last-named predecessor, Ibn Rushd was engrossed in searching for a specific formula defining the mode of man's conjunction (*ittiṣāl*) with the active intellect. Both in his paraphrase on *De Anima* and in his tract on "Whether the Active Intellect Can Be Conjoined to the Material Intellect, While It Is in the Body," he has grappled with this problem. The purpose of the latter tract, he writes, is to "elicit all the clear paths and sound demonstrations which will lead us to the knowledge of

---

52 See *Faṣl al-Maqāl*, ed. A. Nader, Beirut, 1961, 50f. Cf. however, Lerner, *Averroes* 17f.

53 *Faṣl al-Maqāl*, 49f.

54 *Faṣl al-Maqāl*, 52, and Lerner, *Averroes* 16f.

55 See, e.g., *N.E.*, I, 13; VI, 1, 2; X, 7, 8.

the great objective and of ultimate felicity, namely, whether the active intellect can become conjoined to the material while it is still in the body (. . .). This is the question which the Philosopher (Aristotle) promised (to investigate), although his discourse on this subject did not reach us.''[56]

After a brief and approving summary of Alexander of Aphodisias' account of the relationship between the material, the habitual and the active intellects according to Aristotle, he proceeds to specify the function of each of these three intellects. The material (*hayūlānī*) is essentially a potential faculty, fulfilled through the habitual. The active intellect, on the other hand, is that whereby the potential intelligibles are actualized. It has nevertheless two functions; (a) insofar as it is separate from matter (*mufāriq*), it apprehends itself, as befits all the other separate intelligences in which the intellect and its object are one and the same, and (b) it apprehends the intelligibles embedded in the material intellect, by bringing them out from potentiality to actuality. In this respect, this intellect (i.e. the active) is conjoined to man and is to him what form is to matter. However, observes Ibn Rushd, the two functions of this active intellect are inseparable. For to the extent it is conjoined to the 'material' intellect of man, it is able to realize its higher function of self-apprehension. This progression from the lower to the higher level of actualization, he believes, is not only an epistemological necessity, it is a dictate of divine wisdom and justice, which have decreed that no level of reality shall remain unfulfilled.[57]

To fit this dual activity of the active intellect into the ethical framework of moral and intellectual virtues, Ibn Rushd distinguishes in his paraphrase of the *Republic* between two grades of perfection: the first is achieved through the will of the individual, the second through 'conjunction' with the active intellect.[58] In this way a certain autonomy of the will is achieved, in the moral sphere, without abandoning man's ultimate dependence, in the theoretical sphere, on that supermundane agency which dominates the sublunary world, and in 'conjunction' with which man's highest intellectual aspirations are fulfilled. The above distinction between the two functions of the active intellect enables Ibn Rushd to be even more precise: it is through participation in the higher mode of self-apprehension that man's ultimate felicity consists. For his intellectual nature is thereby thoroughly fulfilled, and he becomes a member of that realm of separate intelligences, subsisting eternally in the intelligible world.[59]

---

[56] See *Risālat al-Ittiṣāl*, appendix to *Talkhīṣ Kitāb al-Nafs*, ed. A.F. al-Ahwānī, Cairo, 1950, 119.

[57] *Ibid.*, 122. Cf. *Talkhīṣ Kitāb al-Nafs*, 88.

[58] See Lerner, *Averroes* 93f.

[59] *Ibid.*, 93f. For Averroes' 'conjunction' cf. *Epistle on the Possibility of Conjunction With the Active Intellect by Ibn Rushd, with the Commentary of Moses Narboni. A. Critical Edition and Annotated Translation*, by Kalman P. Bland, New York, 1982. Cf. *In Moralia Nicomachia*, fols. 153–54.

CHAPTER FOUR

NEO-PYTHAGOREAN AND PRAGMATIC ELEMENTS: THE BRETHREN OF PURITY (10th CENTURY)

I. The Genesis and Growth of Moral Traits

Ibn Sīnā's predecessors, the Brethren of Purity, dealt with ethical questions in a more extensive way in a variety of contexts: psychological, cosmological, theological. Considering the somewhat rhapsodic character of their *Epistles*, we do not find in these writings a methodical exposition of these questions, but there is no doubt that their whole outlook is infused with an ethical and didactic spirit.

Two fundamental standpoints are taken in their discussion of ethics, the one anthropological and genetic, the other cosmological. From the first standpoint, man's generation, his acquisition of the diverse traits which make up his character, and his moral and intellectual vocation as God's vicegerent are highlighted. From the second standpoint, his relation to the universe and the analogy of his different faculties and organs to different parts of the universe are meticulously developed, illustrating thereby the Stoic maxim that man, the microcosm, is a replica of the larger universe or macrocosm.

Moral traits (*akhlāq*) are defined by the Brethren as "aptitudes" pertaining to "each of the organs of the body, whereby it is able to readily perform certain actions, works or arts, or to acquire certain sciences or moral qualities (*ādāb*), or political courses of action, without reflection or deliberation."[1] The acquisition of these aptitudes or traits through education, the study of philosophy, and compliance with the religious law (*al-sharīᶜah*) renders the practice of the virtues of courage, temperance and justice easily feasible.

A noteworthy feature of this pliability of man is its association by the Brethren with the aptitudes of the 'absolute man', identified by them with

---

[1] See *Rasāʾil Ikhwān al-Ṣafā*, Beirut, 1957, I, 305. Cf. Kraus, "K. al-Akhlāq li-Jālīnūs," 25 and Miskawayh, *Tahdhīb al-Akhlāq*, 31. Walzer has convincingly argued for the Middle-Platonic affiliation, as interpreted and defended by Posidonius against the Stoic Chrysippus, of this doctrine of the irrational basis of character, transmitted by Galen. See "New Light on Galen's Moral Philosophy," in: *Greek into Arabic*, Oxford, 1962, 147f. and 161f. For the Neoplatonic aspect of the 'purification of the soul' in the Brethren and Miskawayh see Daiber, in: *Orientalistische Literaturzeitung* 76(1981), 46f.

the universal soul, to receive all manner of possible traits and skills. This absolute man in turn is regarded as God's vicegerent on earth, as we have already noted.[2] Aptitude or power is itself ultimately derived, as we shall see later, from God, Who has endowed man, upon creating him, with a group of characteristics which equip him to play his preordained role in the universe. These are: (a) a physical frame possessing the four humors and the nine temperaments in the most moderate way, (b) a spirit (*rūḥ*) which God breathes into him, and (c) a soul which is partly animal, enabling him to move, perceive, understand and perform whatever actions he wishes, and partly spiritual, enabling him to partake of the spiritual virtues of the heavenly bodies, receive all the moral traits, and learn all the sciences and arts that his nature has equipped him to learn or receive.[3] Accordingly, the variations in ethical and psychological traits are due neither to the nature of the 'absolute man', of which every individual is an instance, nor to the divine purpose for which he was originally created. Instead they are due to one or the other of the following factors:

1. Differences in humor or temperament. Thus those of febrile humor tend to be brave, generous or volatile, whereas those of frigid humor tend to be sluggish and ponderous; those of a moist humor, dull and changeable, and those of a dry humor, stable, avaricious and rancorous.

2. Diverse climatic and geographic conditions. Thus people who are born in torrid zones tend to be cold by temperament, whereas those born in colder climates tend to be hotter, "since hot and cold are two contraries which cannot exist in one place in the same way. (...) That is why we find the inhabitants of southern regions, such as the Abyssinians, Nubeans, negroes and Indians manifesting the external effects of heat, whereas the internal parts of their body remain cool. The inhabitants of northern regions, on the other hand, manifest the external effects of cold climate, whereas heat is concealed inside the internal parts of their bodies."[4]

3. Meteorological and astrological conditions. Thus those who are born in fiery zones, dominated by fiery planets such as Mars, tend to be hotheaded and bilious, whereas those who are born in watery zones, dominated by watery planets such as Venus, tend to be phlegmatic and moist, and so on.[5]

The manner of these influences is discussed at some length in the astro-

---

[2] *Rasāʾil*, 306.
[3] *Ibid.*, 297f.
[4] *Ibid.*, II, 303.
[5] *Ibid.*, II, 304.

nomical parts of the *Epistles*. Their secrets, however, are known only to the foremost sages or philosophers, who have been assisted by divine guidance and illumination. They stem, at any rate, from the universal soul, and passing through the fixed stars and the planets, they eventually reach the four elements, and through their intermediary, the mineral, vegetable and animal worlds.[6]

The manner of their transmission is likened by the Brethren to that of light, which emanates from the sun and the planets and is irradiated throughout the whole world. The diverse conjunctions and constellations of the different planets in their heavenly rotations determine the mode of this transmission and accordingly the degree of prosperity or misery befalling individuals in the world of generation and corruption.[7]

4. Cultural, religious and educational determinations. These determinations play a decisive role in the cultivation of those traits which incline one to a life of virtue, nobility, manliness or their opposites. The influence of parents, teachers and elders is as great as the influence of current usages and norms in determining these traits.[8]

Ethical traits may thus be divided into two main groups: (a) natural or ingrained, and (b) acquired or habitual. Some of these traits pertain to the vegetative soul, identified by the Brethren with the appetitive, others to the irascible, identified with the animal, and still others to the human, identified with the rational.[9] To each of these souls correspond a series of faculties or aptitudes: to the first, the desire for food, to the second, the desire for procreation or revenge, to the third, the desire for the acquisition of knowledge or skill. The two ultimate grounds of these powers are the desire for self-preservation and the aversion from self-annihilation, both of which are intended for the ultimate goals of all human endeavor: (a) to endure in this life as long as possible and in the best condition attainable, and (b) to partake in the life-to-come of everlasting bliss.[10]

The virtues conducing to these two goals, the worldly and otherwordly, are arranged by the Brethren according to a religious scheme which is not without historical interest. If one ponders the intelligible world and the central position of the divine law (*nāmūs*) in it, it would appear how this law constitutes a 'spiritual realm' presided over by the lawgiver (i.e. the

---

[6] *Ibid.*, II, 144f.
[7] *Ibid.*, II, 147f.
[8] *Ibid.*, II, 307f.
[9] The source of this identification of the Aristotelian trichotomy of vegetative, animal and human with the Platonic of appetitive, irascible and rational appears to be Galen. See P. Kraus, ed., *K. al-Akhlāq li-Jālīnūs*, 22, 26 and 35.
[10] *Rasāʾil*, I, 316f.

Prophet), who is to his subordinates what number one is to the rest of number. The survival of that realm and its well-being depend on the right order holding together its eight classes: the readers, the transmitters (*ruwāt*), the jurists, the commentators, the warriors, the successors (*khulafāʾ*) of the lawgiver, the pious worshippers and monks, and finally the "scholars charged with interpreting His revelation," namely, the right-guided *imāms* of the realm.[11]

To each of these classes belongs a series of virtues, which contribute to the harmony and well-being of the whole. The virtues of the readers are essentially linguistic and scholastic, comprising eloquence and humility; those of the transmitters of the religious Traditions are punctiliousness, truthfulness and piety; and those of the jurists are knowledge of the commandments and prohibitions laid down by the lawgiver, and the sanctions corresponding to them, as well as knowledge of the principles of analogy (*qiyās*) and their application to particular cases, caution in legal decisions, and avoidance of jealousy, disputatiousness, arrogance and disparagement of rivals. The virtues of the commentators include mastery of the rules of language and perspicacity in comprehending the hidden meaning of the law. The virtues of the warriors are religious fervor, courage and piety; those of the masses of the pious are contentment (*qanāʿah*), abstemiousness, renunciation of vainglory and the constant thought of death. The virtues of the last class, or successors of the Prophet, cannot be given in a single discourse, according to the author of the *Epistles*. Indeed, the whole collection of 51 epistles is an exposition of their virtues, functions and modes of knowledge.[12]

II. Man, the Microcosm

From this analysis, it appears how potent was the religious *motif* in the ethical thought of the Brethren and how organic is their conception of man in his relation to his fellowmen and to the universe at large. The most dramatic expression of the latter relation is their recurrent claim throughout the *Epistles* that man is a *microcosm*, reflecting the *macrocosm* in every particular. This claim is worked out in great detail, and the analogy of the 'small world' to the large is developed at length.

The ancient philosophers, writes the author of the *Epistles*, having carefully surveyed the material world and reflected upon it, "found no part thereof more complete in constitution, or perfect in form, or more analogous on the whole to everything else, than man."[13] For they found his

---

[11] *Ibid.*, 321f.
[12] *Ibid.*, 324f.
[13] *Rasāʾil*, II, 457.

body to be a prototype of the physical world, with its spheres, planets, elements, minerals, plants and animals. They found his soul, on the other hand, to be a prototype of the 'spiritual creation, including angels, jinnees and demons.'

The nine 'substances' of the human body: bone, marrow, flesh, veins, blood, nerves, skin, hair and nail, are analogous to the nine concentric spheres of the heavens. The twelve signs of the zodiac are analogous to the twelve orifices of the body: the two eyes, two ears, two nostrils, two nipples, the navel, the mouth and the two discharge canals. Since six of the zodiac signs are southern and six northern, these orifices are likewise divided into two sets: six right and six left.

To the seven planets which possess each a soul and a body, operating on individual souls or bodies respectively, correspond seven bodily powers in man: those of attraction, cohesion, digestion, discharge, nutrition, growth and representation, and seven spiritual powers: those of hearing, sight, taste, smell, and touch, plus the two powers of speech and reason.[14] The last two correspond to the moon and the sun, for "as the moon derives its light from the sun, as it passes through its twenty-eight phases," so does the power of speech derive from reason the variety of sounds, designated as the twenty letters of the (Arabic) alphabet, as they pass through the throat.[15]

The eyes, on the other hand, correspond to the two stations of Jupiter; the ears, to the two stations of Mercury; the nostrils and the nipples to those of Venus; the two canals to the stations of Saturn; the mouth to that of the sun; and the navel to that of the moon.[16]

Moving downward, the author then develops the analogy between the four elements and the organs of the body: the head, according to him, corresponds to fire by virtue of "the radiations" of sight lodged in it, together with the activities of the senses; the breast corresponds to air by virtue of its breathing; the belly to water by virtue of the 'moistures' filling it up; and the lower abdomen to earth, by virtue of its inherence in it, just as the other three inhere in the earth or rotate around it. From these four elements derive the vapors which cause the phenomena of wind, cloud, rain, as well as minerals, plants and animals.[17]

In a somewhat more metaphorical manner, the author then proceeds to draw more pictorial analogies between man's body and the rest of the physical world. The frame of his body is analogous to that of the globe:

---

[14] *Ibid.*, 464.
[15] *Ibid.*, 464–65.
[16] *Ibid.*, 463f.
[17] *Rasāʾil*, II, 463f.

the bones to mountains, the marrow to minerals, the belly to the sea, the intestines to rivers, the veins to streams, the flesh to earth and the brain to plants. Man's front corresponds to the east, his back to the west, his right side to the south and his left side to the north. His breathing is like wind, his speech like thunder, his voice like the bolt of lightning, his laughter like daylight, and his weeping like rain. The four phases of his life are like the four seasons of the year, and the fluctuations of his fortune like the upward and downward movements of the stars.

As one might expect, the *Epistles* draw an essentially similar picture of social and political stratification or organization, and make somewhat arbitrary analogies between the sun and the king, the commander of the army and Mars, the ministers of the state and Mercury, the judges and Jupiter, and dissident groups (*khawārij*) and the moon.[18]

III. Freewill and Predestination

The author of the *Epistles* never tires of reiterating the moral and religious lessons to be learnt from these psychological and cosmological analogies and comparisons. An important ethical question that he has broached in a number of places is that of freewill and predestination (*qaḍāʾ wa-qadar*). In the fifth religious *Epistle*, he defines the relation of belief in predestination to genuine faith, which, as we have seen, some of the Traditionalists and jurists regarded as inseparable.[19] However, in addition to the divine will or decree (*qaḍāʾ*), the Brethren introduced into the discussion another line of determination, which, grounded in Neo-Platonic cosmology and popular astrology, tended to refer terrestrial phenomena to the influence of the stars. They did not appreciate sufficiently the incompatibility of the two lines of determination, the divine and the astral, and accordingly they laid down as a precondition of genuine faith (*īmān*) joyful acceptance (*riḍā*) of the decree, defined as "the soul's contentedness with what fate shall bring." This fate (*maqādīr*) is determined, according to them, by the determinations of the stars (*aḥkām al-nujūm*), the divine Decree, being simply the "divine foreknowledge of what these determinations shall be."[20] Only those who are fully conversant with the religious law (*nāmūs*), i.e. the prophets and their genuine followers, can partake of this joyful acceptance, commended in the Koran in numerous places. However, examples from secular history are given, such as the heroic submission of Socrates to the sentence of death, rather

---

18 *Ibid.*, 467.
19 See *supra*.
20 *Rasāʾil*, IV, 73.

than that he should flout the laws of the city. Other examples from religious history are Abel, Ḥusayn, the second son of the Caliph ᶜAlī, Christ and Muḥammad, who are all said to have submitted unquestioningly and joyfully to their respective fates, as determined by the 'heavenly decrees'. In such submission, they demonstrated great fortitude, so as to become worthy of the indescribable felicity, comfort and well-being which God has promised His elects.[21]

The author of the *Epistles*, however, is not unaware of the moral and philosophical difficulties which the conflict between the will of man and the power of God involved. He struggles to resolve this conflict which had split the ranks of the jurists and theologians, as we have seen, into the advocates of free will, or Qadarīs and Muᶜtazilah, and the advocates of divine predestination, or Jabriyyah. With the latter, he agrees that God must be affirmed to be the source of all power or capacity which He creates in the agent, with the former, that this 'created power' does not necessarily entail constraint. "For with the same power that enables him to do a certain deed, (the agent) is able to refrain from that same deed."[22] Actions, however, are either performed with comparative ease or comparative hardship. The passions of the soul or the insinuations of the Devil may incline him to take a certain course or its contrary, so that the action, according to him, is not altogether determined, nor altogether free. This verbal compromise is not achieved without a certain amount of quibbling, and the reader is addressed as follows: "Do not imagine, o brother, that an action can be performed by an agent or that he may be directed (*yuyassar*) to do a certain deed or refrain from doing what he has been commanded to do, unless it has been foreknown by God, Whose foreknowledge is called the eternal and inexorable Decree, these two being the two determinants of the course of the stars and the heavenly constellations."[23]

---

21 *Ibid.*, 79.
22 *Ibid.*, III, 499.
23 *Ibid.*, III, 500.

CHAPTER FIVE

YAḤYĀ IBN ᶜADĪ (D. 974), LOGICIAN AND MORAL PHILOSOPHER

I. The Subject-Matter and Aim of Ethics

To the Jacobite logician and theologian, Yaḥyā ibn ᶜAdī (d. 974), we owe one of the earliest systematic ethical treatises; entitled *Tahdhīb al-Akhlāq* (Cultivation of Morals), it was written probably four decades before Miskawayh's more famous treatise of the same title.[1]

The author begins by laying down as a postulate the duty incumbent on man, as a rational being, to acquire every virtuous trait (*shīmah*) and avoid every vicious one, so as to achieve perfection in the refinement of his character. This double task, however, is not easily accomplished without a methodical exposition of the varieties of moral traits (*akhlāq*), their causes, kinds and subdivisions, showing in particular why some of them are commendable, and some are reprehensible, and why he who performs the first type of action is admired, while he who performs the other type is despised.[2] The uses of this exposition are legion: (a) it will guide the morally ambitious, who aspires to emulate the example of the noble and shun that of the ignoble; (b) it will show the way to the practice of virtuous types of action and the renunciation of the vicious; (c) it will portray the man of perfect character, who should serve as a model of morality; and (d) finally, it will enable such a man to shun evil, and derive gratification from the knowledge of his own perfect virtue.[3]

Accordingly, the author engages in an analysis of the nature of character and the way it arises in us. He defines it as "a state of the soul, whereby it is able to perform certain actions, without deliberation or choice,"[4] that is, spontaneously and effortlessly. In some it arises by instinct, in others by training or diligence, so that many people are found to possess the virtuous traits of courage, prudence, temperance and justice by nature, and many others by habit, Vicious traits, however, are more widespread and appear to predominate among people. Evil being man's

---

1 See K. Samir, "Le *Tahḏib al-Akhlāq* de Yaḥya b. ᶜAdī (m. 974) attribué à Ǧāḥiz et à Ibn al-ᶜArabī," in: *Arabica*, XXI (1974), 111–38.

2 Ibn ᶜAdī, *Tahdhīb al-Akhlāq*, ed. G.F. ᶜAwaḍ, Cairo, 1913, 12.

3 *Ibid.*, 12.

4 *Ibid.*, 13. Cf. Miskawayh, *Tahdhīb al-Akhlāq*, 31, and Ikhwān al-Ṣafāᵓ, *Rasāᵓ'il*, I, 305. See *supra* 93, n. 1.

dominant trait, he would be no better than a beast were he to give free rein to his evil propensities and refrain from the use of his reason. In fact, religious laws and political institutions have been established for precisely this purpose, to curb these evil propensities, deter the unjust and punish the wrongdoer.

Now whether we consider the naturally vicious or virtuous, moral education is indispensable for reforming the former and instructing the latter. Some, however, are so recalcitrant that only coercion or intimidation will effectively reform or deter them. Others, because of the intrinsic viciousness of their nature, could never be reformed or deterred, but those fortunately form a small minority of mankind, the majority being on the whole susceptible of reform and occupying an intermediate position between perfect goodness and perfect evil.[5]

The root of all evil, as indeed of all the variations in moral traits, according to Ibn ᶜAdī, is the status of the concupiscent power of the soul, and its relation to the two other powers, the irascible and the rational. To this extent this power is held in check, the agent is temperate or continent; to the extent it is unchecked, he is dissolute or incontinent. The author does not deny, however, that disorders arising in the irascible power can cause moral turbulence, by driving the agent to uncontrollable anger, recrimination or violence. Such anger is the root of all that levity, folly and recklessness which grip those who are unable to control their irascible power. If, however, this power is subordinated to reason and is properly managed, the virtues of high-mindedness and worthy social and political ambition will ensue.[6]

It is, in fact, upon the excellence of the rational soul that genuine virtue depends. Through it, man is able to either acquire the virtues of nobility, high-mindedness, prudence in the conduct of private affairs, benevolence, mercy, frugality (*nusk*), right thinking, and keen understanding, or to hold his two other powers, the concupiscent and the irascible, in check, channel and direct them. It is not, however, altogether free from the disposition to evil, and Ibn ᶜAdī lists as its vices meanness, trickery, deceit, cajolery, cunning, envy and duplicity.[7]

The preponderance of the virtues listed above, or of their opposites, determines the overall character of the individual. Some people, as we have mentioned, are good by nature, others evil, but the influence of habit or example on character is very great. That is why the company one keeps from childhood is decisive, owing to the preponderance of ignorance,

---

[5] *Ibid.*, 15.
[6] *Ibid.*, 17f.
[7] *Ibid.*, 20.

meanness, greed and envy, which are the chief causes of moral corruption.[8]

II. The Table of the Virtues and the Vices

Unlike other ethical writers of the period, Ibn ᶜAdī does not attempt a systematic tabulation of the virtues on the basis of the traditional, Platonic threefold subdivision of the powers of the soul and their corresponding virtues. He gives instead a long list which includes instances of the virtues corresponding to the rational, the irascible and the concupiscent powers, somewhat indiscriminately. The list includes temperance, contentedness, dignity, forgiveness, composure, modesty, friendliness, compassion, loyalty to friends, trustworthiness, confidence-keeping, humility, cheerfulness, truthfulness, purity of intention, generosity, courage, competitiveness, fortitude, magnanimity and justice.

The list of vices, on the other hand, includes profligacy, greed, flippancy, levity, stupidity, lust, cruelty, treachery, treason, divulgence of secrets, arrogance, churlishness, falsehood, meanness, rancor, miserliness, cowardice, envy, fear, pusillanimity and injustice.[9]

A noteworthy feature of Ibn ᶜAdī's analysis of these virtues and vices is his insistence that their status is not independent of the agent or his circumstances. Magnanimity, for instance, is particularly commendable in kings and rulers, just as much as courage, forgiveness, cheerfulness and generosity, whereas pusillanimity, frivolity, churlishness, lying, miserliness and cowardice are particularly reprehensible. These social differentiations of the virtues are so important for Ibn ᶜAdī that he has drawn a list of subsidiary moral traits, which in some are deemed virtuous, in others vicious. They include avidity for praise, which is commendable in the young, but reprehensible in the old, and love of adornment, which is commendable in kings, high public officials and women, but not in monks, ascetics, men of learning and clerics. What is commendable in the latter is "the wearing of rough clothing, aversion from luxury, and constant attendance at houses of prayer."[10] To reward praise is commendable from the former, but reprehensible from the latter; frugality is highly commendable in men of learning or religion, but not in kings or rulers, insofar as it frustrates their social or political aims.

It is characteristic of the virtues that they very rarely exist all together in one person, whereas contrariwise, no one is entirely free from some vice

---

[8] *Ibid.* 21.
[9] *Ibid.*, 22–34.
[10] *Ibid.*, 35.

or other. Accordingly, man's foremost duty is to observe his own state of character and examine his faults, with a view to rectifying them and cultivating the commendable traits. Contrary to the opinion of the vulgar, what sets people apart is their degree of virtue, rather than their wealth or social station. Ibn ʿAdī does not deny that the union of wealth and virtue is highly desirable, insofar as it gives the virtuous the means of extending his help to the needy.[11]

To achieve moral rectitude or uprightness, a series of recommendations, intended to keep the concupiscent power of the virtuous in check, is given by the author.

1. One should constantly remind oneself of the necessity of curbing one's appetites or passions.
2. One should seek the company of ascetics, monks, hermits, people of religious piety and men of learning, and avoid that of the frivolous and merry-makers.
3. One should constantly study books of ethics, politics, and biographies of saints, monks and hermits.
4. One should avoid drunkenness, because it inhibits the power of reason and renders it vulnerable to passion. The continent should quit drinking altogether; if he cannot, he should content himself with very little, consumed in the company of modest companions. One should avoid at all costs drinking at the parties of revellers and boon-companions.
5. One should refrain from indulging one's taste for music and song, especially when performed by painted women or jolly boys. For "singing has a very potent force in stimulating the appetites, especially when coupled with the fact that the singer herself is desirable and uses her wiles to attract attention."[12] If one must attend singing parties, let male singers be chosen.
6. As to eating, one should not be fastidious or gluttonous, since the purpose of eating is nourishment. One should instead confine oneself to simple and unprocessed foods, consumed in quantities sufficient to still the hunger and sate the appetite.
7. One should constantly reflect on the disgrace and opprobrium that attach to incontinence and gluttony, so that one's soul might turn in revulsion from vile desires and yearn after complete continence.

Another series of precepts intended to hold the irascible power in check is given.

---

[11] *Ibid.*, 38.
[12] *Ibid.*, 41.

1. The student of morality should reflect on the ludicrous demeanor of the irate, their stupidity and irrationality when seized by anger.
2. Instead of springing impulsively on the culprit when provoked, he should stop to think what kind of vengeance he would mete out to himself, were he the culprit, and this will inevitably mellow his anger.
3. He should avoid bearing arms at drinking parties or attending to accounts of war and subversion, or keeping the company of violent people or policemen, insofar as they conduce to cruelty and irascibility.
4. He should avoid strong drink, as it excites the irascible power, just as much it excites the concupiscent.
5. He should defer to quiet reflection, and avoid embarking on any course of action before thorough deliberation and reflection, making this the rule of life in all matters.[13]

As to the rational power, upon whose excellence ultimately depends the cultivation of character, as we have seen, our foremost duty is to perfect and strengthen it, through the pursuit of the rational sciences. To the extent the knowledge of these sciences is acquired, particularly that of ethics and politics, the rational soul will be roused to desire virtue and shun vice.

However, the rational sciences include the study of the "sciences of reality", (namely, physics and metaphysics) which is the noblest activity in which man can engage. To ensure progress in this study, the student is urged to emulate the example and mode of life proper to the masters of these sciences.[14]

The impact of this study on the acquisition of the intellectual virtues is, for Ibn ᶜAdī, decisive. These in turn exert an influence on the moral character of the agent, who is able thereupon to recognize the baseness of the concupiscent and irascible propensities of the soul, such as lust, vindictiveness, envy, malice, as well as the futility of actions prompted by these two powers. When one examines oneself rationally, he will realize that the evils consequent upon vicious actions far outweigh their apparent advantages, and that in fact many of these advantages, when carefully considered, will turn out to be disadvantages. Even the advantages will prove ultimately to be fleeting or trivial, and are frequently the occasion of animosity or strife.

The author, finally, urges that in the quest of virtue, our goal should be the highest degree of excellence, and that in fact nothing short of this ideal will do.

---

13 *Ibid.*, 44.
14 *Ibid.*, 47f.

III. The Portrait of the Morally Perfect Man

Accordingly, Ibn ᶜAdī draws up a list of the qualities that should characterise the 'perfect man' (*al-insān al-tāmm*), who is more akin to the angels than to mankind.

1. He should constantly watch over his moral traits, both good and bad.
2. He should be on his guard against the inroads of moral torpitude.
3. He should aspire to every virtue, however lofty.
4. He should be engrossed with the 'form of perfection'.
5. He should delight in every virtuous trait.
6. He should despise vice or public advancement.
7. He should be mindful of the advice of men of virtue and the precepts of ancient philosophers.
8. He should possess a certain eloquence and love of wisdom.
9. He should attend regularly the meetings of the learned and the pious.
10. He should manage his affairs in accordance with a "uniform canon" of moderation and continence, in pleasure-seeking, food or drink.
11. He should look upon wealth as a means, never an end in itself. Accordingly, he should be neither too solicitous in seeking it, nor too miserly in dispensing it for the satisfaction of his needs and those of the weak and the destitute.
12. He should despise anger and irascibility and cultivate the virtue of deliberation.
13. He should cultivate the virtue of love for his fellowmen, compassion and mercy towards them all. "For all men are like a single individual, insofar as they are united in humanity and adorned by the social form."[15] The essence of humanity consists in reason, which is the same in all mankind; by virtue of their rational soul, men are naturally gregarious and charitable. It is only when their irascible soul drives them to arrogance and love of domination that antagonism and jealousy cause them to fall apart.
14. He should exercise benevolence towards all his fellowmen, and should be willing to spend of his own substance in assisting them.
15. He should never forget that none of his vices or shortcomings is concealed from the public eye. Kings and other people in high places may imagine that their faults are not known to the public, because

---

[15] *Ibid.*, 55.

their subordinates and retainers do not proclaim them out of timidity of obsequiousness. Instead of resenting criticism, those people should welcome it, since it is only through criticism that they will be able to correct their faults and achieve by degrees the rank of perfection, which is the token of happiness and good repute.[16]

---

[16] *Ibid.*, 60.

CHAPTER SIX

AḤMAD IBN MUḤAMMAD MISKAWAYH (D. 1030), CHIEF MORAL PHILOSOPHER OF ISLAM

I. Miskawayh's Ethical Writings

Miskawayh's much more substantial ethical theory is embodied primarily in his *Ṭahārat al-Aʿrāq* (Purity of Dispositions), better known, like the work of his predecessor, Ibn ʿAdī, as *Tahdhīb al-Akhlāq*.[1] Whether Miskawayh was actually acquainted with his predecessor's work cannot be readily determined. There are certain similarities of structure and substance which suggest that he may have been familiar with this treatise, which he does not mention anywhere in his writings, as far as I am aware, and it is significant that he refers in his *al-Fawz al-Aṣghar* to al-Ḥasan ibn Suwār (d. ca. 1017), the best-known disciple of Ibn ʿAdī, who is known to have written on psychological and ethical subjects.[2] Moreover, the famous geographer-biographer, Yāqūt al-Ḥamawī (d. 1229), even makes of Miskawayh a 'protegé' (*lāʾidh*) of this al-Ḥasan (alias Ibn al-Khammār) and adds that he was completely taken with the books of Abū Zakariyāʾ.[3]

The *Tahdhīb* was not the only ethical treatise of Miskawayh, but it was undoubtedly the most important. He himself refers in the *Tahdhīb* to a treatise entitled *Tartīb al-Saʿādāt* (The Grades of Happiness), which appears to antedate the former treatise by almost a decade. A short tract on the essence of justice (*Fī Māhīyat al-ʿAdl*) is mentioned in *Kitāb al-Hawāmil wa'l-Shawāmil*, which belongs to the same period as *al-Tahdhīb*.[4]

---

[1] Miskawayh refers to his treatise by the title *Kitāb al-Ṭahārah*. See *Tahdhīb al-Akhlāq*, 91 and 222, et passim. Hereafter *Tahdhīb*. Later MSS. and editions also call it *Tahdhīb al-Akhlāq*, see *Tahdhīb*, 9.

[2] See Ibn Abī Uṣaybiʿah, *ʿUyūn al Anbāʾ*, 429; al-Qifṭī, *Taʾrīkh al-Ḥukamāʾ*, ed. J. Lippert, Leipzig 1903, 164; Ibn al-Nadīm, *al-Fihrist*, 384.

[3] See Yāqūt, *Muʿjam al-Udabā*, Beirut, 1970, V, 5 and 6. Cf. al-Tawḥīdī, *al-Imtāʿ wa'l Muʾānasah*, ed. A. Amīn, Cairo, 1939–44, I, 35f. The text refers to Abū Zakariyāʾ, the *kunya* of Yaḥyā, but this could very well be a corruption of Ibn Zakariyāʾ, the patronymic of the great philosopher and alchemist, al-Rāzī (d. ca. 925). The reference to al-Ḥasan ibn Suwār occurs in *al-Fawz al-Aṣghar*, Beirut, 1319 A.H., 48.

[4] That is 375–6 A.H. (985 A.D.). For the chronology of Miskawayh's writings, see M. Arkoun, *Contribution à l'étude de l'humanisme arabe au IVe/Xe Siècle: Miskawayh, philosophe et historien*, Paris, 1970, 107f.

His most important extant metaphysical treatise, *al-Fawz al-Aṣghar*, is not irrelevant to his ethics insofar as a large part of it is taken up with the discussion of psychological subjects fully pertinent to the acquisition of happiness, at which ethics itself aims. The substantiality and indestructibility of the soul is discussed in greater detail in *al-Fawz* than in *al-Tahdhīb*, and both themes, as we shall see in due course, form the groundwork of his ethics. Other short epistles (*rasāʾil*), *On Pleasures and Pains* and *On the Soul and Reason*, develop these fundamental, psychological themes in some detail.[5] As reported by al-Tawḥīdī, some of his responses in *al-Hawāmil wa'l Shawāmil* on such questions as justice and injustice, moral character, friendship, free will and predestination, and the need for human association are not without moral interest.[6] Finally, *Jāwīdān Khirad*, although not a systematic ethical treatise, consists of a collection of "the maxims (*ḥikam*) of the Persians, the Indians, the Arabs and the Greeks," which he regarded as complementary to the *Tahdhīb*. In that work, he writes, "we have laid down for you all the (general) principles," whereas in this book, our "intention is to give the particular moral maxims, as well as the sermons of the sages of every nation and every cult."[7]

II. Nature and Function of the Soul

The *Tahdhīb* opens with a statement of the author's aim in writing the book. His aim, he says, is twofold: (a) to acquire that moral character or disposition most suited to performing right actions, without effort or inconvenience, and (b) to do that methodically and systematically. To achieve this aim, we should know our selves, or souls, and determine the kind of entities they are and the reason they were created in us, in short "their perfection and purpose, as well as the powers and habits, which if properly used by us will enable us to attain this lofty rank."[8] The conclusions he arrives at in this work correspond roughly to those reached in *al-Fawz al-Aṣghar*, written less than a decade earlier, and in the short epistle *On the Soul and the Intellect*. It appears reasonable to assume that the psychological preamble of the *Tahdhīb* is a summary of an earlier and fuller exposition.

His first major contention in that preamble is that the soul is not body, part or condition of body, accident or temperament (*mizāj*), but a self-

---

5 See M. Arkoun, "Deux épîtres de Miskawayh," in: *Bulletin d'Études Orientales* (Institut Français de Damas), XVII (1961–62), 7–74.

6 See *al-Hawāmil wa'l-Shawāmil*, ed. A. Amīn, Cairo, 1951, 84f; 86f; 131f; 220f; 320f.

7 *Jāwīdān Khirad*, 25.

8 *Tahdhīb*, 2. Cf. Engl. translation by C.K. Zurayk, *The Refinement of Character*, Beirut, 1968, 1. Hereafter Zurayk.

subsisting entity (*jawhar*), which is neither susceptible of death nor destruction. For upon these premises is our resurrection predicated.[9]

To prove that the soul is essentially different from body, Miskawayh argues that:

1. It is self-evident that the body is capable of receiving only one type of form at the same time, whereas the soul is capable of receiving contrary forms (i.e. intelligible forms). These forms—instead of weakening it, as is the case with the body—actually increase its ability to receive additional forms.
2. It is an established proposition that the soul is the principle (*maᶜnā*) whereby man is distinguished from beasts, rather than bodily shape or structure.
3. The (rational) soul is likewise the principle whereby one person surpasses others in point of humanity, rather than the body.
4. The body, with its many organs, is nothing but an instrument or tool (*ālah*), adapted to a specific purpose. It cannot be said, in explaining this 'instrumental' relation, that one part of the body is a tool for another, since that other part is also a tool. Accordingly, the "user" of the tool or tools in question must be other than these tools, that is, something incorporeal and capable of using it or them in a conscious and deliberate way.[10]
5. The yearning of the soul for "the knowledge of divine things" and its search for things other and higher than the body "clearly show that it consists of a substance that is very much higher and nobler than things corporeal."[11]

To prove, on the other hand, that the soul is not an accident, Miskawayh proceeds somewhat circuitously to show that: (a) the soul, which apprehends both classes of sensible and intelligible forms (identified by him with accidents) and is able to discriminate between them, should be sharply distinguished from them;[12] (b) the soul cannot be regarded as a 'material form' or power, equally identified by him with accidents, because material forms or powers, such as the senses of hearing or sight, require bodily organs, and are, in addition, dazzled or dulled by strong sensations, whereas the (rational) soul does not require any bodily organs and is rendered keener by the apprehension of "strong cognitions";[13]

---

[9] See *al-Fawz al-Aṣghar*, 33f. Cf. English trans. by J.W. Sweetman, *Islamic and Christian Theology*, London, 1945, pt. I, vol. I, 118. Hereafter Sweetman. Cf. also *Tahdhīb*, 4, and Arkoun, "Deux Épîtres", 27.

[10] *Ibid.*, 35 (Sweetman, 119f.). Cf. Daiber, *Muᶜammar*, 352f.

[11] *Tahdhīb*, 6 (Zurayk, 8).

[12] *Al-Fawz*, 45 (Sweetman, 128).

[13] *Ibid.*, 46 (Sweetman, 128f). Cf. *Tahdhīb* 6 (Zurayk, 8) and *De Anima*, III, 429^{b}–4.

(c) the soul is capable of apprehending immaterial entities, the first principles of demonstration, the Maker, its own self and many deductive truths about the universe as a whole. None of these apprehensions is derived from the senses or require any material 'instruments'. On the contrary, such instruments are a hindrance to the soul's apprehension of "intelligible forms" in general;[14] and (d) as the bearer of the diverse accidents already listed, the soul cannot be any one of them, since it is an accepted principle that an accident cannot be the bearer of other accidents.[15]

The question whether the soul, as Aristotle had argued, is a form of the body, or more specifically, the "form of life" pertaining to a living organism, is further rejected by Miskawayh on essentially Aristotelian grounds. The soul is independent of the "blunting influence of old age", which affects bodily organs only, as asserted by Aristotle (in *De Anima*, I, 408^b 18f.) and interpreted by al-Ḥasan ibn Suwār. It cannot be a form of body or else it would be dependent on it and would perish with it. The soul, he asserts in distinct Platonic terms, is in fact a living and indestructible substance, which imparts life to the body, superintends its operations and survives its disintegration.[16]

To support the view that the soul is immortal, Miskawayh advances what he believes to be three Platonic arguments, although the second of them is clearly Neo-Platonic:

(a) as the entity which imparts everlasting life to the object in which it inheres, the soul should possess life essentially; it cannot therefore be susceptible to its opposite, i.e. death;[17] (b) being free from matter, privation and corruption, which are all reducible into each other, the soul must be incorruptible, and possess the contrary triplicity of being, goodness and eternal duration;[18] and (c) the soul is a self-moving entity.

Now whatever is self-moving is indestructible. For in *Timaeus* (27D) and *Laws* (4,895B) Plato has identified self-motion with life, and declared it to be distinct from the six natural kinds of motion, on the one hand, and to be above time, on the other. It follows that it is free from all the natural conditions of change, and is incorruptible. This argument is supported by a long quotation purporting to come from the *Timaeus*, in which Plato asserts in answer to the question: What is the generated thing which has no being, and what is the existing thing which is not generated? "The being

---

[14] *Al-Fawz*, 47 (Sweetman, 129).

[15] *Tahdhīb*, 5 (Zurayk, 7), and Arkoun, "Deux Épîtres ...", 27.

[16] See *al-Fawz*, 49f. (Sweetman, 130f.)

[17] *Ibid.*, Cf. *Phaedo*, 105C and *Phaedrus*, 246B.

[18] *Al-Fawz*, 54 (Sweetman, 134). This triplicity appears to derive from Proclus. See Liber de Causis, in: *NeoPlatonici apud Arabes*, ed. ᶜA.-R. Badawī, Cairo, 1955, 6. Cf. Miskawayh, *Risālah fī Māhīyat al-ᶜAdl*, ed. M.S. Kahn, Leiden, 1964, 12f.

that has no generation is that which belongs to those things which are above time, for whatever is above time is also above natural motion, and as such does not enter into the categories of past or future. Its being is most analogous to eternity (*dahr*)."[19]

It follows that the essence of the soul, which has already been identified with substance, is eternal life, and as such that it is indestructible. The motion in which it is involved is the eternal and circular motion, which the heavenly spheres derive from it. Miskawayh, nevertheless, distinguishes in this motion, following Plotinus, between upward and downward; as the soul moves upwards towards Reason, the first emanation from the One, it is filled with beauty and light, and as it moves downwards toward matter, its own light shines upon this matter. The first of these two motions is called by the Holy Law (*sharīᶜah*) the right, and is the source of the soul's felicity; the second is called the left, and is the source of its wretchedness.[20] The detailed discussion of the type(s) of happiness of which the soul can partake in this world and the world-to-come will be attempted in the sequel.

III. Virtue as the Excellence of the Rational Soul

The foregoing account of the soul is intended to serve as a preamble for the discussions of ethical questions proper. The two central questions for Miskawayh, as indeed for most ethical writers in Islam, both philosophical and religious, are the nature and the conditions of virtue, on the one hand, and the attainment (*taḥṣīl*) of happiness, on the other.

Here too the psychological dualism of soul and body derived from Plato and conditioned by Neo-Platonic elements plays a decisive role. By virtue, we are to understand the perfection or excellence (*kamāl*, *faḍīlah*, ἀρετή), as Aristotle has argued in the *Nicomachean Ethics*, of that part of the soul which constitutes the essence of man and sets him apart from other animals, i.e. reason or deliberation. To the extent an individual cultivates the perfection of this part or faculty, shunning at the same time those activities associated with the body, he excells his fellowmen in humanity and virtue. In fact, he writes, "the yearning (of the soul) for its specific activities, by which I mean the different modes of knowledge and cognition, and the shunning of those activities proper to the body constitute its virtue or excellence. This virtue increases in proportion as man attends to his soul and keeps away from those matters which hinder it from its

---

[19] *Al-Fawz*, 57 (Sweetman, 137). Cf. *Timaeus*, 35A and *Laws*, X, 895B.
[20] *Ibid.*, 58 (Sweetman, 138f). Cf. e.g. Koran, 56: 7–8, 24, 41, 90–91.

goal (. . .), i.e. corporal matters, sensations and related matters.''[21]

However, Miskawayh's classification of the virtues follows Platonic and late Peripatetic lines. Starting from the Platonic trichotomy of the soul, he assigns to each of the three faculties or parts (used indifferently) a cardinal virtue to the rational, wisdom, to the irascible, courage, and to the concupiscent, temperance. When these parts act in harmony, the fourth Platonic virtue, justice, arises. The common characteristic of each of these virtues is moderation (*i ᶜtidāl*); accordingly, Miskawayh describes each of them in Aristotelian fashion as a mean between two extremes, each of which is a vice. The mean, according to him, is the farthest point from the two extremes, and may be compared in that respect to the center of the circle in relation to the circumference.[22]

This fourfold scheme is then developed with some ingenuity, each of the cardinal virtues serving as a stem on which a series of branches is grafted, but contrary to one's expectations, the Aristotelian table of intellectual and moral virtues is not conformed with. Thus the subdivisions of wisdom are given as intelligence, retention, prudence, lucidity, sound judgement and easy comprehension. Those of courage are magnanimity (μεγαλοφυχὶα), fearlessness, fortitude, steadfastness, patience, self-assurance, manliness and endurance. Those of temperance are modesty, meekness, self-control, liberality, honesty, contentedness, equableness, self-discipline, good disposition, docility, composure and piety. Finally, those of justice are friendship, concord, kindness to one's kin, reciprocity, honest dealing, gracious dispensation, affability and worship.[23]

None of these tables appears to have a precise Greek predecessor, although as Richard Walzer has shown recently, it was common for Stoic and Peripatetic authors in late Greek antiquity to develop similar schemes, as attested, for instance, by the cases of Arius Didymus and the unknown author of the spurious Aristotelian *De Virtutibus et Vitiis*.[24]

---

[21] *Tahdhīb*, 9f. (Zurayk, 10). Cf. *N.E.*, I, 1097^b, 24f.

[22] *Ibid.*, 16 and 25 (Zurayk, 16f and 23f). On a pseudo-Platonic source for Miskawayh, see H. Daiber, ''Ein bisher unbekannter pseudoplatonischer Text über die Tugenden der Seele in arabischer Überlieferung,'' in: *Der Islam* 47 (1971), 34–42.

[23] *Tahdhīb*, 19f. (Zurayk, 20f.).

[24] See Walzer, *Greek into Arabic*, 222f. Cf. Stobaeus, *Eclog.* II, 60 (Wachsmuth) and Von Arnim, *Stoic. Vet. Frag.*, III, 63–72. Lists of these subsidiary virtues are attributed to minor Peripatetic and Stoic authors in an Arabic tract on ethics, apparently written by Nicolaus of Laodicea (4th century). It reproduces some of the sub-virtues of the spurious *De Virtutibus et Vitiis*. See M.C. Lyons, ''A Greek Ethical Treatise,'' in: *Oriens*, XIII–XIV (1960–61), 50f. For pseudo-Aristotle, *De Virtutibus*, Syriac-Arabic translations, see edition by Mechtild Kellermann, *Ein pseudoaristotelischer Traktat über die Tugent. Edition und Übersetzung der arabischen Fassungen des Abū Qurra und des Ibn aṭ-Ṭayyib*, thesis, Erlangen, 1965.

IV. Justice

Of the whole group of virtues and sub-virtues given above, two stand out as pre-eminent: justice and friendship. Miskawayh's general conception of justice, as we have seen, is essentially Platonic, but he appears to encounter no difficulty in fitting it into an Aristotelian framework. Thus it is defined as "the perfection and fulfillment" of the three (Platonic) virtues of wisdom, courage and temperance, resulting from the right equilibrium (*iᶜtidāl*) or proportion (*nisbah*) of the three faculties of the Soul.[25] This equilibrium is then interpreted in Pythagorean and Neo-Platonic terms as a mode of unity, which is the ultimate principle of order and subsistence in the world, a 'surrogate' or 'shadow' of unity.[26] For to the extent an entity partakes of unity and is free from multiplicity, he explains, it is higher in the order of reality and virtue. Unity is in fact synonymous with the "perfection of being", which is in turn synonymous with "perfect goodness". The difference between these three terms is purely semantic: being, whose perfection is unity, when conceived as the object of desire is simply designated as goodness.[27]

Miskawayh's deduction of the concept of justice from that of unity appears, as we mentioned, to reflect Pythagorean theories, but is not without intrinsic interest. In his tract *On the Essence of Justice*, he explains that because physical objects are never free from plurality; by reason of their diverse dimensions, proportions and contrary forms, they can never fully partake of unity, but only of its nearest 'similitude' or surrogate, which is equality. Through this equality, physical objects receive a certain unity or equilibrium which ensures that they retain their own identity or integrity and are not dominated or destroyed by other objects. This in fact is the essence of that natural justice, without which the whole universe would fall to ruins.[28]

To this natural or physical justice, Miskawayh opposes a divine justice which "exists in the realm of metaphysics and of everlasting entities."[29] It differs from physical justice, which is also eternal, in that its object is the immaterial, whereas that of physical justice is the material only. Accordingly, the Pythagoreans illustrate this concept in terms of number, for when "number is abstracted from what is numbered, it is found to possess

---

25 *Tahdhīb*, 16 (Zurayk, 17).

26 *Ibid.*, 112 (Zurayk, 101).

27 See *R. fī Māhīyat al-ᶜAdl*, 17.

28 *Ibid.*, 16f. Cf. *Tahdhīb*, 112f. (Zurayk, 100f.) In *Vita Pythag.*, 130–1. Jamblichus reports that Pythagoras had identified justice with proportion, harmony or equilibrium, which he interpreted mathematically. Cf. A. Delatte, *Essai sur la politique pythagoricienne*, Liège-Paris, 1922, 57f. For *iᶜtidāl* (*wasaṭ*) see Daiber, in: *Der Islam* 47 (1971), 38f.

29 *R. fī Māhīyat al-ᶜAdl*, 20.

in itself certain essential properties and a certain order which are not liable to change."[30]

Two other divisions of justice are given by Miskawayh in this tract, namely, conventional and human. The former is subdivided into general and particular and is said to be the attribute of those modes of legislation or action which are either universally approved by the whole of mankind, or particularly by a given state, nation or household. The norms of conventional justice are neither immutable nor absolute. For the lawgiver lays down, in accordance with the circumstances and customs prevalent in his day rather than in accordance with immutable principles, certain rules which are regarded during his reign as just.[31]

As for human justice, designated by him as voluntary, it is defined as the manner in which the powers of the soul are at peace with each other, and are neither in mutual strife nor oppression. It is to the body what health is to the soul.[32] Strangely enough, Miskawayh contends that it cuts across the other three already-mentioned subdivisions of justice.[33]

When he proceeds to develop the social implications of this ethical concept, the Platonic conception of justice as 'psychic harmony' is modified along familiar Aristotelian lines. Like Aristotle, he argues that the truly just man is not only one who achieves equilibrium or harmony within himself, but "seeks that in whatever transactions or honors are external to him", for the sake of the virtue of justice itself and nothing else.[34] In this respect, we can distinguish three spheres of justice corresponding to the three spheres of human activity: (a) that of distribution of goods and honors, (b) that of voluntary transactions, and (c) that of (involuntary) transactions involving violence or oppression.[35]

With regard to (a), justice is determined by arithmetical proportion, called by Miskawayh discontinuous, as in the ratio 1:2 = 2:4. With regard to (b), it is determined by harmonic proportion (called by him continuous), as in the proportion of A (a tailor) to B (a cobbler) = a (a garment)

---

30 *Ibid.*, 20.
31 *Ibid.*, 19.
32 *Ibid.*, 19.
33 *Ibid.*, 12.
34 *Tahdhīb*, 112 (Zurayk, 100).
35 *Ibid.*, 114 (Zurayk, 101). Cf. *N.E.*, V, 1130b 29f, where Aristotle divides 'particular' acts of justice into:
1. those involving distribution of goods and honors;
2. those involvoing rectification of wrongs either in
   a) voluntary transactions
   b) involuntary transactions, which are
      either (i) clandestine, or
      (ii) violent.

to b (a pair of shoes).[36] With regard to (c), justice is determined by geometrical (*misāḥiyyah*) proportion. If a man, for instance, had a certain proportion or relation to another that was disturbed by an act of injustice or injury, justice would require that a "similar injury be inflicted on him, so that the (original) proportion may be restored."[37] Hence the just may be defined in this case as one who restores equality, with respect to unequal things.

A key concept in the whole discussion of proportion, both for Aristotle and Miskawayh, is that of a measure or norm. In social or political relations, the law (*sharīᶜah*) is the measure in one sense, whereas it is the ruler in another. In economic relations, on the other hand, the measure is money, which is the principle regulating and equalizing commercial transactions. After commenting on the etymological kinship of the word for law (*nomos* = *nāmūs*) in Greek with that for money (*nomismos*),[38] Miskawayh goes on to quote a statement from the *Nicomachean Ethics* purporting to assert that of the three norms, the highest is the law emanating from God. Even the second norm, the ruler, acts on behalf of God.[39]

Now to these three laws correspond three modes of justice. For he who clings to the divine law will act in accordance with the precepts of justice and thereby acquire perfection of character and happiness. He who deals with his fellowmen equitably in money matters will contribute to the prosperity of the state, and this is the essence of 'political justice'. (Likewise, he who submits to the authority of the ruler is just.) Contrariwise, he who flouts the divine law, repudiates the authority of the ruler (identified by Miskawayh with the *Caliph* or *Imām*), or appropriates what is not his own is unjust;[40] the three types of injustice, corresponding to the three types of justice already discussed, are identified in the sequel, on the basis of Aristotle's alleged statements, with our duty to God, our superiors or equals and our ancestors.[41]

V. Friendship

The second generic virtue upon which Miskawayh dwells at some length is friendship or love.[42] Some have maintained, he says, that the moral

---

[36] *Tahdhīb*, 114 (Zurayk, 102). Cf. *N.E.* V, 1131a, 15f.

[37] *Ibid.*, 12. Cf. *N.E.* V, 1132a 20f.

[38] See *N.E.* V, 1133a 30.

[39] *Tahdhīb*, 115 (Zurayk, 103). The Aristotelian source of this alleged statement is uncertain.

[40] *Ibid.*, 116 (Zurayk, 104).

[41] *Ibid.*, 119 (Zurayk, 106f). In the spurious *De Virtutibus et Vitiis*, 5, 1250b, Aristotle actually gives a fivefold division of justice: towards God, demons (spirits), the fatherland, parents, and the dead.

[42] The two terms, *ṣadāqah* and *maḥabbah* are used almost interchangeably, although

disposition of justice arises in the soul, simply because the noble disposition of friendship cannot be achieved. For when men are held together by the bond of friendship, justice can be readily dispensed with,[43] both being to some extent regulative social principles.

The bond of friendship, however, is the primary principle of social association. Because of his imperfections and insufficiency, the individual cannot fulfill his essential needs without the cooperation of his fellowmen. In this cooperation, and the harmony attendant upon it, men are "as one person, whose many organs combine to carry out the one action advantageous to him."[44]

The divisions of friendship are given by Miskawayh as four, based not on the different goals of the relationship, as suggested by Aristotle, but rather on its comparative durability: (1) the type of friendship which is quick to develop, but equally quick to dissolve; (2) the type which is quick to develop, but slow to dissolve; (3) that which is slow to develop, but quick to dissolve; and, (4) that which is slow to develop and slow to dissolve. This fourfold division corresponds to the threefold division of human goals or objectives: aiming at the pleasant, the good and the useful, to which a combination of the three may be added.[45]

Friendship for the sake of pleasure corresponds to (1), according to Miskawayh, that for the sake of goodness to (2), that for the sake of utility to (3), and that for the sake of a combination of the three to (4), provided it includes the good as an ingredient.

Insofar as they involve will and deliberation, these varieties of friendship can only arise among human beings, and are attended by punishment or reward. However, a species of friendship which is really a mode of affinity (*ilf*) can hold irrational animals, which are similar, together. As to inanimate objects, such as minerals and rocks, the only relationship between them is the natural tendency towards their centers, although discord (*munāfarah*) and concord (*mushākalah*), depending on the mixture of the original elements making them up, can arise between them. When the mixture accords with one of the three relations laid down in the sciences of arithmetic and harmony, i.e. the harmonic, the arithmetical and the geometrical, concord prevails; when it accords with their contraries, discord arises.[46]

Miskawayh appears to be concerned more with the Aristotelian *philia* than the Platonic *eros*.

[43] *Tahdhīb*, 133 (Zurayk, 118). Cf. *N.E.*, VIII, 1155a 25.

[44] *Ibid.*, 135 (Zurayk, 123).

[45] *Ibid.*, 136 (Zurayk, 123). Cf. *N.E.*, VIII, 1155b and II, 1104b 30. However, Aristotle reduces the list to two basic goals: the good and the pleasant.

[46] *Ibid.*, 136 (Zurayk, 124). In *al-Hawāmil wa'l-Shawāmil*, friendship is divided by

Like Aristotle, Miskawayh holds that only that friendship grounded in virtue is truly durable, the nature of good being constant, unlike that of utility or pleasure which is continuously changing. The rapid fluctuations attendant upon the friendship of utility is due to the warring inclinations caused within man by the 'contrary properties' making him up, one bodily pleasure conforming with one property, while another conflicting with it.[47]

The case of 'intellectual pleasure' is different. For there exists in man a simple and divine substance which is unmixed with any of the other natural properties; accordingly, he is able to partake of this intellectual pleasure, which is entirely different from corporeal pleasure. This is a simple pleasure which can reach the intensity of passionate love (*ᶜishq*), is analogous to mystical rapture (*walah*), and identical with the "divine love" which some divine men (*mutaᵓallihūn*) claim to have experienced.[48]

This divine love is characterized by Miskawayh in essentially Neo-Platonic terms, which bear none but the remotest relation to Aristotle's view, to which it is nevertheless alleged to be affiliated. Once the divine substance in man has been cleansed of its sensuous accretions, it yearns for its like, and perceives with the eye of reason the Pure and First Good. Thereupon, it hastens to meet Him, and the Pure Good reciprocates by imparting to it His light, causing it to partake of a pleasure which is unequalled and to attain a degree of union which is the goal of the truly divine man.[49]

We will consider in due course the divine level of happiness corresponding to this divine love. Miskawayh, having taken us to the pinnacle of this supernatural friendship or love, now turns to the consideration of the more mundane forms of friendship, those for the sake of utility or plea-

---

Miskawayh into essential and accidental. The former is described as a proportion (*nisbah*) between two entities, either of specific mixture, soul or nature, the second as a relationship between rational beings involving habit, affinity, utility, apparent utility, pleasure, hope, joint trades, opinions or beliefs, or kinship (*ᶜaṣabīyah*). See *al-Hawāmil wa'l-Shawāmil*, 131f. For the ethics of its author see Marc Bergé, *Pour un humanisme vécu: Abū Ḥayyān al-Tawḥīdī*, Damascus, 1979, 303ff. For the ethics of his contemporary Abū Sulaymān al-Sijistānī see J. Kraemer, *Philosophy in the Renaissance of Islam*, Leiden, 1986, 267ff. Aristotle has described friendship as a certain likeness ('ὁμοιότητα τινα), holding like things (Empedocles) or unlike things (Heraclitus) together. See *N.E.*, VIII, 1155a 32f.

47 *Ibid.*, 138 (Zurayk, 126).

48 *Ibid.*, 138f. (Zurayk, 126).

49 *Ibid.*, 139 (Zurayk, 126). Cf. Uthūlūjiyā in *Plotinus apud Arabes*, ed. ᶜA.-R. Badawī, Cairo, 1955, 34f. and 116f. The source of this mystical love (or *eros*) is Porphyry, who is criticized for using 'pictorial, poetic, and mystical' language in his account of the union of the soul with its object. See *Avicenna's De Anima* (Arabic text), ed. F. Rahman, London, 1959, 239f. and R. Walzer, "Porphyry and the Arabic Tradition," 294f.

sure. Their subdivisions are numerous. In the first place, we have the natural gregariousness binding us to our fellowmen, which is the basis of all forms of friendship or love. Congregational meetings and banquets have been instituted either by religion or 'refined convention' to enhance this gregariousness (*uns*). It was for this reason that the (*Islamic*) call to the worshippers to meet five times a day in the mosque, and particularly on Friday, to assemble twice a year on feast-days, and, finally, to meet once in a lifetime at the Holy Place in Mecca, arose.[50]

Secondly, we have the love of husband and wife, which is rooted in the enjoyment of mutual pleasures and advantages which both derive from their conjugal union. This love is liable to dissolution as a consequence of the failure of either party to live up to the expectations of the other. Analogous to it is the love of lover and paramour and that of rich and poor, master and subordinate, ruler and subject, and father and child.[51]

Thirdly, we have the love of man for his Creator which is the prerogative of the man of 'divine learning' (*ᶜālim rabbānī*), since it is impossible for one to love what he does not know, except by dissimulation. This love is attended by obedience for and glorification of God, and is akin to the child's love for his parents, or the disciple for his master. The latter of these two is the nobler, for teachers are responsible for refining our souls and are the "causes of our genuine existence", as well as our supreme happiness. Accordingly, we should accord them the same veneration we owe to God, the teacher being "a spiritual father and a human lord (*rabb*)."[52]

It is a mark of the truly virtuous man who has attained this rank that he discriminates between the different types of friendship and deals with every class of friends, as well as his own self which is his genuine friend (*maḥbūbah*), in accordance with the precepts of justice and benevolence (*iḥsān*). He will not be satisfied either with the life of honor or pleasure, but will seek the highest good, which is the good in itself, to which the 'divine part' in him is referred.[53]

Nevertheless, Miskawayh insists that man's supreme happiness cannot be achieved without the fellowship of friends and associates, for being a 'political animal' by nature, he could not fulfill himself in solitude. Accordingly, a list of precepts for choosing one's friends and dealing with them virtuously is given.

1. You should, he argues, choose your friends carefully and avoid in particular association with the ungrateful and the slothful.

---

[50] *Tahdhīb*, 141 (Zurayk, 127f.)
[51] *Ibid.*, 142f. (Zurayk, 129f.)
[52] *Ibid.*, 147f. (Zurayk, 134).
[53] *Ibid.*, 152f. (Zurayk, 138f.).

2. Approach your friend in a spirit of affability and consideration, as well as readiness to share his joys and sorrows.

3. Do not withhold from your friend any knowledge, wealth or advantage that you may have, but deal with him generously.

4. Castigate your friend gently for his faults, but do not listen to columniators, and always be willing to volunteer friendly advice.[54]

VI. Happiness, its Object and Grades

Friendship, like the other moral virtues, should be conceived, according to Miskawayh, as a means to man's ultimate goal, or happiness. Like Aristotle, he argues that the exercise of these virtues requires certain external goods, such as money and other material objects, as well as the assistance of associates and friends.[55] This is particularly true of the exercise of justice, which is the essential condition of human (social) existence. That is why we reckon laziness and sloth among the vilest vices and reproach the adepts of asceticism "if they cut themselves off from mankind and dwell in mountains and caves." For how can he who leads a solitary life practise temperance, justice, liberality and courage, and should he not be regarded as no better than the inanimate, or even the dead?[56]

However, he recognizes that man as a composite being partakes of a composite activity: practical and intellectual. To the former corresponds a practical, or moral perfection (*kamāl khuluqī*); to the latter a cognitive one (*kamāl ᶜālimī*).[57] The second is to the first what form is to matter, and the perfection or happiness corresponding to it is proportionately higher.

In making these distinctions, Miskawayh remains on solid Aristotelian grounds, but when he proceeds to characterize the cognitive perfection of man, he suddenly shifts his ground and describes it, in the manner of Ibn Sīnā and other Muslim Neo-Platonists, in terms of 'conjunction' or contact (*ittiṣāl*) with the intelligible world, without sacrificing, however, the 'moral perfection' which simply serves as a prelude to it. "When you have attained these grades (i.e. cognitive coupled with orderly action)," he writes, "you become a world apart, and you deserve to be called a small world (microcosm), because the forms of all existing entities would have become realized within you, so that you would have become in a sense

---

54 *Ibid.*, 157f. (Zurayk, 141f).
55 *Ibid.*, 167f. (Zurayk, 149f) Cf. *N.E.* I, 1098b 30f. and X, 1178a 25f.
56 *Ibid.*, 168 (Zurayk, 150).
57 *Ibid.*, 39f. (Zurayk, 36f).

identical with them."[58] It is in the attainment of this ultimate intellectual and supermundane condition that man's genuine happiness actually lies; the moral perfection injected into the argument by Miskawayh serves at best as an intermediate phase. Attended by the trials and tribulations or terrestrial existence, and clouded by the deceptions and frustrations of bodily pleasure, the latter can never be the ultimate object of human quest. Only by rising above it and achieving the intellectual perfection of wisdom will man be able to join the higher spiritual realm (*al-malaʾ al-aʿlā*) and receive the illumination of the "divine light". When man has attained that condition, he will become immune to suffering, "fully pleased with himself and content with his condition and the emanations be receives from the light of the One. He will derive no other pleasure save from these conditions, is delighted with nothing save these beauties, and is not jubilant save at the prospect of revealing that wisdom to those who are worthy of it."[59]

Man's "ultimate and uttermost happiness" is said by Miskawayh to lie in this intellectual condition. It is significant, however, that he recognizes beyond it a third and higher condition, designated as divine. This is a condition in which all man's actions are divine, that is, directed to the pure good (identified by him with God or the 'divine reason' in man) and are performed as befits the divine mode of action for the sake of the action itself. This indeed is the mark of divine activity, that it has no object outside or beyond itself. "Thus the Creator, may He be exalted, acts for His own sake, rather than for the sake of something else extraneous to Him."[60] It follows that in achieving this condition man is able to partake of the divine perfection or achieve that state of self-divinization compared to which all his natural desires, anxieties and aspirations are sheer vanities.

Although the account of this 'divine condition' is alleged by Miskawayh to derive from an Aristotelian tract "On the Virtues of the Soul", which is clearly other than the spurious *De Virtutibus et Vitiis* of the Aristotelian corpus, its Plotinian, mystical ring is unmistakable. In it, he says, on the alleged authority of Aristotle also, the truly happy sage (*ḥakīm*) partakes of that happiness pertaining to God, "the perfectly happy sage", and accordingly has no proportion to humanity or the 'natural life', being "a divine gift which the Creator, Whose greatness is vast, bestows on whomsoever of His servants He chooses."[61] However, despite his obvious ob-

---

[58] *Tahdhīb*, 41 (Zurayk, 37). Cf. Ibn Sīnā, *al-Najāt*, Cairo, 1938, 293 and *Aḥwāl al-Nafs*, 130f. and appendix A.
[59] *Tahdhīb*, 85 (Zurayk, 77).
[60] *Ibid.*, 89 (Zurayk, 79).
[61] *Ibid.*, 171 (Zurayk, 152).

session with it, Miskawayh continues to struggle with the problem of reconciling it to the "unmixed life" already mentioned. His insistence on the composite nature of man and the 'mixed life', we believe, is purely verbal. Man's ultimate happiness has been explicitly stated by him to be intellectual, spiritual or divine, however one might interpret these terms, the concessions made to the moral or practical perfection being at best aporetic.[62] The intellectual perfection of active thought is attended by a happiness which nothing terrestrial or bodily can mar; neither the pleasure of the flesh nor the vicissitudes of fortune will have any dominion on the happy man who has achieved that self-mastery and equanimity born of genuine wisdom.[63] Even death will have no terror for him who knows that death is nothing but the liberation of the soul, an immaterial and indestructible substance, from the bondage of the body, and that the resultant breaking of the bond between soul and body is the goal of all genuine philosophy.[64]

In *Tartīb al-Saᶜādāt*, mentioned four times in *Tahdhīb al-Akhlāq* and antedating it apparently by two decades,[65] Miskawayh wrestles with this same antithesis between the two modes of perfection. The title of the treatise itself is instructive: happiness is spoken of in the plural and its different grades admit of an orderly arrangement (*tartīb*). The moral and intellectual perfections of man are qualified in this tract as proximate and ultimate, the proximate consisting in the "emanation from him of outward actions, through deliberation and will, and their ordering according to the dictates of reason."[66] The ultimate happiness, on the other hand, attainable only by the privileged few, is achieved only subsequently to the former and once self-sufficiency and leisure have been secured. The marks of the man who has achieved this second stage of happiness are:

1. Energy
2. Optimism and confidence
3. Fortitude
4. Equanimity
5. Non-conformism
6. Self-contentment

The last characteristic is perhaps the keynote of this condition of happiness on which Miskawayh dwells so insistently. The happy man (*saᶜīd*),

---

62 Arkoun recognizes Miskawayh's "oscillation" on this point and the absence of "une definition coherente du Bonheur Supreme." See *Contribution à l'étude*, 289.

63 *Tahdhīb*, 95f. (Zurayk, 85).

64 *Ibid.*, 216 (Zurayk, 191). Miskawayh quotes in this passage al-Kindī's tract on *The Art of Dispelling Sorrows*, an essentially Socratic tract. Cf. *Phaedo*, 66D.

65 See Arkoun, *op. cit.*, 107.

66 See *Kitāb al-Saᶜādah*, Cairo, 1928, 34.

he writes, "is self-contented, because he perceives certain immutable realities, which neither change or are liable to change. He sees everything he sees with the eyes of one who does not err or stumble, and is not liable to corruption (. . .)[67] He is like a traveler who is headed for a country (*waṭan*) that he already knows and clings to in spirit, and every time he passes a mansion leading to it, or enters upon a grade bringing him closer to it, his energy, peace of mind and joy are heightened. This condition of confidence and self-assurance is not simply a matter of report (*khabar*), unconfirmed by actual vision (*muᶜāyanah*). The soul does not rest in it until the truth has been grasped."[68]

This mystical language is pursued with some relentlessness and the mode of vision in question compared to the sight of the eye, with this difference that the physical eye is weakened by prolonged observation, whereas this 'spiritual' eye increases in strength and keenness in proportion as it engages in extended observation, until the point is reached when it is able to comprehend what originally it deemed unintelligible.

Despite the obvious un-Aristotelian character of this experience, Miskawayh feels confident that it can be fitted into the Aristotelian scheme of practical and theoretical wisdom, and he concludes the discussion with a list of the chief parts of the Aristotelian corpus purporting to derive from Paul the Persian's letter to Anushirwan (Chosroes I), outlining the order and method to be adopted in seeking the two modes of wisdom.[69] He finds once more in the Aristotelian distinction between the two components of human nature the key to that 'divine happiness' which belongs to the divine part in man, and consists, according to him, of the "love of wisdom", dedication to intellectual activities and the "use of divine opinions". Whoever has attained that stage, which is identical with the pure good, will be relieved from the stresses and strains of natural desire or passion and will join the company of the blessed spirits and associate with the angels closest to God.[70] In support of this view, he invokes the authority of Aristotle as interpreted no doubt by Neo-Platonic authors, notably Porphyry, to whose lost commentary on the *Nicomachean Ethics* we have already referred, and concludes that the culmination of this happiness, according to Aristotle, is the love of God, of which only the truly virtuous and happy man can partake. Aristotle's famous response in *Nicomachean*

---

[67] The blank stands for a part of the text which is not intelligible to me.

[68] *K. al-Saᶜādah*, 43. Cf. *al-Fawz*, 71, where Miskawayh refers to the mansions (*manāzil*) and stations (*maqāmat*) of mystical experience.

[69] *Ibid.*, 45–60. Cf. D. Gutas, "Paul the Persian on the Classification of the Parts of Aristotle's Philosophy: A Milestone Between Alexandria and Baġdād" in: *Der Islam* 60, (1983), 231–267.

[70] *Tahdhīb*, 169 (Zurayk, 151).

Ethics X, 1177b 30f. to "those who advise us, being men, to think of human things" is then reproduced in support of this 'divine happiness', as follows: "Man's aspirations should not be human, though he be a man, nor should he be content with the aspirations of mortal animals, though he himself be mortal. He should strive with all his powers to live a divine life; for man, though small in bulk, is great in wisdom and noble in intellect."[71]

If we are justified in describing this line of reasoning as mystical, it would follow that there are really three strains or layers in Miskawayh's theory of happiness: (a) a mystical or Plotinian strain, expressed in experiential or visionary terms, (b) an intellectualist or Aristotelian strain, in which happiness is described in line with *N.E.* X, 7, as a mode of self-divinization, and (c) a realistic and dualistic strain, affiliated to the more mundane tendencies in Aristotle's psychology and ethics and the farthest removed from the Platonism which served as the groundwork of Miskawayh's ethics, but was in fact at the heart of the Platonism of the *Protrepticus*.

Accordingly, the tensions in Miskawayh's thought arising from (a) and (b) can be fitted into an Aristotelian developmental framework, i.e. the transition from the Platonism of the *Protrepticus* to the 'Aristotelianism' of the *Eudemian* and *Nicomachean Ethics*.[72] Both elements are reflected, as we have seen, in the general outline of his ethics, as well as the extensive quotations from the spurious *Virtues of the Soul*, which apparently reached Miskawayh through an unknown Neo-Platonic medium.[73] What would be particularly difficult to accommodate to genuine Aristotelianism is the duality of soul and body, on which the substantiality and immortality of the soul are predicated. These two propositions are stated by Miskawayh in almost exclusively Platonic terms. His attempt to extract from Aristotle's comments on Solon's words in *N.E.* I, 1100a 10f. that "we must see the end" a positive theory of immortality, although ingenious, must be declared abortive.[74] So much in the mature Aristotelianism of the *Nicomachean Ethics* and the *De Anima* militates against the thesis of immortality that Aristotle should be exonerated from the charge.

---

71 *Tahdhīb*, 171 (Zurayk, 152).

72 For the development of Aristotle's ethics, see W. Jaeger, *Aristotle, Fundamentals of the History of his Development*, Oxford, 1948, 79f., 229f., 426f. Cf. *Aristotle's Protrepticos*, ed. and Engl. transl. by Ingemar Düring, Göteborg, 1961, B85–B100.

73 S. Pines, "Un texte inconnu d'Aristotle en version arabe," in: *Archives d'histoire doctrinale et littéraire du moyen âge* (Paris), 1955, 5–43 and 1959, 295–99.

74 See *Tahdhīb*, 97 (Zurayk, 86f.). Aristotle clearly implies in this passage that certain actions or affections, such as honors or dishonors and the good or bad fortune of offspring, can affect the happiness of their ancestors. See *N.E.* I, 1100a 10f.

VII. Moral Therapy

A large part of the *Tahdhīb* is concerned with the cultivation of character, or the manner in which the different parts or faculties of the soul are brought into harmony, and is directed towards the chief goal of human activity, i.e. happiness. This cultivation may be called, by analogy with medicine, the art of preserving the health of the soul. The concluding part, appropriately enough, turns on the manner in which those powers may run amock, and as a result threaten the moral harmony or health of the soul, calling thereby for the special skills of moral therapy, or the restoration of moral health.[75]

To preserve the moral health of the soul, it is essential to engage in the pursuit of practical and theoretical disciplines, designed to keep firmly established in the soul the moral and intellectual traits without which 'moral relapse' is inevitable, and to guard against their loss through disuse or sloth. Should these 'treasures' be allowed to be lost, their owner is greatly to be reproached, since unlike the external goods and honors, even those of royalty, they "are inseparable from us, being gifts of the Creator," Who has commanded us to put them to constant use, and thereby be assured of infinite blessing leading us ultimately to eternal happiness.[76]

In a more specific way, Miskawayh informs us that he who wishes to preserve his moral health should take particular care not to stimulate his concupiscent and irascible powers by dwelling on the memory of the pleasurable sensations experienced by him and yearning after their recurrence. To do so would be like unleashing ferocious beasts, and having excited them, trying to curb and keep them at bay. This indeed is the way of fools, who do not understand that the sole function of these two powers is to subserve the rational, as God has decreed, rather than allow them to enslave us.[77]

Moreover, he should guard against being driven by the force of habit to do what in the light of rational deliberation he had resolved not to do. Let him in that event chastize his soul for succumbing to the temptation of a pleasurable sensation, by privation or reproach, and for outbursts of displaced anger, by humbling himself before men of virtue, or allowing himself to be humiliated at the hand of the innocent. Or let him give some money in alms, as an atonement for his transgressions. If he should suspect that he is guilty of sloth, let him impose on himself additional, onerous tasks or prolonged penances and acts of charity.[78]

---

[75] See *Tahdhīb*, 175 (Zurayk, 157f.)
[76] *Ibid.*, 183 (Zurayk, 163).
[77] *Ibid.*, 185 (Zurayk, 165).
[78] *Ibid.*, 187 (Zurayk, 167).

Furthermore, he should emulate those kings who are known for their sagacity and far-sightedness in fortifying their realm against attack. For it is to the extent that we have held our passions in check, and have fortified our souls against the onslaughts of anger or lust in advance, that we are able to ward them off when they do assail us.[79]

He should also examine his own shortcomings with the greatest diligence, and should not be satisfied with the recommendations of Galen in his tract on *Man's Recognition of His Own Shortcomings*.[80] Galen advises him who is solicitous to identify these shortcomings, to take a sincere friend into his confidence and to urge him to inform him about any faults he observes in him. Whenever he refrains, he should lampoon him for betrayal and prefer an enemy to him, as Galen has argued in another tract entitled *That the Virtuous Benefit from their Enemies*.[81] Al-Kindī has put it even better where he says: "The seeker after virtue ought to look upon the forms of all his acquaintances as so many mirrors, showing him the form of each one when afflicted with those pains which generate vices."[82] Observing a transgression in one of them, he will reproach himself for it, as though it was his own deed, and will review at the end of every night and day all his actions, so as to take stock of each one of them without exception.

Another part of the therapeutic art, as we have seen, is the restoration of health. The 'diseases' which afflict the soul are the many vices corresponding to the four cardinal virtues and their subdivisions, which we have already discussed. Altogether, we have eight generic vices constituting either an excess or a defect in relation to the original virtues: (a) recklessness and cowardice, corresponding to courage, (b) self-indulgence and insensibility, corresponding to temperance, (c) frivolity and stupidity, corresponding to wisdom, and (d) oppression and servility, corresponding to justice.

In diagnosing these diseases, it is necessary to determine in the first place their causes and grounds. Now recklessness and cowardice, like courage, are grounded in the irascible power of the soul; when it is overstimulated by anger, or the desire for vengeance,[83] the intellectual faculty is clouded and rendered immune to criticism or advice. The "originative causes" of this disturbance of the soul are arrogance, vanity, duplicity, disputatiousness, frivolity, conceit, derision, perfidy, oppression and

---

79 *Tahdhīb*, 187 (Zurayk, 167).

80 *Ibid.*, 188 (Zurayk, 168).

81 See Ibn al-Nadīm, *al-Fihrist*, 419. Cf. "A Diatribe of Galen," in: R. Walzer, *Greek into Arabic*, 142–74.

82 *Tahdhīb*, 190 (Zurayk, 169f). Cf. Ibn al-Nadīm, *al-Fihrist*, 419.

83 The definition of anger is given, as in *De Anima*, I, 403a 30f., as "the boiling of the heart's blood out of a desire for vengeance." *Tahdhīb*, 193 (Zurayk, 172).

competitiveness, whereas the 'final cause' (*ghāyah*) of all these is the desire for vengeance; their consequences are remorse, ill-humor, the contempt of friends and the rejoicing of enemies.[84]

The cure of these ills consists in eradicating their principal causes, i.e. passionate anger and arrogance. The essence of the latter is "a false opinion of one's self, as deserving a higher rank than the one it has earned."[85] Therefore by forming a right opinion of one's self and its many faults, and understanding that the object of arrogance is something external to one, one would take pause and abate his arrogance. The former is a species of injustice, or incontinence, which can only be remedied by the recognition of the folly and futility of fitful anger, and the cultivation of the virtues of forbearance (*ḥilm*) and courage, which help to hold the irascible power in check.[86]

The antithesis of anger is the abating of the passion for revenge, which is the cause of cowardice, servility, laziness and vacillation. To remedy these ills, it is necessary to arouse in the irascible power the contrary passions of self-composure and docility, sometimes to an inordinate extent, so as to achieve the intermediate condition of courage.[87]

The other principal disease of the irascible soul is fear, which is caused by the anticipation of a disaster or the expectations of a calamity. Now anticipation and expectation relate to future occurrences, which are either great or small, necessary or contingent. Of contingent events, either we ourselves or others are the cause, and in neither case does the reasonable man have cause to take fright. First, contingent events may or may not happen, and it is a mistake to determine in advance that they shall and accordingly to fret at the prospect of their happening. Secondly, one should face the future with hope and refrain from dwelling in thought on the terrible things it may have in store for us. Thirdly, should our future miseries be caused by our own miscalculation or wrongdoing, the obvios antidote of the fear or suffering they occasion is to refrain from the offences which are their root-causes.[88]

As for the fear of necessary occurrences, such as the onset of old age and its attendant woes of disease, bereavement or loneliness, its antidote is the knowledge that he who welcomes a long life must surely welcome old age and its natural consequences. He who understands these consequences and accepts their preconditions initially, will not fear them, but instead

---

[84] See *Tahdhīb*, 195f. (Zurayk, 170f.)
[85] *Ibid.*, 195 (Zurayk, 174).
[86] On *ḥilm* and its Arabic-Islamic background, see *Encyclopaedia of Islam*^{2}, art. ḥilm.
[87] *Tahdhīb*, 202f. (Zurayk, 179f.)
[88] *Ibid.*, 207 (Zurayk, 183f.)

anticipate and hope and even pray to God Almighty for them.[89]

The greatest fear that man is afflicted with, however, is the fear of death. As al-Kindī had argued, this fear is born either of: (a) the ignorance of the reality of death, (b) the ignorance of the destiny of the self (*dhāt*) after the dissolution of the body, (c) the belief that death is attended by great pain, other than that of the diseases which may have caused it, (d) the punishment ensuing upon it, (e) the uncertainty of our condition after death, or, finally, (f) grief at the loss of wealth and other acquisitions left behind.[90]

Now all these are groundless fears. For to him who is ignorant of the reality of death or the destiny of the soul after the dissolution of the body, we need only say that "death is nothing more than the soul's relinquishing the use of its instruments, i.e. the organs whose sum-total is called the body, in very much the same way as the craftsman relinquishes the use of his tools."[91] The soul itself, which is neither a corporeal substance nor an accident, is clearly incorruptible.[92]

As for him who fears death because he does not know whither his soul shall ultimately repair, or believes that once his body has dissolved, his self would disintegrate also, being ignorant of the immortality of the soul and the mode of its resurrection, he does not in reality fear death, but is ignorant of what he ought to know. It is ignorance therefore that is the cause of his fear, and it is to escape this ignorance that the philosophers have engaged in the search for learning and renounced the pleasures and other allurements of this world. For they realized that these indeed were the active ingredients of death, and have accordingly assured us that death, like life, is of two types, voluntary and natural; thus Plato has commanded the seeker of wisdom: "Be dead by will, and you will live by nature."[93]

In fact, he who understands the reality of death has no cause to fear it, but should instead yearn for it. For death is "the fulfillment (*tamām*) of man's essence;" man being defined as a living, rational and dying animal, it follows that death is his fulfillment and perfection (*kamāl*). It is therefore the height of folly to fear the fulfillment of his nature, or to think that his destruction is bound up with his genuine life or his imperfection with his fulfillment. Moreover, he who understands his genuine humanity, must understand that man is a generable entity, and that everything generable (*kāʾin*) is *eo ipso* corruptible. "Therefore he who wishes not to

---

[89] *Ibid.*, 208f. (Zurayk, 184).
[90] *Ibid.*, 209. (Zurayk, 185).
[91] *Ibid.*, 209f. (Zurayk, 185).
[92] *Ibid.*
[93] *Ibid.*, 212 (Zurayk, 18), cf. *Phaedo*, 66D. and F. Rosenthal, "On the Knowledge of Plato's Philosophy in the Islamic World," in: *Islamic Culture*, XIV (1940), 409, note 1.

perish, wishes in fact not to be (*yakūn*), and he who wishes not to be, wishes that his soul should perish. It is as though he wished both to perish and not to perish, or as though he wished both to be and not to be, and this is absurd."[94]

He who imagines that death is attended by a great pain which is different from the pain of the diseases preceding or leading up to it, should realize that this imagining is false, and that pain can only affect the living. When the body has been separated from the soul as a result of death, it can no longer experience sensation or pain, which are affections of the soul only.

He who fears death on account of the punishment following in its wake should be reminded that it is in fact the punishment he fears rather than death. He should accordingly quit the sins which he acknowledges as the basis of this punishment, and should address himself to the study of the different states of character identified as virtues or vices. It is wisdom, in short, which emancipates us from those pains and false opinions caused by ignorance.

The same is true of him who fears death because he is ignorant of what death holds in store for him. To cure him of his fear, it is enough to cure him of his ignorance. Once he knows, he will be reassured and will have discovered the true path of happiness.

Finally, he who claims that he does not fear death, but simply grieves at the prospect of leaving kin, children and worldly existence, should be informed that grief is the premonition of pain over a calamity which cannot be averted. Man, as we have seen, being a generable being, must by definition be corruptible. Moreover, it is entirely futile to expect that, in this world of generation and corruption, the satisfaction of our wants and the ownership of our worldly goods should be permanent. Only in the intelligible world is such permanence to be expected.[95] Let him train himself to accept joyfully what he has been granted and not to fret over what he has missed. He would then discover the true meaning of contentment and trust in God, Who has said (in Koran 10: 61): "Verily God's friends have nothing to fear, and they shall not grieve."[96] Indeed, death being the fate meted out to mankind by their just and wise Creator, it follows that the fear of death or the vain expectation of eternal life is an instance

---

[94] *Tahdhīb*, 215 (Zurayk, 190). Cf. al-Kindī's statement that "death is the fulfillment of our nature. For where there is no death, there would be no man at all, since the definition of man is the living, rational and dying (being)." See *al-Ḥīlah li-Daf^c al-Aḥzān*, 44f. and supra, 70.

[95] *Tahdhīb*, 217f. (Zurayk, 192f). Cf. al-Kindī, *al-Ḥīlah li-Daf^c al-Aḥzān*, 37f.

[96] *Ibid.*, 218f. (Zurayk, 192f).

of the fear of His justice and wisdom, as indeed of His bounty and munificence.[97]

Let one, finally, consider what would have happened had our predecessors not been eliminated by death. The world would have been too small to contain the ever-increasing throngs of newborn generations, and we ourselves would never have seen the light. Imagine, for instance, an illustrious ancestor, such as ᶜAlī ibn Abī Ṭālib, who lived four hundred years ago, and imagine that his children and grandchildren have continued to increase without any of them being eliminated by death; their sum-total today (i.e. the year of writing the *Tahdhīb* in 985 A.D.) would exceed ten million, their actual number, despite the assassination and decimation to which they have been subjected, being more than two hundred thousand.[98] If we multiply this figure by the number of people living at that time throughout the globe, their numbers today would be innumerable, and there would be no standing room left for them or for their urban and agricultural activity, or even for movement.[99]

In conclusion, Miskawayh paraphrases al-Kindī's words in the *Art of Dispelling Sorrows*, reproaching those who grieve at the loss of material possessions, which are neither essential for genuine happiness nor permanent. Were they to consider that the causes of their grief are by no means necessary, they would soon come to realize that grief is neither necessary nor natural, and that whoever has brought upon himself this condition will soon be comforted and return to his natural state. For even people who have been afflicted by the loss of their children or their dearest friends and relatives, and have in the process experienced the greatest grief, have in time returned to their natural condition of enjoyment, as though they had never grieved before.[100]

Moreover, let them consider, as al-Kindī has also argued, that material goods are not private gifts which we can hold forever; they are instead the common possessions of mankind, which are temporarily entrusted to us by God. Only the thankless and the envious (*ḥasūd*) will wish to own them forever, thereby depriving others of the opportunity of owning or making use of them for a while. The only genuine goods which are given to us freely and permanently, and which we may guard jealously for ourselves, are the soul, reason and the virtues. These are gifts which can never be withdrawn or given back. If he is to avoid the occasion of grief, man should

---

97 *Ibid.*, 216 (Zurayk, 191). By eternal life, Miskawayh obviously means life on earth, since he has consistently asserted the indestructibility of the soul and its eternal life in the intelligible world.

98 *Tahdhīb*, 215 (Zurayk, 190).

99 *Ibid.*, 216 (Zurayk, 190f.).

100 *Ibid.*, 219f. (Zurayk, 194).

not covet earthly goods. Asked how he was able to keep his good cheer and equanimity, Socrates replied: "I have not owned anything the loss of which could be the occasion of grief."[101]

In these Stoic and Cynic terms, fathered on Socrates by Miskawayh and other Arabic authors, the most important ethical treatise of Islam closes. And although the Greek sources of these Stoic-Cynic elements cannot be determined, the role of Porphyry, who in his lost commentary on the *Nicomachean Ethics* must be presumed to have exploited to the full the ingenious methods of synthesis characterizing his school, should be constantly kept in view. In fact, it is no exaggeration to say that the subtle way in which Miskawayh has woven together such diverse Stoic, Cynic, Platonic, Neo-Platonic, Aristotelian, Neo-Pythagorean and Arabic-Islamic elements in his eclectical ethical system could have only been successfully achieved, in the first instance, by a scholar whose knowledge of the Greek ethical tradition must have been very extensive. Porphyry, the great logician and editor of Plotinus, was surely such a scholar. Miskawayh must therefore be assumed to have had more than a casual knowledge of the subject-matter of the lost commentary of this Neo-Platonic philosopher on Aristotle's ethics, known to us from Arabic sources only.

---

[101] *Ibid.*, 221 (Zurayk, 196). Cf. al-Kindī, *op.cit.*, 40, and M. Fakhry, "Al-Kindī wa-Suqrāṭ," 33.

CHAPTER SEVEN

NAṢĪR AL-DĪN AL-ṬŪSĪ (D. 1274)

I. Ethics in Relation to the Other Sciences

A measure of the importance of Miskawayh's contribution to philosophical ethics is not only the fact that it had hardly an equal predecessor in Arabic, as we have seen, but equally the fact that it became in due course the model of almost all moral compositions. Thus two centuries later, the great Shīᶜite astronomer and philosopher Naṣīr al-Dīn al-Ṭūsī (d. 1274) wrote at the instance of his Ismāᶜīlī patron Naṣīr al-Dīnᶜ Abd al-Raḥīm Ibn Abī Manṣūr, governor of Qulistan, a Persian recension of the *Tahdhīb al Akhlāq* called after the patron, *Akhlāq-i Nāṣirī*.

In the preamble, al-Ṭūsi informs us quite candidly what his intent in writing his ethics really was: to Persianize Miskawayh's *Kitāb al-Ṭahārah* (Book of Purity) as he calls the *Tahdhīb*, and to supplement it with a discussion of 'household management' (*ᶜilm tadbīr-i manāzil*) and politics (*ᶜilm siyāsat-i mudun*), which in fact Miskawayh had omitted altogether.[1]

More concerned perhaps than Miskawayh to popularize and systematize his subject, al-Ṭūsī begins by a consideration of the relation of ethics to the other philosophical sciences. First, he defines philosophy as "the knowledge of things as they are and the fulfillment of one's functions as one should, according to human capacity, so that the human soul may arrive at the perfection to which it is directed."[2] Its two major divisions are speculative and practical wisdom, each of which admits of a threefold division corresponding to the well-known Aristotelian-Avicennian scheme of the sciences, first developed in the Arabic tradition by al-Fārābī in *Iḥṣāʾ al-ᶜUlūm* which appears to be at the basis of al-Ṭūsī's own classification.

Practical philosophy, of which ethics, household management and politics are the principal divisions, is concerned with the knowledge of voluntary activities or skills insofar as they conduce to human felicity. The principles of such activities or skills are either natural or conventional. In the first case, they are arrived at by human insight or sagacity, the prerogatives of the philosopher or sage; the second arise either from the consensus

---

[1] See al-Ṭūsī, *Akhlāq-i Nāṣirī*, Teheran, 1344 A.H. 20f. Cf. Engl. transl. by G.M. Wickens, London, 1964, 25f. Hereafter Wickens. On al-Ṭūsī's dependence on Miskawayh, but also on Ibn Sīnā and al-Fārābī, cf. W. Madelung, "Naṣīr ad-Dīn Ṭūsī's Ethics Between Philosophy, Shiᶜism and Sufism," in: R.G. Hovannisian, ed., *Ethics in Islam*, Ninth Giorgio Levi Della Vida Biennial Conference, Malibu, 1985, 85–101.

[2] *Akhlāq-i Nāṣirī*, 22f. (Wickens, 26f.)

of the community and are called manners or conventions (*ādāb u rusūm*), or from the injunctions of a great man favored by 'divine support' (*taʾyīd-i ilāhī*), who is the Prophet or Imām, and are termed 'divine laws' (*nawāmis-i ilāhī*).[3]

The subdivisions of 'conventional' practical activity are stated by al-Ṭūsī to consist, like those of 'natural' practical philosophy, of three: (a) devotions and ordinances governing individual actions, (b) actions and transactions regulating the relations of members of the same 'household', and (c) stipulations (*ḥudūd*) and modes of political organization (*siyāsāt*) governing whole cities or provinces. The science which investigates the principles of these three types of activity is jurisprudence, but insofar as these principles are conventional and as such liable to change, it follows that, strictly speaking, their study falls outside the purview of philosophy, which is concerned exclusively with universal and immutable principles.

II. The Soul and its Powers

The substance of the ethical core of the *Akhlāq-i Nāṣirī* differs little from that of its prototype, Miskawayh's *Tahdhīb al-Akhlāq*. After defining the object of this part of practical philosophy, al-Ṭūsī examines the essence of the soul and its faculties and the manner in which man is to be regarded as the noblest creature in this world. A noteworthy feature of al-Ṭūsī's psychology is its dependence on Ibn Sīnā's Aristotelian scheme, especially as regards the subdivisions of the soul, in which Miskawayh tended, as we have seen, to follow the Platonic threefold model.[4] Some of his arguments for the substantiality of the soul are more reminiscent of Ibn Sīnā than of Miskawayh. He had, it will be recalled, written an important commentary on Ibn Sīnā's *al-Ishārāt*. The existence of the rational soul, according to him, requires no proof, insofar as the most manifest or self-evident entity for a rational being is his own essence or reality, known intuitively without any intermediaries.[5] Its independence of sense-organs is demonstrated by the fact that the soul knows itself and knows that it knows itself, whereas the sense-organs are not capable of knowing themselves, but corporeal objects only. Sense-organs, like other parts of the body, are only used by the soul as instruments.[6]

The powers of the soul are given by al-Ṭūsī, following Ibn Sīnā, as vegetative, animal and human, each of which has a series of subdivisions

---

3 *Akhlāq-i Nāṣirī*, 26f. (Wickens, 27f.)

4 See *supra*, 112.

5 *Akhlāq-i Nāṣirī*, 36 (Wickens, 36). Cf. Ibn Sīnā, *al-Ishārāt wa'l-Tanbīhāt*, ed. S. Dunyā, Cairo, 1960, II, 319f. and *Avicenna's De Anima*, 16. Cf. also, al-Ṭūsī's commentary on this passage in the margin of *al-Ishārāt*, II, 321.

6 See *al-Najāt*, 157f. and *De Anima*, 39f.

corresponding to the Avicennian table. The Platonic trichotomy is artfully fitted into this scheme, the irascible and concupiscent powers being regarded as instances of the motive faculty, which is a part of the animal soul. Together with the rational, these two powers are the bases of praiseworthy or reprehensible actions, and correspond in fact to the Koranic trichotomy of commanding (*ammārah*), reproachful (*lawwāmah*) and quiescent (*muṭmaʾinnah*) soul respectively.[7] However, like Miskawayh, al-Ṭūsī refuses to engage in a detailed discussion of these powers on the grounds that this discussion belongs to 'natural science' rather than to ethics.[8]

III. Happiness and the Virtues

After reviewing Aristotle and Miskawayh's views of the good, al-Ṭūsī distinguishes between relative and absolute good, and then proceeds to defend the thesis that good is to be identified with the ultimate human perfection or good proper to every activity or entity. Aristotle's predecessors, Pythagoras, Socrates and Plato, contended, according to him, that the good of man or his happiness (*saʿādah*) consists in cultivating the four cardinal virtues of wisdom, justice, temperance and courage. These virtues belong exclusively to the soul; corporeal virtue is entirely irrelevant to this happiness, and the hardships and tribulations of this world will not touch him who has achieved that happiness.[9] Aristotle himself divided the different modes of happiness, corresponding to the various aspirations of the generality of mankind into: (a) physical well-being or health, (b) material wealth and influence, (c) a good name or virtue, (d) success or prosperity, and (e) sound judgement or sagacity. Complete happiness, although it does not exclude material well-being or success, consists, according to the moderns (i.e. Miskawayh and his followers), in attaining the degree of proximity to the higher or intelligible world, whereby man becomes akin to the angels. Like Miskawayh, al-Ṭūsī regards this view as accordant with that of Aristotle and quotes in support of this Neo-Platonic view the long passage from the spurious *Virtues of the Soul*, which Miskawayh, as we have already seen, had also quoted.[10]

---

7 See *Akhlāq-i Nāṣirī*, 72f. (Wickens, 57). Cf. Koran 12:53; 75:2; 89:27.

8 *Ibid.*, 47 (Wickens, 42) *et passim*. In the Aristotelian-Avicennian scheme of the sciences, psychology formed part of physics, as is well known.

9 *Akhlāq-i Nāṣirī*, 81 (Wickens, 61f). The view that bodily traits, such as life and health, are morally neutral is ascribed by Hecato to Zeno, who identified the four cardinal virtues with the good. See *Diogenes Laertius*, Hicks trans., Loeb Library, VII, 207f. The view that worldly misfortunes will not affect the wise was a fundamental tenet of Stoic ethics. See e.g. Marcus Aurelius, *Meditations*, I,1,17; VIII, 1, etc.

10 See *supra*, 120.

The table of the virtues and their subdivisions differs little from Miskawayh's. Basing himself perhaps on a different manuscript tradition, al-Ṭūsī tends to extend the list of subdivisions given in the *Tahdhīb*, sometimes rather redundantly. For instance, to the eight subdivisions of justice given in that work, four are added by al-Ṭūsī: loyalty (*wafāʾ*), compassion (*shafaqah*), resignation (*taslīm*) and trust (*tawakkul*).[11]

An interesting aspect of Miskawayh's ethics developed by al-Ṭūsī is the consideration of 'mock virtues' manifested in the actions of individuals who are not truly virtuous or happy. Thus a person may act justly, bravely or temperately without actually possessing the corresponding virtue, because he has not fulfilled one of the essential preconditions of genuine virtue, namely, that the action should be done for the sake of virtue rather than some other extraneous factor, such as anticipated profit or advantage, or simply by virtue of the sluggishness of his will or the dullness of his desires.[12] Like Aristotle, these two authors appear to be concerned to underscore in this connection the organic correlation between the outward action and the inner disposition of the will, or the fact, as Aristotle has put it, that action should flow from a firm and unchangeable character.[13] Otherwise, the action is a mock counterpart of the virtue corresponding to it. Both, however, possibly under the influence of Porphyry, have developed in some detail the implications of this Aristotelian maxim.

The ethical part of *Akhlāq-i Nāṣirī* closes, like Miskawayh's *Tahdhīb*, with a 'pathology' of the virtues and the measures that moral 'therapy' should resort to in order to ensure that the health of the soul, once lost, may be restored. Al-Ṭūsī's arguments are supported by quotations from or references to 'Master Abū ʿAlī' (Miskawayh), al-Kindī and al-Ghazālī.

IV. Household Management

Al-Ṭūsī's genuine contribution consists perhaps in broadening the scope of 'ethical' enquiry to include household management and politics. Although, as he himself informs us, his political ideas are derived for the greater part from the works of the principal political philosopher of Islam, Abū Naṣr al-Fārābī, it is not without interest that his treatise underscores better than any other Islamic treatise that organic correlation between ethics and politics which was a distinctive feature of the Platonic and

---

[11] See *Akhlāq-i Nāṣirī*, 117f. (Wickens, 84).
[12] See Miskawayh, *Tahdhīb*, 105f. (Zurayk, 95f.) Cf. *Akhlāq-i Nāṣirī*, 126f. (Wickens, 89f.)
[13] See *N.E.*, II, 1105a 33.

Aristotelian traditions.[14] To insure the preservation of the human species and to provide for the necessities of life, "divine wisdom," he writes, "has decreed that every man should take a mate, who will both attend to the care of the household and its contents and through whom the work of procreation will be accomplished."[15] This household, starting initially as a partnership between husband and wife, will eventually develop into a community comprising parents, children, servants and assistants. Such a community requires, in addition to a dwelling-place, a mode of organization which will ensure that the primary purpose of human association is fulfilled in the most effective manner. In developing the principles of household economy, al-Ṭūsī relies on the tract of the Neo-Pythagorean Bryson and that of Ibn Sīnā on the same subject.[16] He argues that the basic principles of regulating the household are three: (a) to preserve the equilibrium of the household once it has been established, (b) to restore it once it has been disturbed, and (c) to promote the welfare of every member individually as well as that of the whole household collectively. In this respect, the household may be compared to the human body and its master to the physician, who attends both to the preservation of the health of the body as well as its restoration.[17]

With the principles governing property, children and servants, we need not concern ourselves here, but al-Ṭūsī's very pertinent reflections on the principles regulating conjugal relations may be briefly reviewed. As we have said, the purpose of taking a wife is the preservation of property and the procreation of children. Hence the two primary qualities a wife should possess are thrift and fertility. In addition, she should be affable, modest, continent, obedient and pious. Her beauty should not be the chief incentive for marrying her, rather the contrary. Due to her weak intelligence, the beauty of a woman is often a snare and a cross.[18]

The attitude of the husband to his wife should be determined by three rules: he should inspire awe, honor her and keep her mind fully occupied. By inspiring awe is meant that the husband should dominate; should this relationship be reversed, the husband will be reduced to slavery and become the object of the wife's whims and fastidiousness. By honoring her is meant that he should confer on her those favors and responsibilities which render her satisfied with her estate and devoted to him. He should

---

14 See *Akhlāq-i Nāṣirī*, 278 (Wickens, 187).

15 *Ibid.*, 224 (Wickens, 153).

16 Bryson's tract is mentioned by Miskawayh in *Tahdhīb*, 55 (Zurayk, 50). Cf. M. Plessner, *Der Oikonomikos des Neupythagoreers "Bryson" und sein Einfluss auf die islamische Wissenschaft*, Heidelberg, 1928, and *al-Mashriq* (Beirut), XIX (1921), 161–181.

17 *Akhlāq-i Nāṣirī*, 227 (Wickens, 155f).

18 *Ibid.*, 239 (Wickens, 162).

not prefer to her a woman of superior beauty or wealth, arousing thereby her jealously. "For women are moved by the jealousy rooted in their natures, together with the deficiency of their intelligence, to give vent to abominations and ignonimies" which are bound to cause untold suffering and lead eventually to the destruction of the household.[19] By occupying her mind is meant that the wife's mind should be kept constantly on the responsibilities of the household and the business of everyday living, so that she will not occupy herself with vanities.

However, in showing solicitude for the welfare of his wife, the husband should avoid three pitfalls: (a) showing excessive affection, (b) consulting her on issues of major importance, and (c) allowing her to engage in foolish pastimes or malicious gossip.[20] The 'philosophers' have stated that a good wife is like a mother, a companion, and a mistress; whereas a bad wife is like a tyrant, an enemy and a bandit. Proximity to an unworthy woman is worse than proximity to wild beasts or serpents.[21]

V. The Principles of Political Science

The political part of the *Akhlāq-i Nāṣirī* pursues the same theme of orderly association, as a precondition of the happy life, laid down in the 'domestic' part. Without this association, coupled with mutual assistance dictated by the diversity of needs and capabilities, civilized existence becomes impossible. That is what the 'philosophers' mean by saying that man is by nature a political animal.[22]

Because of the conflicting aspirations, greed and lust for power that impel human beings to act, a mode of civil authority or management (*tadbīr*) is essential and is at the root of genuine political organization (*siyāsāt*). If conducted in accordance with the 'rule of wisdom', this management is called 'divine government' (*siyāsāt-i ilāhī*); otherwise it is named after the principle or goal determining its genesis. Aristotle has distinguished three modes of government: monarchy (*siyāsāt-i mulk*), tyranny (*siyāsāt-i ghalabah*) and democracy (*siyāsāt-i jamāᶜah*).[23] Of these forms, it is the first that al-Ṭūsī regards as the ideal one, which, like Plato, he tends to identify

---

[19] *Ibid.*, 242 (Wickens, 163).

[20] *Ibid.*, 242 (Wickens, 164).

[21] *Ibid.*

[22] See *Akhlāq-i Nāṣirī*, 283 (Wickens, 190).

[23] This list derives actually from Plato's *Republic*, VIII and IX. Aristotle reduced the 'good constitutions' to three: monarchy, aristocracy and constitutional polity, as against the 'bad constitutions' of tyranny, oligarchy and democracy. The fourfold table is adopted by al-Fārābī and other political philosophers in Islam, such as Ibn Bājjah (d. 1138). See Aristotle, *Politics*, III, 6–13 and al-Fārābī, *al-Madīnah al-Fāḍilah*, 109f.

with aristocracy or 'rule of the virtuous' (*siyāsāt-i fuḍalāʾ*), with important Shīʿite interpolations. Thus the monarch is favored with 'divine inspiration' and is called the religious lawgiver (*al-shāriʿ*).[24] His office is relegated to that of the Imām, or spiritual head of the community, identified by al-Ṭūsī with 'Plato's' world leader (*mudabbir-i ʿālam*) and Aristotle's 'statesman' (*insān madanī*).[25] Some (i.e. the Ismāʿīlīs), he argues,, refer to the spiritual leader as the speaker (*nāṭiq*), to distinguish him from the political leader, designated by them as the foundation (*asās*).

However, as laid down in general Shīʿite doctrine, it is not necessary, according to al-Ṭūsī, for the lawgiver or Imām to exist visibly in every age, but the existence of the political ruler (*mudabbir*) is essential for the administration of justice and the preservation of mankind at all times. The authority of this ruler, however, is purely vicarious (*wilāyāt-i taṣarruf*).[26] It follows that the science of politics is the study of universal (secular) laws, designed to serve the best interest of the community in accordance with the universal principles of right and wrong, and should for that reason be regarded as the master science. It is to the other practical sciences what metaphysics is to the theoretical, and its practice is essential for the exercise of virtue, the preservation of justice and order in the world, and, once they have been disturbed, for their restoration.[27]

The types of association (*ijtimāʿ*) range from the household to the locality, city, nation and world at large. Each type must have a head (*raʾīs*), who is subservient to the head of the larger type, until we reach the 'head of the world', who is the 'head of heads', 'absolute king', or 'absolutely obeyed one' (*muṭā-i muṭlaq*) and 'exemplar of the species' (*muqtadā-i nawʿ*).[28]

In view of the fact that association is the precondition of virtue, it follows, according to al-Ṭūsī, that the life of solitude, whether that of hermits, ascetics or vagrant beggars, is contrary to the moral life, which does not consist, as some might think, in total abstension from all human enjoyment or endeavor, but only in avoidance of that excess or defect which is the essence of virtue. In fact, the lot of those people who have willfully cut themselves off from the world altogether is no better than that of inanimate objects or corpses.[29]

---

24 *Akhlāq-i Nāṣirī*, 285 (Wickens, 191).

25 The Greek source of these terms cannot be determined; it appears, however, that the concept of world leader derives from Stoic literature, and that of *insān madanī* from Platonic or Neo-Platonic sources. Al-Fārābī had already identified him with the monarch. See *Fuṣūl Muntazaʿah*, 24 and 35.

26 *Ibid.*, 286. (Wickens, 192).

27 *Ibid.*, 286f. (Wickens, 192). Cf. *Nicomachean Ethics*, I., 1094^{a} 28f., for the status of politics among the sciences.

28 *Ibid.*, 288f. (Wickens, 193f.).

29 *Ibid.*, 290f. (Wickens, 194f.).

What holds people together and welds them into a single community is the bond of love. This bond, grounded in natural union, is superior to justice, which is grounded in artificial union, and only where love is wanting, does the need for justice arise.[30]

After a short digression on the all-pervading character of love as a cosmic force which holds the whole universe together as well as the elements making it up, in the manner of Empedocles' *Philia*, al-Ṭūsī turns to the consideration of the divisions of human love. Its two major divisions, according to him, are natural and voluntary. Voluntary love is then divided, along lines suggested by Miskawayh and derived ultimately from Aristotle, as interpreted or modified by Porphyry, into: (a) that which arises and dissolves quickly, (b) that which arises quickly but dissolves slowly, (c) that which arises slowly but dissolves quickly, and, finally, (d) that what arises and dissolves slowly.[31] The objects of love are given, along the already mentioned lines also, as pleasure, utility or goodness, and this threefold classification is woven into the previous fourfold one along familiar Aristotelian lines. Of the three kinds, the last is the noblest and the most enduring, being affiliated to the pure good, which is not corruptible or changeable. The pleasure to which it gives rise is not, however, unmixed, unlike the higher 'divine love' of which man partakes by virtue of the divine element in him and which is attended by an extraordinary pleasure analogous to that of mystical rapture (*walah*). The words of Heraclitus (or rather Empedocles), as reported by Aristotle in *Nicomachean Ethics*, VIII, 1155^{b} 4f., are quoted in an almost unrecognizable form to support this view of universal love.[32]

The more mundane forms of love discussed by al-Ṭūsī include the love of spouse, love of paramour, that of subject to ruler, that of father to child, that of pupil to teacher and, finally, that of ruler to subject. All these forms of love are liable to the vicissitudes of time and circumstance and are vitiated by selfishness and vanity. Only the love of God, of which the genuine philosopher partakes, is free from all vicissitudes and imperfections and is attended by that unalloyed blessedness which God confers on those of His servants that He has elected, as a divine favor. According to Aristotle, al-Ṭūsī observes, this is the highest mode of happiness of which man can partake, for although he is small in bulk, he is great in wisdom and intelligence. Therefore, he must not content himself with human aspirations, but should strain every nerve in his nature to achieve that divine condition of which he is truly worthy.[33]

---

[30] *Ibid.* Cf. *supra*, 116, for Miskawayh and Aristotle's view.
[31] *Ibid.*, 294f. (Wickens, 197).
[32] *Ibid.*, 297 (Wickens, 198).
[33] *Ibid.*, 316 (Wickens, 210). Cf. Aristotle, *N.E.*, X, 1177b 30f. and *supra*, 123.

Cities or states are then classified along essentially al-Fārābian lines, although the basis of classification is more explicitly ethical. To virtuous activity corresponds the virtuous city, to unvirtuous actions, the unvirtuous cities, which are so many perversions of the virtues with which ethics is concerned. They include the ignorant city (*jāhilah*), whose inhabitants are devoid of the use of the rational faculty; the wayward (*fāsiqah*), in which the rational faculty is made subservient to the other lower faculties of the soul; and the erring (*ḍāllah*), in which erroneous notions of virtue are entertained.[34] Each of these non-virtuous cities admits of endless ramifications or subdivisions.

The ultimate purpose of the virtuous city, according to al-Ṭūsī, is doubly ethical and theoretical: to achieve the varieties of good and eliminate evil, on the one hand, and to attain the knowledge of man's beginning and end (*mabdaʾ-i u maʿādi-i*), as well as the ultimate realities, on the other. Now considering the great diversity of aptitudes and activities of the inhabitants of the city, no unanimity is possible in the fields of belief or action, and accordingly it belongs to the lawgiver to insure that, as a Muḥammadan Tradition has put it, everyone is addressed according to the measure of his intelligence. The social station of every group will depend on the aptitudes and achievements of its members, as directed by the supreme ruler. However, despite the divergences between them, the groups which make up the state form a single and closely-knit community held together by the bond of mutual love, rooted in religion and kinship.[35]

The classes making up the virtuous city and administering it are given as follows:

1. The perfect philosophers, whose function is to determine the sound beliefs and convictions.
2. The 'linguists', who assist the philosophers to disseminate those beliefs through the sciences of theology (*kalām*), jurisprudence (*fiqh*), elocution, rhetoric, poetry and calligraphy.
3. The 'assessors' (*muqaddirān*), who superintend the just distribution of goods and services through the sciences of arithmetic, geometry, medicine and astronomy.
4. The 'holy warriors' (*mujāhidān*), who defend the city's ramparts against the aggression of non-virtuous cities.

---

34 *Ibid.*, 320 (Wickens, 211). Cf. al-Fārābī, *al-Madīnah al-Fāḍilah*, 109f. Al-Fārābī's table includes a fourth type, the renegade (*al-mubaddilah*), which, originally virtuous, changes in time into its opposite.

35 *Akhlāq-i Nāṣirī*, 325 (Wickens, 215).

5. The 'financiers' (*māliyān*), who oversee the levying of taxes and the distribution of provisions and financial resources.[36]

The non-virtuous cities are subdivided into six: the necessary, the ignominious, the base, the timocratic, the despotic and the democratic, which differ, as in al-Fārābī's scheme, according to the objectives they seek, namely, provision of material needs, wealth, pleasure, honor, conquest or freedom, respectively.

Certain unruly or parasitic elements arise within the virtuous city and mar its perfection, without, however, causing its complete perversion. They are called by al-Ṭūsī, following al-Fārābī, 'outgrowths' (*nawābit*) and include hypocrites (*murāʾiyān*), deviates (*muḥarrifān*), rebels (*bāghiyān*), heretics (*māriqān*), and sophists (*mughāliṭān*).[37]

VI. The Attributes of the Imām and his Duties to his Subjects

The qualities which should characterize the ruler of the virtuous city or Imām are seven:

1. Good descent
2. Nobility of character
3. Sound judgement
4. Single-mindedness
5. Steadfastness or fortitude
6. A certain affluence
7. Reliance on dependable aides

This ruler is to the state what the physician is to the body. The two ills which he ought to attend to are despotic rule and its antithesis, anarchy. The first appears to resemble monarchy, but is in fact its opposite; the second violates the general political principle that agreement is the cornerstone of genuine government; so long as the conditions of agreement and the unity attendant upon it prevail, the state will continue to grow. When that agreement is destroyed through insurrection or strife, the state is weakened and becomes an easy prey to aggression.[38]

To ensure the rule of order and justice, the ruler should keep the different classes making up the state in equilibrium. He should not, however, ignore the principles of social and political discrimination, but

---

[36] *Ibid.*, 326f. (Wickens, 215f). Cf. al-Fārābī, *Fuṣūl Muntazaʿah*, 65f. A somewhat different list is given on p. 351 (Wickens, 231) and includes: people of the pen, men of the sword, businessmen and agriculturalists. This list appears to be a practical simplification of al-Fārābī's list and its subdivisions include such classes as judges, accountants, astrologers, doctors, military men, craftsmen, tax-collectors and farmers.

[37] *Ibid.*, 343 (Wickens, 226). Cf. al-Fārābī, *al-Siyāsāh al-Madaniyyah*, 104f.

[38] *Ibid.*, 349f. (Wickens, 229).

should arrange his subjects according to a rising scale of merit, comprising the following groups:

1. Those who are naturally good and whose goodness is communicable.
2. Those who are naturally good, but whose goodness is not communicable.
3. Those who are naturally neither good nor bad.
4. Those who are evil, but whose wickedness is not communicable.
5. Those who are naturally evil and whose wickedness is communicable.

The ruler should treat the first two classes with the greatest deference and should select his assistants and advisors from the first of them. The second two should be treated with tact or contempt and continually exhorted to shun their evil ways. The fifth class should be reformed, but if their reform is not possible, they should be disciplined or held in check in one of three ways: imprisonment, restraint or banishment. Whether capital punishment should be imposed in extreme cases is a matter of dispute among the philosophers, according to al-Ṭūsī.[39]

Thirdly, he should observe the principle of justice or equity in distributing goods and honors, according to individual ability or merit.

Fourthly, he should guarantee the lawful enjoyment of these goods and honors, and whoever is forcefully despoiled of his share should be compensated.

Fifthly, having satisfied the conditions of distributive and rectificatory justice, the ruler should practice benevolence and charity (*iḥsān*) towards his subjects; for next to justice, no virtue inclines the hearts of the subjects towards their king or holds them together better than charity.[40]

The other precepts by which the king or ruler should order his life illustrate the subtlety and sagacity of the author. He should not keep petitioners at a distance, should not listen to slanderers or informers, and should not occupy himself with pleasure-seeking or idle pastimes. He should not seek his own aggrandizement, but should concentrate on the conduct of the affairs of state.

However, should the ruler, despite all these counsels, neglect his constitutional duties and give himself up to licence, the well-being of the state would be jeopardized and it will be necessary, once more, to seek out the 'true Imām', who is the just king and genuine ruler of the state. Whether the overthrow of the unjust king by force is permissible or not, we are not informed, but judging from Shīᶜite political history, such a dire course would appear to be justified.[41]

---

39 *Ibid.*, 363 (Wickens, 231).

40 *Ibid.*, 356 (Wickens, 233). Cf. Miskawayh, *Tahdhīb*, 129. (Zurayk, 115).

41 *Ibid.*, 357 (Wickens, 234). The Imām, being in temporary concealment (*mastūr*), the

With respect to the conduct of war, the ruler, according to al-Ṭūsī, should do everything in his power to learn the plans of his enemies, so as to foil them, whenever possible, through vigilence and stratagem rather than open warfare. This warfare should be undertaken as a last resort in self-defence rather than aggression, unless the ruler is compelled to initiate hostilities "for the sake of the pure good and the quest of religion." However, in that event the king should be assured of victory and the general support of his subjects.[42]

This part of *Akhlāq-i Nāṣirī* closes with a series of bits of advice, which from the time of Ibn al-Muqaffaᶜ (d. 759), author of *al-Adab al-Kabīr*, had become a feature of political writings, directing the retainers or ministers of the king to act with great discretion and caution in their dealings with their master. These writings are marked by great psychological and practical insight, but do not actually belong to the *genre* of political or ethical philosophy with which most of this treatise is concerned.

Another group of precepts for choosing one's friends and dealing with them, as well as dealing with the different classes of men, whether friendly or unfriendly, follows the political section. Finally, a postscript purporting to consist of Aristotle's testament to his master, Plato, concludes the whole discussion. Like many such testaments or 'epistles' attributed to this philosopher and addressed to his master Plato or his pupil Alexander, this version is highly conditioned by Islamic otherworldly elements, which had become by the time of al-Ṭūsī a characteristic feature of Platonic-Aristotelian ethics as interpreted by Muslim authors.

---

temporal ruler, as we have seen, acts as his vicar until his return (*rajᶜah*).

42 *Ibid.*, 359 (Wickens, 235).

CHAPTER EIGHT

JALĀL AL-DĪN AL-DAWWĀNĪ (D. 1501)

I. Man's Position in the Universe

The Persian contribution to ethics is best illustrated by al-Ṭūsī's paraphrase and elaboration of Miskawayh's *Tahdhīb al-Akhlāq* in the thirteenth century, just discussed. This contribution had certain remarkable advantages over the prototype: it recognized the organic correlation of ethics and politics and supplemented the ethical framework of Miskawayh's thought, which tended to remain introverted and esoteric, by the injection of a social and political spirit into it, thereby greatly broadening its scope.

Two centuries later, another Persian author, Muḥammad ibn Asᶜad Jalāl al-Dīn al-Dawwānī (d. 1501) wrote an ethical treatise which follows closely the *Nāṣirean Ethics* of al-Ṭūsī. It is called *Lawāmiᶜ al-Ishrāq fī Makārim al-Akhlāq* (Flashes of Illumination on the Nobility of Character) and is popularly called *Akhlāq-i Jalālī*, after its author.

The book is divided like its Persian model into three parts: the ethical, the domestic and the political, and is infused with a more pronounced otherworldly and Shīᶜite spirit. Thus it opens with a preamble purporting to determine man's position in the universe and the function God assigned to him in the Koran as His vicegerent (*khalīfah*). Al-Dawwānī quotes a series of verses which assert that God did not create mankind in vain (Koran 23:117), but, as the 'epitome' of the whole universe, man was intended to serve as His vicegerent on earth (Koran 2:30).

This function was rightly earned by man, since of all the creations in heaven and on earth, he was the only being who was willing to assume the divine 'trust' (*amānah*) proferred to the whole universe by God (Koran 33:72). Man reflects in this capacity of vicegerence the dual character of the Divine Nature, the inner and the outer, the spiritual and the corporal, and better than any other creature, including the angels, can be described as the 'image' of God, who is capable of the 'direct vision' (*mushāhadah*) of the higher realities. On this point the philosophers and the Ṣūfīs alike are in agreement.[1]

---

[1] Of the philosophers, Aristotle, Plato and Ibn Sīnā are quoted; of the Ṣūfīs, Ibn al-ᶜArabī (d. 1240), al-Suhrawardī (d. 1191), al-Tustarī (d. 986) and Abū Saᶜīd ibn Abi'l-Khayr (d. 1049) and al-Bisṭāmī (d. 874) are mentioned. See *Akhlāq-i Jalalī*, Calcutta, 1911, 11f. Cf. W.F. Thompson, *Practical Philosophy of the Muhammadan People*, London, 1839, 25f. Hereafter Thompson.

A second theme with which the preamble is concerned is the degree to which human character is liable to change. The author reviews certain 'physiological' theories which appear to imply the constance of moral disposition or character, rooted as it is in the physiological properties or humors. His review is supported by a series of Traditions which appear to imply the unalterability of character.[2] To this is opposed the ancient (Manichean) view that man was produced out of a base substance in which light and darkness are mingled, but instruction and breeding (*taᶜlīm* or *taᵓdīb*) will cause the light element to dominate. Galen is also mentioned as holding the intermediate view that some people are by nature good, others evil. The majority of mankind, however, are neither, but are rendered good or evil by virtue of the company they keep.[3]

Aristotle and the moderns, who include al-Ṭūsī and ibn Sīnā, are said to be of the view that by education people are rendered good or evil, and although al-Dawwānī rejects the arguments from observation advanced by al-Ṭūsī in support of this view, he tends to agree with him on the general thesis that moral dispositions are liable to change or correction. Even when such change or correction proves difficult, we are urged by the Koran and the Traditions to persevere in our effort to bring it about.[4]

II. The Principal Virtues

The analysis of the virtues, their nature, subdivisions and simulations follow familiar lines defined by Miskawayh and al-Ṭūsī, whom al-Dawwānī follows, on the whole, more closely. His references to al-Ghazālī and to ᶜAlī, the fourth Caliph, and his quotations from their writings, the Koran and the Traditions tend on the whole to be more copious. In any case, it will be pointless to attempt a review of this analysis which adds little to that of his two predecessors.

The principal virtue, according to him, is justice, which Aristotle did not regard as a single virtue, but rather as the sum-total of all the individual virtues, due to its all-pervading character.[5] It is related to equilibrium or proportion (*iᶜtidāl*) which is the 'shadow' of unity, of which equality

---

[2] See *Akhlāq-i Jalālī*, 18 (Thompson, 37). One Tradition reads: "The metals making up man are like the metals of gold and silver; the foremost of you in pre-Islamic times (*jāhiliyyah*) are the foremost in Islam, if they would understand." Cf. A.J. Wensinck, *Concordance et indices de la tradition musulmane*, Leiden, 1936 and 1962. See *Jāhiliyyah*, *Maᶜādin*.

[3] *Akhlāq-i Jalālī*, 19 (Thompson, 40f.) Cf. Miskawayh, *Tahdhīb*, 32f. (Zurayk, 30) and *Akhlāq-i Nāṣirī*, 102 (Wickens, 75f.).

[4] *Ibid.*, 22 (Thompson, 49f.)

[5] See *Akhlāq-i Jalālī*, 56 (Thompson, 136). Cf. *N.E.* V, 1129^{b} 30f, Miskawayh, *Tahdhīb*, 117 (Zurayk, 104) and al-Ṭūsī, *Akhlāq-i Nāṣirī*, 127f. (Wickens, 96).

is simply the surrogate. Of these three categories, unity is regarded by him in Neo-Platonic and Neo-Pythagorean fashion as the noblest, and is said to be manifested in the mathematical, the physical and the moral realms as harmony (*munāsabah*). Manifested in the body, it is called moderate temperament (*iᶜtidāl-i mizāj*); in musical tones, it is called pure tonality; in outer movement, grace; in language, eloquence; in the limbs, physical beauty; and in the dispositions of the soul or character, justice.[6]

The three divisions of justice into distributive, commercial and rectificatory correspond to those given by Miskawayh and al-Ṭūsī, and are stated to be equivalent to discrete or mathematical, sometimes to discrete and sometimes to continuous, and finally to continuous (or geometrical), respectively. To preserve this justice a criterion (*mīzān*) must exist enabling mankind to determine the mean in which justice consists, as well as to ensure its application. The highest criterion or law (*nāmūs*, νὸμος) is that of the divine law (*sharīᶜah*), the second is the just ruler and the third is money. This is borne out by the authority of the Koran which states in verse 57: 25: "And We sent down with them the Book and the Balance so that men might uphold justice. And We sent down iron, wherein is great might, and many uses for men" (trans. Arberry). The Book, according to al-Dawwānī, refers in this verse to the divine law, the Balance to any means of estimating quantities including money, and iron to the sword which is grasped by the law-enforcing ruler.[7]

It follows from this threefold subdivision of justice that its opposite, injustice, is of three types: (a) that of the infidel (*kāfir*) or sinner (*fāsiq*) who violates the divine law, (b) that of the rebel (*bāghī*) or aggressor (*ṭāghī*) who disobeys the ruler, and (c) that of the robber (*sāriq*) or swindler (*khāᵓin*) who violates the norms of equitable transactions involving money. The first two types are the most grievous, for it is impossible for him who flouts the authority of the divine law to act justly in any respect, and he who disobeys the ruler violates the divine precept in the Koran (4:59 and 47:33): "Obey God and obey the Apostle and those in authority among you."[8] In support of this view, Aristotle is reported to have divided justice into three types: (a) towards God, (b) towards our fellowmen or superiors, and (c) towards our predecessors (*aslāf*).[9]

The detailed discussion of our obligations to God given by Aristotle and

---

[6] See *Akhlāq-i Jalālī*, 51 (Thompson, 122f.). Miskawayh, *Tahdhīb*, 113 (Zurayk, 100f.).

[7] *Akhlāq-i Jalālī*, 53 (Thompson, 128f.). Cf. *Akhlāq-i Nāṣirī*, 131f. (Wickens, 98).

[8] *Akhlāq-i Jalālī*, 53 (Thompson, 129) and *Akhlāq-i Nāṣirī*, 142f (Wickens, 98).

[9] *Akhlāq-i Jalālī*, 57 (Thompson, 138). Cf. Miskawayh, *Tahdhīb*, 119 (Zurayk, 106). In the spurious *De Virtutibus et Vitiis*, 5, 1250^b, Aristotle actually gives a fivefold division of justice: (1) towards the Gods, (2) towards demons (spirits), (3) towards the fatherland, (4) towards parents, and (5) towards the dead.

'a later group of philosophers' that al-Ṭūsī engages in, using it as an occasion for introducing mystical elements into the discussion, is not pursued by al-Dawwānī, but his account is embellished by numerous Traditions commending the excellence of justice and our duty to God, His Apostle and our fellowmen.[10]

III. Household Management

The second part of *Akhlāq-i Jalālī*, like that of *Akhlāq-i Nāṣirī*, is concerned with domestic science and like it deals with the need for the household as an indispensable means of managing provisions and money, the 'government' (*siyāsāt*) of wives, that of children, servants, etc. Three precepts are laid down for the management of wives, two of which, dignity and affability, correspond to al-Ṭūsī's, whereas the third is different. The husband should be deferent and cordial in dealings with his wife's friends and relatives; he should also refrain from taking another wife, except in the event of the first's depravity. Indeed, the plurality of wives is not permissible, except in the case of royalty.[11]

Three prohibitions are then laid down: (1) not to show excess of affection towards the wife, (2) not to consult her on paramount matters, and (3) not to allow her to engage in idle pastimes or frivolities. The 'philosophers' have said, he informs us, that a good wife is like a mother, a mistress and a friend, all three combined in one, whereas a bad wife is a tyrant, an enemy and a thief.[12]

IV. Political Science

The third part of this treatise deals with the 'management of states' (*tadbīr-i mudun*) and opens with a preamble on man's need for the cooperation of his fellowmen in the provision of his essential wants and the consequent call for life in the city, or civilized existence (*tamaddun*). However, due to the divergent natures of individuals and their conflicting interests, the pursuit of one's advantage often clashes with that of others. Therefore, some provision for restraining people from encroaching on the rights of others becomes necessary and this is what is designated 'supreme government' (*siyāsāt uẓmah*). That is how the need for the three criteria of law, ruler and money, already referred to in connection with justice, has arisen.[13]

---

[10] *Akhlāq-i Jalālī*, 57f. (Thompson, 138f.). Cf. *Akhlāq-i Nāṣirī*, 150f. (Wickens, 103).
[11] See *Akhlāq-i Jalālī*, 99 (Thompson, 266). Cf. *Akhlāq-i Nāṣirī*, 241 (Wickens, 163).
[12] *Ibid.*, 101 (Thompson, 272f.), and *Akhlāq-i Nāṣirī*, 243f. (Wickens, 164f.).
[13] *Akhlāq-i Jalālī*, 117 (Thompson, 322). Cf. *Akhlāq-i Nāṣirī*, 283f. (Wickens, 191).

The political ruler is a person assisted by 'divine inspiration' and charged with the direction of ritual observances (*ᶜibādāt*) and practical transactions (*muᶜāmalāt*) conducing to the welfare of the citizens in this life and the life-to-come. The ancient philosophers designated this ruler as the life-to-come. The ancient philosophers designated this ruler as the 'master of the law' (*ṣāḥib-i nāmūs*), whereas the moderns designate him as the prophet or lawgiver (*shāriᶜ*). Next to him comes the personal ruler (*ḥākim-i shakhṣī*), who is also favored with divine support, whereby he is able to further the welfare of his subjects. The philosophers call him the king, pure and simple, the moderns the *imām*; Plato called him the 'world ruler', Aristotle the 'statesman' (*insān madanī*).[14] His foremost duty is to preserve the ordinances of the Law (*sharīᶜah*) and to conduct the affairs of state in accordance with universal principles and the requirements of the times. He is for that reason God's 'shadow' and His vicegerent in the world, as well as the vicar (*nāʾib*) of the Prophet. Like a doctor, his duty is to preserve the health of mankind and he might therefore be referred to as the 'world physician' (*ṭabīb-i ᶜālam*).[15]

The closing sections of the political part of *Akhlāq-i Jalālī* consist of a digression on the varieties of love and friendship which hold together the different classes of the state, as well as the subjects and rulers, students and teachers, and finally creatures and Creator. This is followed by a discussion of the different constitutional forms, both virtuous and non-virtuous, along essentially al-Fārābian and al-Ṭūsean lines. The manner of dealing with friends and foes, the right attitude towards our superiors and our subordinates, and our duties to the weak and the strong put the final touches on the moral and intellectual course to be followed by the seeker after virtue who aspires to the rank of divine vicegerence (*khilāfat-i ilāhī*).[16] A series of aphorisms attributed to Plato and Aristotle finally closes the discussion.

---

[14] *Ibid.*, 117 (Thompson, 325).
[15] *Ibid.*, 118 (Thompson, 326). Cf. *Akhlāq-i Nāṣirī*, 286 (Wickens, 192).
[16] *Akhlāq-i Jalālī*, 160 (Thompson, 448f.)

PART FOUR

RELIGIOUS ETHICS

CHAPTER ONE

RELIGIOUS MORALITY AND THE ASCETIC IDEAL

I. Religious Ethics Defined

Despite the difficulty of drawing a sharp line of demarcation between theological and religious ethics, we believe the distinction to be sufficiently important to justify a separate treatment. In the first place, the theologians, whether Muᶜtazilite or non-Muᶜtazilite, dealt with ethical questions, as we have seen, in a 'dialectical' spirit, and were either concerned to support certain rationalist theses ultimately affiliated to Greek philosophy, such as the nature and grounds of right and wrong, religious obligation (*taklīf*) and the like, or to question them. Secondly, many of the questions with which they were concerned were largely methodological; they were anxious to determine the logical status of ethical propositions rather than develop a substantive theory of morality. Thirdly, the tone of theological discussions of ethics tended on the whole to be polemical; their authors either inveighed against the 'traditionalists' and determinists, as was customary in Muᶜtazilite circles, or against the philosophers or philosophically inspired authors, as the Ashᶜarites and the Ḥanbalites tended to do.

Religious ethics, more firmly grounded in the Koran and the Traditions, tended on the other hand to dispense with 'dialectical' or 'methodological' subtleties and to concentrate on eliciting the spirit of Islamic morality in a more direct way. As was natural in the circumstances, religious writers, especially during the earliest period, dwelt on the key Koranic concepts of faith (*īmān*), piety (*waraᶜ*) and obedience (*ṭāᶜah*), and were often simply content to quote the Koran and the Traditions in support of their moral or religious disquisitions.

II. Ethical Traditionalism: Al-Ḥasan al-Baṣrī (d. 728) and Ibn Abi'l-Dunyā (d. 894)

A good example of this type of ethical compilation is *Kitāb Makārim al-Akhlāq* of Abū Bakr ᶜAbdallāh ibn Abi'l-Dunyā (d. 894), which, although somewhat historically late, continues a long line of such treatises.[1] The author follows the conventional method of Traditionists (*al-*

---

[1] See James A. Bellamy, "The Makārim al-Akhlāq by Ibn Abī'l-Dunyā (A Preliminary Study)," in: *The Muslim World*, LIII (1963), 106f.

muḥaddithūn), which consists in reporting the Tradition of the Prophet with its complete chain of transmission (*isnād*), with hardly any attempt at commentary or discussion. The selection of morally relevant utterances of the Prophet or his companions is not determined by theoretical or discursive considerations, but rather by a Tradition attributed to ᶜĀᵓishah, wife of Muḥammad, summing up the virtues or 'traits of good character' under ten headings: truthful report, steadfastness in obeying God, almsgiving, rewarding good deeds, kindness to the kin, returning of trusts, kindness to the neighbor, consideration for friends, hospitality and modesty.[2]

More discursive is the ethical contribution of the great jurist and divine of the seventh/eighth century, al-Ḥasan al-Baṣrī (d. 728), who is a key figure in the development of *kalām*, moral theology and mysticism. Because of the intensity of his religious pathos, many Ṣūfī authors acknowledge him as a pioneer in the fields of religious asceticism and piety, and hardly a single moral or mystical collection has omitted mentioning his name or quoting his profoundly moving aphorisms. We are naturally concerned here with the morally relevant utterances of this scholar, as well as his contribution to the Qadarī movement destined to develop in due course into the Muᶜtazilite school in theology, which, according to the traditional account, stemmed in fact from al-Ḥasan's own circle at Baṣrah.[3]

Miskawayh has given in his ethical collection *Jāwīdān Khirad* a good sample of these utterances, which underscore the otherworldy strain in his thought, as appears from those statements which condemn engrossment in the affairs of this world, grasping and attachment to material possessions.[4] A somewhat lengthy quotation illustrates further this strain and the duty incumbent on the believer to concern himself with personal moral rectitude and self-examination, and to disregard the faults of others. Because of its articulate character, this quotation may be paraphrased in full.

No one deserves to be called a true believer, he is reported as saying, until he quits reproaching others for faults of which he himself is not free, or ordering others to right their own faults before he has righted his own. A man who attends to his own faults will soon discover many faults equally deserving of correction, and this will lead him gradually to mind his own business and overlook the faults of others. The righteous should dwell on his own actions carefully, appraise their rightness or wrongness, without overlooking any part thereof, however small.

How instructive a teacher is death! "It has exposed the vanity of this

---

[2] Se Ibn Abi'l-Dunyā, *Makārim al-Akhlāq*, ed. James A. Bellamy, Wiesbaden, 1973, 8.
[3] See M. Fakhry, *A History of Islamic Philosophy*, 44.
[4] See *Jāwīdān Khirad*, 117, 130, 151 and 153.

worldly life, in which no man of intelligence has found any cause for joy. God have mercy on him who looks, and looking understands and takes stock of his condition. O, son of man, remember God's words (Koran 17:13–14): 'And every man—We have fastened to him his bird of omen upon his neck; and We shall bring forth for him, on the Day of Resurrection, a book he shall find spread wide open. Read thy book! Thy soul suffices thee this day as a reckoner against thee' (trans. Arberry). For, by God, he has indeed treated you justly, who has appointed you as your own judge (*ḥasīb*). Man is indeed neglectful of his lot in this world; o, son of man, you should understand that you cannot dispense with your lot in this world, although you are in greater need of your lot in the next."[5]

In the Ṣūfī tradition, al-Ḥasan al-Baṣrī is represented as the paragon of asceticism, as we have already mentioned, and of the total reconciliation of the human and divine wills. The method he proposed consised of reflection (*fikr*), self-examination and total submission to God, resulting ultimately in a state of inner contentment or joy (*riḍā*).[6] Thus in *al-Risālah al-Qushayriyyah*, al-Ḥasan is reported as saying that a grain of pure piety (*wara*ᶜ) is far better than a thousand weights of fasing and prayer.[7] This piety (*khushū*ᶜ) is defined as fear constantly clinging to the heart;[8] asceticism, on the other hand, is defined as hatred for the world and everything in it, whether it be people or material goods.[9] Asked what is the most useful part of the science of morals in this life and the next, he replied, thorough religious knowledge (*tafaqquh*), asceticism and the realization of your debt to God. This realization, he argued, is tantamount to perfect faith.[10] Finally, he regarded modesty and benevolence as the two foremost virtues.[11]

Equally noteworthy is al-Ḥasan's position in the history of the Qadarī controversy, to which we have already referred.[12] A famous letter addressed to the Umayyad Caliph, ᶜAbd al-Malik (685–705), in response to a query he had directed to this venerable divine concerning the question of *qadar*, illustrates the great regard in which he was held and the earnestness with which he grappled with this problem at the behest of the Caliph. In his letter, ᶜAbd al-Malik is anxious to elicit al-Ḥaṣan's stand on this

---

5 See *Jāwīdān Khirad*, 164–65.

6 See L. Massignon, *Essai sur les origines du lexique technique de la mystique musulmane*, Paris, 1922, 168f.

7 See al-Qushayrī, *al-Risālah al-Qushayriyyah*, Cairo, 1966, 288.

8 *Ibid.*, 399.

9 *Ibid.*, 296.

10 *Ibid.*, 560. Cf. al-Sarrāj, *al-Luma*ᶜ, eds. ᶜA.H. Maḥmūd and Ṭ. Surūr, Cairo and Baghdad, 1960, 194.

11 See Ibn Abi'l-Dunyā, *Makārim al-Akhlāq*, 24.

12 See *supra*, 152.

question, and in particular to determine whether this stand stemmed: (a) from a report (*riwāyah*) emanating from the Companions of the Prophet, (b) his own judgement, or (c) the authority of the Koran. The Caliph acknowledges the pre-eminence of al-Ḥasan in that field as the first dialectician (*mujādil*) and speaker (*nāṭiq*) on the subject of *qadar*.[13]

In his response, al-Ḥasan begins by explaining how the original consensus of the 'ancestors' (*al-salaf*) on the justice of God was shattered as a result of the rise of heresy and controversy. The Koran itself has clearly spelt out the relation between divine grace (*niᶜmah*) and human endeavor; the author of grace is God, it is man who turns it into infidelity (*kufr*) and sin (Koran 14:28–29). Now God, according to the Koran, is displeased with infidelity and sin (Koran 7:33). It follows that "were infidelity the result of God's decree and preordination (*qaḍāᵓ wa qadar*), He would be pleased with its perpetrator, but God could not issue a decree and then show displeasure at His own decree. Indeed, injustice and wrongdoing are not part of God's decree; for His decree consists in commanding the right (*al-maᶜrūf*), justice, charity and kindness to kin and in prohibiting vileness, wrongdoing (*munkar*) and oppression."[14] The Koran abounds with passages which speak of God's guidance and admonition to mankind to refrain from evil; it is the light which enlightens man, ensuring that "whosoever perished might perish by a clear sign (*bayyinah*), and by a clear sign he might live who lived" (8:42, trans. Arberry). Moreover, the Koran has in numerous places, such as the oft-quoted verses 91:7–10, understored the soul's capacity for piety and impiety, and implied that God "has instilled in the nature of mankind by inspiration (*ilhām*) the knowledge of impiety and piety."[15] It has also clearly underscored the fact that guidance (*hudā*) is from God, whereas error (*ḍalāl*) is from man or from the Devil (Koran 3:75–76; 17:53; 20:79; 28:15–16; 33:67; 41:17,29; 92:12–13).

Those who question this view refer to Koran 13:27, which states that God "leads astray or guides whomsoever He pleases," without taking note of what precedes this verse or follows it, such as the reference in verse 14:27 to God leading the "evildoers" and in 2:26–27 and 10:33 to His leading the "sinners" astray. Or they refer to such verses as 57:22, which

---

[13] See H. Ritter, "Studien zur Geschichte der islamischen Frömmigkeit, I," in: *Der Islam*, XXI (1933), 67. Cf. J. Obermann, "Political Theology in Early Islam," in: *Journal of the American Oriental Society*, LV (1935), 138f. For the history and authenticity of this letter, see H. Ritter, *op. cit.*, 59f. Al-Shahrastānī (d. 1153), who states that he saw a copy of that letter, nevertheless doubts its authenticity on transparent doctrinal grounds. See *al-Milal wa'l-Niḥal*, I, 47.

[14] *Ibid.*, 69.

[15] *Ibid.*, 71.

speaks of material and personal afflictions (*maṣāʾib*) as pre-recorded in a 'Book', interpreting it to imply predestination. In fact, this verse, according to al-Ḥasan, simply informs us that these afflictions are ways by means of which God tries His servants in this world, so that they may not be grieved at what they miss or rejoice at the allurements of this life.

Other verses cited by the advocates of predestination, such as 11:105, speak of the segregation of mankind on the Day of Judgement into the happy and the wretched. They extract from them mistakenly the view that this segregation is decreed by God while the creature is in its mother's womb. However, were this the case, "God's [revealed] Books and Prophets would mean nothing, and the call of the Apostles to them to be pious and their exhortation to righteousness would equally mean nothing, but would indeed be in vain."[16] Now what this and similar verses mean is that those who have complied with God's commands will be happy on the Last Day, those who flouted them will be wretched.

Moreover, the advocates of predestination contradict in practice their avowed belief in the irreversibility of the divine decree, since they continue to take risks in trade and guard their property or persons against robbers or aggressors.[17]

Another classic argument of these advocates is presented and refuted by al-Ḥasan al-Baṣrī. The foreknowledge by God of the impiety and wickedness of the creature predestines him to be wicked or impious, just as God's foreknowledge of his color, form and personal traits irrevocably determines that he possess them. The analogy between the two objects of foreknowledge, i.e. physical traits and moral traits, is false; piety and impiety, like other voluntary actions, are the outcome of the free will (*ikhtiyār*) of man, whereas physical traits are the product of God's predetermination, and over these man has no control. With respect to a certain voluntary action such as infidelity (*kufr*), God simply knows that the human agents "have chosen it at will, as He knows that, had they not wished it, they would have quit it," and that in addition they are capable (*qādirūn*) of doing it "by virtue of the capacity (*istiṭāʿah*) that He has created in them, in order to test them in the ways of faith and justice."[18] This is borne out by numerous Koranic verses, of which 9:42; 18:65 and 18:84 are examples. The many other verses, such as Koran 4:78–79; 11:32 and 11:34, which appear to imply God's responsibility for the misdeeds of the impious, simply underscore the desire of the hypocrites (*munāfiqūn*), whenever they are visited by adversity or misfortune, to impute the

---

[16] *Ibid.*, 75.
[17] *Ibid.*, 75f.
[18] *Ibid.*, 77.

responsibility for it to God, as they impute the responsibility for their infidelity, wrongdoing and vile actions to Him also. God has admonished them in the Koran to keep themselves pure and therefore He will not accept their excuses or repentance, once His verdict has been pronounced.[19]

The recurrent theme of guidance and misguidance, which was in fact at the center of theological controversies in which Muᶜtazilite and Ashᶜarite theologians from the earliest times were involved, figures prominently in al-Ḥasan al-Baṣrī's anti-predestinarian arguments. Those verses of the Koran which, like 6:125, speak of God guiding people to embrace Islam willingly or not embrace it, should be properly understood. It is absurd to assume that God has singled out some for belief without any prior good works, while he predestined others for disbelief without any prior infidelity or impiety, for ''our Lord is too merciful, just and benificent to do this to His servants.'' This is borne out by those verses which, like 2:181, deny that God can demand the intolerable, and those which, like 5:16, assert God's readiness to guide those who ''abide by His good pleasure (*riḍwān*)'' and bring them out from the darkness and lead them upon the ''straight path'' (*ṣirāṭ mustaqīm*).[20] The intent of this and other verses, such as 5:65–66; 7:96 and 39:18, is clear. ''God did not impose things necessarily (*ḥatman*) on His servants,'' writes al-Ḥasan al-Baṣrī, ''but He simply said [in the Koran]: If you do this, I will do that to you, and if you do that I will do this to you, rewarding them according to their actions, after having ordered them to worship and call upon Him and seek His assistance. So that, were they to seek what He has ordered, He would add a new form of aid to His previous aid, and new prosperity to His previous prosperity, enabling them to choose the right actions (*ḥasanāt*) and avoid the wrong (*sayyiᵓāt*).''[21]

The historical significance of this epistle is very great. Whether, as asserted by a later authority, al-Ḥasan, ''who had engaged in some aspects of discussing free will (*qadar*)'', did in fact recant (*rajaᶜa ᶜanhu*),[22] or not, cannot be easily determined in our present knowledge of early theological controversies. What is particularly noteworthy is that this epistle set the stage for the epoch-making discussions within Qadarī and post-Qadarī circles on the subject of free will and predestination. The method

---

[19] *Ibid.*, 78f. On personal guiltiness and responsibility of man in al-Ḥasan al-Baṣrī and his pupil Wāṣil Ibn ᶜAṭāᵓ, cf. H. Daiber, *Wāṣil Ibn ᶜAṭāᵓ als Prediger und Theologe*, Leiden, 1988 = Islamic Philosophy and Theology. Texts and Studies 2, 12, 17, 46 n. 91, 58 n. 209, 61 n. 248.

[20] *Ibid.*, 80.

[21] *Ibid.*, 81.

[22] See Ibn Qutaybah, *al-Maᶜārif*, ed. Th. ᶜUkāsha, Cairo, 1969, 441.

adopted by al-Ḥasan, as we have seen, was partly discursive, but the arguments advanced against the predestinarians of the time are all grounded in the Koran. There is hardly a single argument which al-Ḥasan does not support by a Koranic quotation, and hardly a single predestinarian thesis which did not in turn emanate from the Koran. These arguments and counter-arguments, as well as their Koranic grounds, remained for centuries to come the stock-in-trade of predestinarian and anti-predestinarian polemicists, from al-Ḥasan's disciple Wāṣil ibnᶜAṭā' (d. 748) down to al-Ashᶜarī (d. 935), who revolted against the Muᶜtazilite school founded by Wāṣil. A significant development, however, came in the wake of founding that school: the gradual rationalization of methods of proof and the eventual predominance of the syllogistic process over the more traditionalist process, so well illustrated by al-Ḥasan al-Baṣrī's *Epistle*, with its almost total reliance on the text of the Koran and omission of the Traditions.

CHAPTER TWO

OTHERWORLDLY AND MUNDANE TRENDS: ABU'L-ḤASAN AL-MĀWARDĪ (D. 1058)

I. Traditionalism Tempered by Rationalism

Al-Ḥasan al-Baṣrī and Ibn Abi'l Dunyā illustrate well the traditionalist approach to moral discussion, with its thorough reliance on the Koran and the Traditions. Other religious moralists, who relied equally on these two sources of Islamic doctrine, tended nevertheless to exploit somewhat the discursive method.

A key figure in the history of this type of religious ethics is Abu'l Ḥasan al-Māwardī, who studied jurisprudence (*fiqh*), Traditions and, although his biographies are silent on these two branches of learning, theology and philosophy, with a number of scholars, pre-eminent among whom was Abu'l-Muẓaffar al-Isfarāyīnī (d. 1027). His travels were extensive and he served as religious judge at different provincial cities, returning eventually to Baghdad to serve the Caliph al-Qādir (991–1031).[1]

His writings include a commentary on the Koran, a voluminous work on Shāfiᶜī jurisprudence, linguistic treatises, an anthology of aphorisms (*K. al-Amthāl wa'l-Ḥikam*), etc. His major ethical work, however, is *Adab al-Dunyā wa'l-Dīn* (The Right Conduct in Matters Worldly and Religious), to which should be added his best-known work, a treatise on government, *al-Aḥkām al-Sulṭāniyyah* (Government Ordinances).

As we have already noted, this author is not concerned in the above-mentioned ethical treatise with methodological questions, but rather with an analysis of what he regarded as primarily Islamic moral and religious virtues. His method, although to some extent discursive, is much more narrative and didactic. His major themes are supported by an abundance of quotations from the Koran, the Traditions, the sayings of the Orthodox Caliphs, especially ᶜAlī, and venerable scholars, renowned for their sagacity or orthodoxy, like al-Ḥasan al-Baṣrī, as well as numerous unnamed and unidentified 'philosophers' (*ḥukamā*ᵓ), rhetoricians (*bulaghā*ᵓ) and poets.

---

[1] See al-Khaṭīb al-Baghdādi, *Tārīkh Baghdād*, ed. M.A. al-Khānjī, Cairo 1931, 12, 102 and Yāqūt, *Muᶜjam al-Buldān*, II, 15 and III, 245. Cf. al-Subkī, *Ṭabaqāt al-Shāfiᶜīyah al-Kubrā*, Cairo, n.d., III, 303f. and Aḥmad M. Akhṭar, "Al-Māwardī: A Sketch of His Life and Works," in: *Islamic Culture*, XVIII (1944), 283–300.

II. The Excellence of Reason

The first major theme with which al-Māwardī deals, in the manner of contemporary theologians and religious writers, is the virtue or excellence (*faḍl, sharaf*) of knowledge (*ᶜilm*), especially religious knowledge, and the manner in which one can progress in the acquisition of this knowledge. This discussion is preceded by an account of the excellence of reason (*ᶜaql*), which is the foundation of all the virtues, as well as the mainstay of religious obligation (*taklīf*). To illustrate the importance of reason, he divides obligation into: (a) what reason stipulates as necessary and is merely confirmed by revelation (*al-sharᶜ*), and (b) what reason regards as purely admissible (*jāᵓiz*), but revelation stipulates as necessary. Stated differently, the foundation of religious obligation is for him the conformity with reason "in matters which revelation does not prohibit' and the conformity with revelation in matters which reason does not prohibit. For it is impossible that revelation should enjoin what reason prohibits, or that reason should be deferred to in matters prohibited by revelation. That is why religious obligation is addressed to people of sound reason only.[2] The role of reason is decisive in relation to both types of obligation, a thesis which al-Māwardī supports by quotations from the Traditions, the sayings of the Caliph ᶜUmar, al-Ḥasan al-Baṣrī, 'some philosophers', men of letters and poets.[3] His insistence on this role of reason as the source of religious truth, subsequently confirmed or stipulated (*awjabahā*) by revelation, as well as the faculty which discriminates between right and wrong, would appear to confirm al-Māwardī's Muᶜtazilite sympathies. The attempt of Shāfiᶜī doctors like Ibn al-Ṣalāḥ and Ibn Ḥajar al-Asqalānī to exonerate him from the charge of Muᶜtazilism is understandable, but by no means conclusive.[4]

The two divisions of reason are given, following contemporary scholars, especially Ashᶜarite authors, as instinctive or inborn (*gharīzī*) and acquired. The first is the primary division and is concerned with "the knowledge of necessary objects of cognition," which are of two types: sense-perceptions and the intuition of primary truths.[5] The etymology of the term reason (*ᶜaql*) is given along generally accepted linguistic lines as deriving from that of 'knee-hobbling the she-camel', insofar as reason inhibits man from indulging his base appetites.

Acquired reason, on the other hand, is grounded in instinctive or neces-

---

[2] See *Adab al-Dunyā wa'l-Dīn*, Cairo, 1955, 78.

[3] *Ibid.*, 3f and 78f.

[4] See A.M. Akhṭar in: *Islamic Culture*, XVIII (1944), 290f.

[5] *Ibid.* Cf. al-Bāqillānī, *K. al-Tamhīd*, 6f.; al-Baghdādī, *Uṣūl al-Dīn*, 8 and al-Juwaynī, *al-Irshād*, 8.

sary reason and is concerned with the cultivation or perfection of theoretical knowledge, the sound management (*tadbīr*) of one's private affairs and right thinking. It is indefinable, since it grows with use and wanes with disuse, so long as it is not foiled by passion or desire. That is why age and experience are praised in literature, including poetry, because they sharpen this mode of knowledge and refine it.[6]

If we ask now in what does the perfection of this noble faculty of reason, with its theoretical and practical functions, actually consist, the answer given by al-Māwardī is not without interest: it consists in the union of native intelligence and keenness of intuition, sharpened by prolonged use. He in whom these traits coalesce is truly virtuous, as the Traditions themselves attest.[7]

Virtue, however, being a mean, as a well-known Tradition of Muḥammad and a saying of ᶜAlī attest,[8] the question may be asked whether excess of acquired reason is not a defect, since it often conduces to cunning (*dahāᵓ*) and malice (*makr*). Al-Māwardī's answer is that the excess of reason is nothing but excess of knowledge and sound judgement; it can never, therefore, be a vice, in the strict sense. The analogy with certain practical virtues, such as courage and generosity, is not valid here, for what renders cunning or malice actually reprehensible is simply the evil use to which it is put. It is of the nature of genuine reason that it is always attended by piety and the fear of God, and cannot therefore be an instrument of evil. This is supported by some Traditions of the Prophet and by certain lines of verse purporting to be written by ᶜAlī, the fourth Caliph, giving the ten components of noble character as: reason, religion, knowledge, patience (*ḥilm*), generosity, rightdoing (*ᶜurf*), piety, patience, gratitude, and gentleness.[9] The antithesis of reason is passion (*al-hawā*), which has been decried by the Prophet, the Companions, philosophers and others.

Despite its nobility, reason remains for al-Māwardī a tool for acquiring practical and religious knowledge, and not as it was for the Muslim Neo-Platonists, such as al-Fārābī and Ibn Sīnā, a supermundame entity, "conjunction" with which is the ultimate goal of man's moral and intellectual endeavors.[10] Thus of the many branches of learning commended by the

---

[6] See *Adab al-Dunyā*, 6.

[7] *Ibid.*, 11. A man is praised in the presence of the Prophet, who asks: "But how is his reason?" He is told about his piety, and his many good deeds, but he continues to ask about his reason, concluding: "The stupid worshipper causes more harm through his ignorance than the profligate through his profligacy. Verily, people come closer to their Lord through their reasons."

[8] "The best actions are always those which are means" and "The best actions are those pertaining to the intermediate course (*al-namaṭ al-awsaṭ*)", respectively.

[9] *Ibid.*, 13.

[10] *Ibid.*, 28. See Appendix A, The Contemplative Ideal in Islamic Philosophy: Aristotle and Avicenna.

Koran, the Traditions and the philosophers, the noblest are, for him, the religious sciences. It is noteworthy, however, that without knowledge, religion, according to him, is incomplete. The Prophet is quoted as saying: "The excellence of knowledge is greater than the excellence of worship." For worship divested of genuine knowledge of the circumstances and prerequisites of its proper performance is dubious worship. The Prophet is again quoted as saying: "The best portion of my community are its men of learning (*ᶜulamāᵓ*); the best of these are men of religious learning (*fuqahāᵓ*)."[11]

Some religious indifferentists, he then goes on to argue, have inclined to the 'rational sciences' and gone so far as to consider them superior to the religious, either on account of the onerous character of religious obligations, or out of contempt for religious rituals and observances. Reason itself proves, however, that upon religion depends the regulation of human relations, and the curbing of the natural propensity of mankind for animosity and strife, so that it appears unquestionable that reason is the very foundation (*aṣl, uss*) of religion.[12]

The primary virtue which genuine knowledge generates, according to al-Māwardī, is that of guarding one's self (*ṣiyānah*) and cultivating the quality of moral abstinence (*nazāhah*).[13] The learned man should cultivate in addition the virtue of humility and shun arrogance, frequently born of insufficient knowledge. He should not be ashamed of admitting his ignorance, or seeking constantly to add to his stock of knowledge. For, as some sages have said (here he writes in obvious reference to Socrates): "I have no virtue in matters of knowledge except the knowledge that I know not."[14]

Furthermore, the man of genuine knowledge should combine theory with practice and refrain from preaching what he does not practise. He should not deny the earnest student the fruits of his own knowledge, by guarding them jealously to himself. For the great advantage of instruction is not simply to impart knowledge to the learner, but also to increase and deepen the knowledge of the teacher.[15]

III. Rules of Religious Conduct (*Adab al-Dīn*)

With this well-balanced analysis of the three key concepts of reason, knowledge and religion, as well as their relationship and function, as a

---

11 *Adab al-Dunyā*, 28.
12 *Ibid.*, 29.
13 *Ibid.*, 30f.
14 *Ibid.*, 67. Cf. Plato, *Apology*, 21 E.
15 *Ibid.*, 72.

preamble, al-Māwardī proceeds to discuss the rules of religious conduct (*adab al-dīn*), mundane conduct (*adab al-dunyā*) and, finally, personal conduct (*adab al-nafs*). However, the lines of demarcation between the three forms of conduct are not always sharply drawn by this author.

Thus the opening sections of the first part of his treatise develop further the theme of religious obligation, along lines which, despite the protestations of his Shāfiᶜī supporters, reflect, as we have already mentioned, his definite Muᶜtazilite sympathies. God has revealed His will to mankind and laid down His religious obligations without any advantage accruing to Him, or any necessity constraining Him to do so; "He only intended to profit them, through His gracious bounty," manifested through the infinite graces (*niᶜam*) He has conferred on them.[16] A measure of His bounty and compassion is that none of the three types of obligations He has imposed on them, in the form of beliefs, commands and prohibitions, is beyond their capability. Each of these types of obligation, although divinely ordained, is rationally commendable, and the wisdom of enjoining it clearly discernible by right reason. This is particularly true of commands and prohibitions. "For He has only commanded as obligatory what is right (*maᶜrūf*), and prohibited what is wrong (*munkar*), so that commanding the right might confirm His orders and prohibiting the wrong might exhibit His displeasure."[17]

The fulfilment of these obligations, though essential for righteousness, serves at best as a means of eternal felicity in the life to come. It is therefore essential that the agent should train himself to cut himself off from the world (*al-dunyā*) in one of three ways:

First, by turning his thoughts away from the love of this world, insofar as it distracts him from yearning for the next. Jesus is then quoted as saying: "The world is like a bridge; cross it and do not linger on it." ᶜAlī, the fourth Caliph, is quoted as saying: "Woe to the world! Its beginning is trouble, its end is destruction. What is permitted (*ḥalāl*) in it is an object of retribution, and what is prohibited an object of punishment. Whoever is healthy is safe, whoever falls sick is sorry."[18]

Secondly, by understanding that the satisfaction of his desires and the attainment of his willful objectives are never achieved except at the cost of rectitude or peace of mind.

Thirdly, by dwelling on the thought of his mortality, so that he will not

---

[16] *Ibid.*, 78.

[17] *Ibid.*, 85. As already mentioned, commanding what is right or approved, as well as prohibiting what is wrong or disapproved, was a key concept of Muᶜtazilite ethics. *Supra*, 31f.

[18] *Ibid.*, 99.

be distracted by vain hopes and expectations. This theme, which the author supports by profuse quotations from the Traditions of the Prophet, the sayings of ᶜAlī, ᶜĪsā (Jesus), Alexander the Bihorned, and miscellaneous Ṣūfīs, philosophers and poets, was, as we have already noted, a fundamental feature of that otherworldly ideal which philosophers, religious divines and Ṣūfīs, such as al-Ḥasan al-Baṣrī, placed at the center of their moral and religious concerns, claiming a basis for it in Greek (especially Socratic-Platonic) philosophy, the Koran and ascetic literature in general.[19]

IV. Rules of Mundane Conduct (*Adab al-Dunyā*)

The part dealing with 'mundane conduct' develops along essentially similar otherworldly lines, the theme of man's frailty and insufficiency. Thanks to this frailty and insufficiency, man is guarded against arrogance and compelled to turn to God, both for guidance and the actual satisfaction of his needs, such satisfaction being achieved through the use of his reason and common sense, but only to the extent God has decreed and piety will permit. The general rule here too is not to cling to this world and neglect the other, but rather to satisfy one's mundane needs in moderation and never to lose sight of the otherworldly felicity which is in store for the virtuous.

However, because of the diversity of human aptitudes and estates, worldly order (*ṣalāḥ al-dunyā*) requires that six conditions be fulfilled:

1. An established religion, whereby man's passions are held in check and peace and order are secured.

2. A powerful ruler (*sulṭān*), dedicated to the enforcement of the principles of peace and justice. For neither religion nor reason is by itself sufficient to bar people from wrongdoing or injustice, unless they are coerced by the superior authority of a strong ruler.[20]

3. The reign of universal justice to ensure mutual love and submission to authority, as well as the prosperity of the land and the security of the ruler.

The three aspects of justice without which political order will disintegrate are: (a) justice towards one's subordinates, (b) justice towards one's superiors, including God, and (c) justice towards one's equals.[21] This latter aspect takes one of three forms: (a) refraining from overbearing

---

[19] *Ibid.*, 106f. Cf. *supra*, 152f.

[20] *Ibid.*, 120f. This theme is further developed in al-Māwardī's treatise on government. See *al-Aḥkām al-Sulṭāniyyah*, Cairo, 1966, 5–21.

[21] *Ibid.*,, 106. Cf. Miskawayh, *Tahdhīb al-Akhlāq*, 119f.

demeanor, (b) refraining from arrogance and (c) refraining from causing others injury. Here al-Māwardī states, in the manner of Miskawayh and other Muslim ethical philosophers, that justice consists in moderation or equilibrium (*iᶜtidāl*), as its etymology actually suggests, and like the other cardinal virtues of courage, wisdom, temperance, serenity, loyalty, liberality, etc., it is a mean between two extremes.

4. The reign of law and order, resulting in a universal sense of security, without which social existence becomes virtually impossible.

5. General economic prosperity or well-being, rooted in abundance of resources as well as revenue.

6. Vast hope, the precondition of any productive activity or endeavor, and of the cumulative achievements of civilization and of continuous progress.[22]

The importance of mutual love or affinity (*ulfah*) for social solidarity is particularly stressed; without it, human existence would indeed be wretched. Its causes are five: religion, good pedigree (*nasab*), kinship through marriage, friendship and piety. Both the Koran and the Traditions urge Muslim believers to band together and avoid strife and animosity. Direct and indirect kinship is an essential bond of union, and so is friendship. This latter virtue is divided into two kinds: (a) involuntary friendship, based on natural or conventional affinity, and (b) voluntary friendship, based on choice. The two motives of the latter are asserted along essentially Aristotelian lines to be the desire for the company of men of virtue and the need for association with one's fellowmen. Al-Kindī is reported as saying in an obvious variation on Aristotle's conception of the friend as an *alter ego* in *Nicomachean Ethics*, IX, 1166ª 30: "Your friend is another, who is yourself, but is nonetheless other." A similar saying, al-Māwardī informs us, is attributed to the first Caliph, Abū Bakr.[23]

Piety (*birr*), a key concept in Koranic ethics, as we have seen in Part One, is discussed at length. It is a basic element in mutual love or solidarity, since it causes the heart to "bend in love and compassion" and is an element in gracious dealings with our fellowmen. That is why it has been commanded by God (in the Koran and the Traditions). Its two subdivisions are: charity (*ṣilah*) and right action (*al-maᶜrūf*). Charity consists in giving of one's substance for a good cause, without the expectation of any return. It presupposes generosity, which is a mean between the two extremes of extravagance and miserliness, both of which are denounced in the Koran and the Traditions. Right action, on the other hand, is of two

---

22 *Ibid.*, 130.
23 *Ibid.*,, 148f.

kinds: complaisance in discourse, and good will and succor towards those in need without stinting or complacency.[24]

V. Rules of Personal Conduct (*Adab al-Nafs*)

The third part of al-Māwardī's *Adab al-Dunyā wa'l-Dīn* deals, as we have already noted, with 'personal conduct', and may be said to be concerned with the analysis of the individual virtues of humility, good manners, modesty, self-control, truthfulness, and freedom from envy, as well as a series of social virtues, such as the rules of speaking and keeping silent, elocution, patience and fortitude, good counsel, keeping confidence and decorum. This analysis abounds, like the rest of this treatise, with acute psychological observations and reflections, supported with copious quotations from the Koran and the Traditions, the sayings of the Caliphs, especially ᶜAlī, the poets and the philosophers. The key moral concept for al-Māwardī is nobility of character (*murūʾah*), a fundamental concept in Arabic morality which appears to antedate the Islamic period.[25] It is defined by al-Māwardī as "consideration for the circumstances (of the action), so that the soul may be in the best condition possible, neither manifesting ill-will deliberately, nor becoming the object of deserved reproach."[26] The Traditions and quotations given in support of this cryptic definition suggest that, like Aristotle's justice, the term is used as a synonym for 'complete virtue'.[27] In contrast to reason or common sense, which commands us to do what is most useful, nobility of character commands us to do what is most beautiful. Such a virtue must be cultivated diligently, for it can only be achieved through sustained effort and a solicitous regard for the soul, its needs and inclinations. Two virtues or dispositions of character facilitate its acquisition: magnanimity (*ᶜulūw al-himmah*) and dignity (*sharaf al-nafs*). Its preconditions or prerequisites are too numerous to list; "the whole content of this book," writes the author, "forms part of the requirements and conditions of the virtue of nobility."[28] The virtues which stem from it fall into two categories: (a) those pertaining to the self, and (b) those pertaining to others. Under

---

[24] *Ibid.*, 184f.

[25] *Ibid.*, 290. Cf. M. Arkoun, "L'éthique musulmane d'après Māwardī," in: *Revue des Études Islamiques*, XXXI (1963), 3f. It has been reprinted in: *Essais sur la pensée islamique*, 3rd ed., Paris, 1984 (= Islam d'hier et d'aujourdhui 24), 251–282. Cf. also H. Laoust, "La pensée et l'action politiques d'al-Māwardī (364–450/974–1058)," in: *Revue des Études Islamiques* XXXVI (1968), 11–92.

[26] *Ibid.*, 290.

[27] See *N.E.*, V, 1129^{b} 25f.

[28] *Adab al-Dunyā*, 315.

(a) the author gives: temperance, abstinance and guarding one's self, "once the ordinances of religion have been fulfilled." Under (b) he gives: mutual assistance, latitude, and benevolence.

The two subdivisions of temperance are abstention from religious prohibitions (*maḥārim*), on the one hand, and moral transgressions (*maʾāthim*), on the other. The two subdivisions of the virtue of abstinence (*nazāhah*) are shunning base acquisitions and suspicious occasions. Those of guarding oneself are: questing for material sufficiency and avoiding the humiliation of asking.

The virtues which stem from nobility admit of many subdivisions also. Mutual assistance is of two kinds, depending on the station of its author: (a) assistance in prosperity, and (b) assistance in distress. The latter is either obligatory or voluntary; it is obligatory in relation to one's relatives, friends and neighbors, and it is voluntary in relation to everybody else.

As to latitude, it is of two kinds also: (a) pardoning the offences of others, and (b) writing off our own rights, either contractual, financial or political. The latitude attendant upon these traits is an essential condition of mutual trust and social-religious solidarity, as well as the rooting out of animosity, envy and strife.

Finally, bounty is of two kinds: (a) spontaneous, or aimed at friends and associates, and (b) 'preemptive', or aimed at the envious and the thankless, so as to ward off calumny or ill-will.[29]

The following table of the ramifications of the cardinal virtues of nobility and its two preconditions will give a diagrammatic representation of the whole network of the virtues of personal morality.

The whole treatise closes with a discussion of a series of practical precepts directing one to conduct oneself with decency and decorum in matters of food, drink, personal appearance and the management of one's domestic affairs, in accordance with the 'customs of the times' and 'the conventions of its people', seeing that these precepts vary from time to time and from place to place. In all these matters, one should conduct one's self with great prudence and avoid engaging in any activity before a careful consideration of its possible consequences. A particularly noteworthy admonition of the author is the constant practice of self-examination. Every evening one should make an honest review of the actions of the previous day, so as to determine whether one has fulfilled one's object, missed it altogether, fell short of it or exceeded it. Thereby one will be better equipped on the morrow to undertake afresh one's many activities in a spirit of responsibility, and to avoid the occasions of failure or transgression.[30]

---

[29] *Ibid.*, 316f.
[30] *Ibid.*, 326.

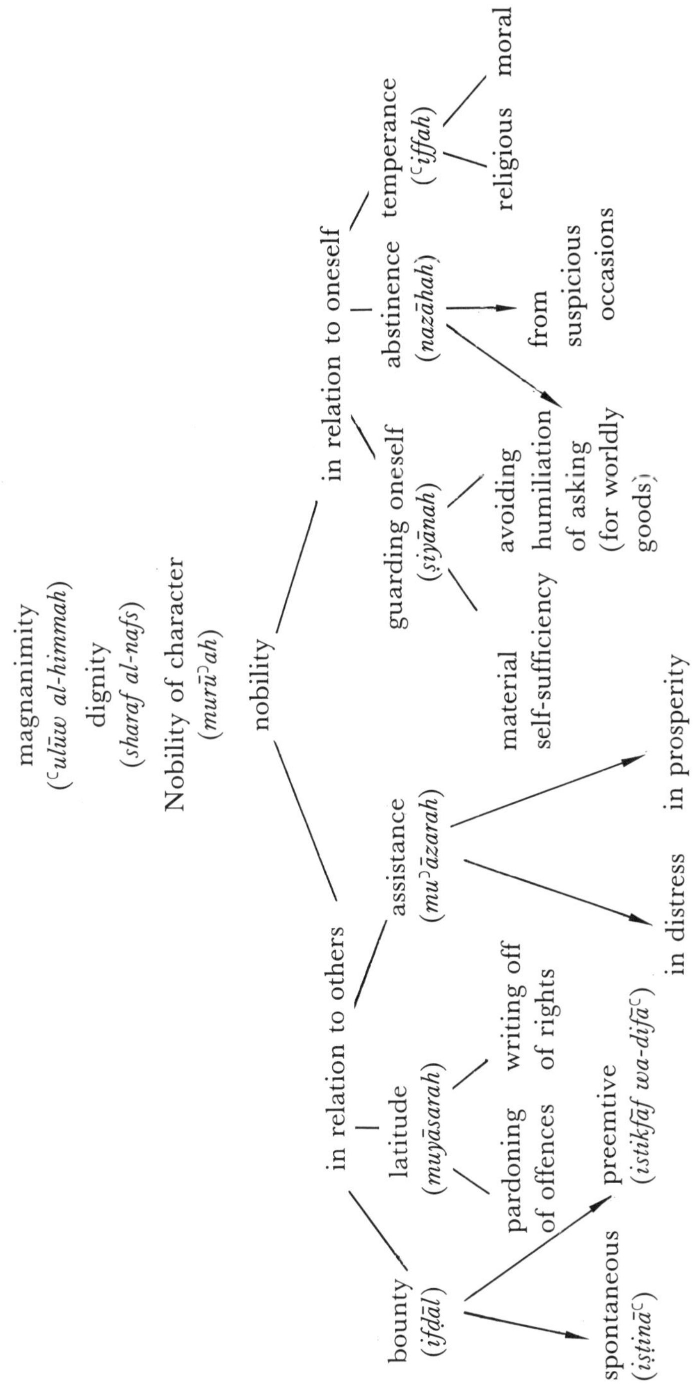
magnanimity
(ʿulūw al-himmah)
dignity
(sharaf al-nafs)
Nobility of character
(murūʾah)
nobility
in relation to oneself
in relation to others
guarding oneself
(ṣiyānah)
abstinence
(nazāhah)
temperance
(ʿiffah)
religious
moral
material self-sufficiency
avoiding humiliation of asking (for worldly goods)
from suspicious occasions
bounty
(ifḍāl)
latitude
(muyāsarah)
assistance
(muʾāzarah)
spontaneous
(iṣṭināʿ)
preemtive
(istikfāf wa-difāʿ)
pardoning of offences
writing off of rights
in distress
in prosperity

CHAPTER THREE

TRADITIONALISM AND PRAGMATISM: ᶜALĪ IBN AḤMAD IBN ḤAZM (D. 1064)

I. The Ẓāhirī Ethical Dilemma

The literalism of certain traditionalists, like Ibn Ḥazm of Cordova, raised the crucial question of the significance of religious obligation, on the one hand, and that of moral responsibility, on the other. If the Koran and Traditions are, as the literalists actually do assert them to be, the two ultimate sources of religious truth, it is obvious that religious piety and moral virtue are not only identical, they can only consist in strict observance of the dictates of the law as defined in these two sources, so that in fact all piety or virtue is nothing other than ritual compliance.

The crux of Ibn Ḥazm's literalism is the rejection of all methods of deduction (*istidlāl*) and analogy (*qiyās*) which over the years had been applied by many theological schools to juridical and theological questions, in some form or other. It is true, some early theologians, like Aḥmad ibn Ḥanbal (d. 855), had rejected the use of these methods altogether, but the complex question of reconciling religious obligation (*taklīf*) with moral responsibility made it imperative, as we have seen in the case of many theological authors, such as al-Ḥasan al-Baṣri, al-Māwardī and others, to mellow this rigid traditionalism. Apart from this 'methodological' difficulty, there was the equally rigid attitude of the traditionalists to the question of free will (*qadar*). Many of the early jurists, as we have already seen, accepted almost unquestioningly the position of the early Determinists such as al-Najjār, Jahm ibn Ṣafwān and others.[1]

True to type, the great Ẓāhirī jurist and heresiographer, starting from the grand thesis of unqualified divine omnipotence, asserts that God has not only created man by a sheer act of divine fiat (*amr*), but has completely predetermined his actions. Having created both good and evil, which depend entirely on the determinations of His will, man has been robbed of the ability to plumb these two mysteries through his own natural lights; he can only derive his knowledge of them from the Koran and the Traditions. Any attempt at giving a rational justification of God's ways, His prescriptions or prohibitions, should be abandoned as entirely futile[2]

---

[1] See *supra*, 47.

[2] See Ibn Ḥazm, *al-Fiṣal fi'l-Milal wa'l-Ahwā*ᵓ *wa'l-Niḥal*, Cairo, 1317 A.H., II, 81, 116, 121.

God, Who is fully unanswerable for His actions, as the Koran itself has put it (21:23), can torture or reward whomever He pleases, having Himself guided them aright (*hadā*) or led them astray (*aḍalla*) in the first place.[3]

These extreme theological affirmations notwithstanding, Ibn Ḥazm, who was actively involved in the political squabbles of his time and led an active scholastic and public life, was compelled to record his moral reflections gained over many troubled years, so that his readers might profit from them in "the reformation of their evil characters and the healing of the ills of their souls," as he tells us in his major ethical work.[4]

The twofold purpose of the author is achieved by the double use of the discursive and the reflective method; his attempt at systematism is counterbalanced by his tendency to slip into the literary or hortatory style. Three key ethical concepts, however, permeate the discussion: (a) the all-pervasiveness of anxiety (*hamm*), (b) the futility of worldly ambition, and (c) the universal character of love or friendship.

II. Repelling Anxiety (*Ṭard al-Hamm*)

Drawing upon his own rich store of personal experience and trial, Ibn Ḥazm states that he looked assiduously for an objective which all men concurred in approving and searching for, but could find no other common objective than repelling anxiety. When he reflected further on this phenomenon, he became convinced that this was not only the sole common objective of all mankind, but the sole motive unterlying all their actions; "they do not make a single move unless they expect thereby to repel anxiety, and do not utter a single word except insofar as they strive to turn it away from themselves."[5] There are some who, being devoid of religious faith, do not seek the bliss of the hereafter; others who, being incorrigibly wicked, do not wish to see goodness, security or justice done; and still others who, being naturally slothful, have no desire for a good name. Prophets, ascetics and philosophers shun wealth, the vulgar prefer ignorance to knowledge, and there are those boors who are naturally repelled by pleasure and despise its seekers. However, there has not been a single person, from the beginning of Creation to its end, who will welcome anxiety and does not wish to be rid of it.

Having made this discovery through divine illumination, as he tells us,

---

[3] *Ibid.*, III, 100–105 and 128.

[4] *K. al-Akhlāq wa'l-Siyar*, ed. and French trans. Nada Tomiche, Beirut, 1961, 12 (Arabic text).

[5] *Ibid.*, 14. (Arabic text).

Ibn Ḥazm proceeded to determine the best means of repelling this anxiety and found that it only consisted in "turning towards God, by working for the hereafter."[6] This otherworldly featue of Ibn Ḥazm's thought will be considered in the next section; in the meantime we will examine his arguments in support of the thesis that all human endeavors are directed towards repelling anxiety. Thus the seeker of wealth in fact seeks to repel through it the anxiety of poverty; the seeker of fame is primarily concerned to repel the anxiety of subordination or subservience; the seeker of pleasure simply wishes to repel the anxiety of missing its enjoyment. This rule can be generalized to apply to every human endeavor, according to Ibn Ḥazm; even the seeker of knowledge is concerned to repel the anxiety of ignorance. He who seeks the company of others in fact wishes thereby to repel the anxiety of solitude and the fear of being passed by the world. In short, he who eats, drinks, practices sex, clothes himself, plays, and performs acts of piety is concerned simply to ward off the opposite modes of action.

Other subsidiary forms of anxiety attendant upon all of these pursuits arise either by reason of the unattainability of their goals, by their eventual loss, or by occasional failure to achieve them by reason of some incapacity or other. Add to these the anxiety which assails the agent who has achieved these goals, but is troubled by the fear of rivals, the criticism of the envious, the constant threat of despoliation or enmity, and, finally, the fear of reproach or sin.[7]

The negative ideal of repelling anxiety is reminiscent of the Epicurean ideal of *ataraxia*. Epicurus' letter to his disciple Menoeceus appears to have been at the basis of the moral reflections of al-Kindī and al-Rāzī on the fear of anxiety and of death, as we have seen.[8] However, Ibn Ḥazm is not satisfied with this purely negative ideal and modifies it somewhat by stressing the positive motive of the soul's quiescence (*uns*). The root of all virtue and vice, as well as pious and impious actions, "is the revulsion of the soul or its quiescence. The happy man is he whose soul aquiesces in the practice of virtues and acts of piety, and is repelled by vices and acts of impiety, whereas the wretched man is he whose soul acquiesces in vices or acts of impiety, and is repelled by virtues or sins."[9] The excellence of knowledge consists, among other things, in that it dispels those wearying thoughts and futile expectations, which can only breed anxiety and painful thoughts. The man of learning should consider the humiliation he is

---

[6] *Ibid.*, 14 (Arabic text).
[7] *Ibid.*, 15 (Arabic text).
[8] See *supra*, 76.
[9] *Kitāb al-Akhlāq*, 18 (Arabic text).

spared at the hands of the ignorant, and the anxiety which the flight of truth from him, as well as the joy which the discovery of truths hidden from others, has generated; he will be truly grateful to God and exultant at his knowledge and eager to add constantly to it.[10]

III. The Futility of Worldly Ambition and Self-Conceit

What makes anxiety particularly poignant, according to Ibn Ḥazm, is the fact that it is wedded to worldly ambition and solicitude, the root of all misery in the world. For the world is like a succession of shadows cast by a series of dummies mounted on a wheel which is continually turning round. Man's idle wishes will not cause this wheel to stop or its direction to be reversed. However, most men in their folly bring upon themselves the greatest anxiety and wretchedness by maliciously wishing the misfortune or destruction of their enemies. They wish that prices might rise, so that others might starve; that injury befall their fellowmen, so that they may derive a certain advantage over them. They do not understand that these idle wishes will neither bring about these desired ends nor hasten them, and that they only compound their own anxiety in this world and bring upon themselves deserved punishment in the next. Were they to dedicate themselves instead to wishing their fellowmen well, their reward in the hereafter would be compounded and their own well-being in this life increased. In fact, it is the mark of the truly rational man that he is troubled by the widespread injustice and oppression he observes in the world and his own inability to proclaim the truth publicly, that he finds relief only in shunning the superfluous goods of this world which the rest of mankind is preoccupied with seeking.[11]

The vanity of worldly ambition is such that man's only real portion of it is the present or the now, but this present is nothing but the line of demarcation between two portions of time, past and future, neither of which actually exists. It is the height of folly to trade the hereafter which is eternal for the present which is shorter than the twinkling of an eye.[12]

As further evidence of this vanity, it is enough to consider how in sleep all the cares which trouble us while we are awake simply vanish; the sleeper no longer cares or yearns for anything he held so dear while he was awake, neither kin nor child, social station or political office, poverty, wealth or disaster.[13] If only one were to use his reason properly, he would

---

[10] *Ibid.*, 21 (Arabic text).

[11] *Ibid.*, 19f., 28f. and 59f.

[12] *Ibid.*, 20. Cf. *Fiṣal*, I, 14f. For this concept of the 'now', see Aristotle, *Physics*, IV, 220^a-5 and 222^a-10f.

[13] *Ibid.*, 20 and 59.

realize the folly of clinging to this world. Reason (*ᶜaql*) is defined as the practice of piety and virtue, as well as the avoidance of impiety and vice. Its opposite is folly (*ḥumq*), which is the practice of impiety and vice; between these two attitudes, there is only that of stupidity (*sukhf*), which consists in doing or speaking to no avail, either in matters religious or worldly. To imagine that reason consists in seeking worldly success or in conviviality in our dealings with our fellowmen, with a view to some advantage or gain, or in using every device to accumulate wealth or enhance our social position, is a mistake. Such action is sometimes referred to as cunning (*dahāʾ*), but is far from deserving to be designated as reason; the Koran itself has identified the wicked with those who 'do not reason' (Koran 67: 10–11).[14]

A major vice born of ignorance or stupidity is that of self-conceit (*ᶜujb*). It is in fact the mark of the ignorant that he does not recognize his faults, whereas the reasonable man is by definition he who, having acknowledged his faults, proceeds to fight and repress them. He who does not perceive his faults is worse than the worst of the vile; his foremost duty is to search for his faults and to avoid self-conceit, on the one hand, and preoccupation with the faults of others or with public calumny, on the other.

Moreover, the self-conceited has on reflection no cause to pride himself on any of his alleged advantages. If he prides himself on his reason, let him consider all the evil or idle thoughts that flit through his mind, or the false opinions he entertains and which far exceed the right ones, and he will understand the inferiority of his intelligence. If, on the other hand, he prides himself on the goodness of his actions, let him recall his transgressions or shortcomings, and then he will realize how much they exceed his commendable actions.[15]

Should the self-conceited pride himself on his knowledge, he should be reminded that knowledge is indeed a divine gift, which God can withhold at will by afflicting him if He wished with a disease which could cause him to lose it altogether.[16] To prove this fact, it is enough to consider how some diligent searchers for learning have devoted themselves assiduously to study without making much progress in that field. Moreover, he should consider how far greater is the part of learning of which he is ignorant than that of which he has partaken, and this will give him cause to despise him-

[14] *Ibid.*, 55f.
[15] *Ibid.*, 63f.
[16] *Ibid.*, 65. In support of this argument, the author cites an attack of temporary amnesia which afflicted him, as well as a more lasting loss of memory which afflicted a certain ᶜAbd al-Malik ibn Ṭarīf, reputed for his learning.

self, rather than be puffed up with pride. If he considers likewise how his knowledge is a valid ground for reproach whenever he fails to practice what he knows he should, he will realize how much less vulnerable to criticism the ignorant are, and that accordingly it would have been safer for him to be ignorant.[17]

None of the customary grounds for self-conceit, such as social station, good looks, personal courage, or good birth, are justified; each of these boons are divine gifts for which one has no cause to pride oneself or think that thcy can be enjoyed in an unadulterated or perfect way, seeing that human life is constantly threatened by poverty, sickness, disaster or old age.[18]

IV. The Principal Virtues

Like other Muslim moralists, Ibn Ḥazm accepts the fourfold division of the principal virtues derived ultimately from Plato. However, his fourfold table consists of justice, intelligence (*fahm*), courage and generosity, upon which all the other virtues are based. He does, however, include in his list of major virtues temperance (*ᶜiffah*), which he regards as a species of justice and generosity.[19] In his analysis of these virtues, he is less dependent on philosophical ethics, especially Plato's, than one might expect; in fact, certain moral Islamic elements condition his account of these and related virtues. Thus generosity (*jūd*) is defined by him as "the act of spending the whole surplus [of our substance] in acts of righteousness (*birr*), especially in assisting a needy neighbour, a poor relative, a person whose substance has been wasted, or one who is in very urgent need." To withhold giving in all these cases is a form of miserliness, whereas giving in other ways is a form of reprehensible prodigality. Beyond this is the virtue of munificence, or the act of giving up your own portion to one who is in more dire need than yourself.[20]

Courage, on the other hand, is defined as "the act of offering one's self to the point of dying [in the defense] of religion, womenfolk (*ḥarīm*), an abused neighbour, an oppressed man calling for help, injustice in matters of money, honor and other forms of right, regardless of whether opposition is great or small."[21] Defect in carrying out these obligations is cowardice, and wasting one's energies in seeking the vanities of this world is sheer rashness and stupidity. Worse still is the case of the man who

---

[17] *Ibid.*, 66.
[18] *Ibid.*, 68.
[19] *Ibid.*, 57.
[20] *Ibid.*, 30.
[21] *Ibid.*, 30.

strives to oppose right doing in matters affecting him or others, or he who strives haphazardly, siding now with X, then with Y. For not knowing for what purpose they fight, such fortuitous friends are senselessly destroyed.[22]

The essence of temperance is to refrain from indulging your eye-sight or any other of your senses in the enjoyment of what is not lawful (*lā yaḥill*); the excess of such indulgence is lasciviousness (*ᶜihr*), and its defect impotence. This virtue, as we have seen, is for Ibn Ḥazm a species of justice, defined as "the act of giving of your free accord what is due and to take it" when it is due to you. Contrariwise, injustice consists in taking, but not giving what is due. Magnanimity (*karam*) on the other hand, consists in giving what is due to others freely, while being prepared to give up what is due to you, although fully capable of wresting it. The latter is a form of benevolence (*faḍl*) which is analogous to generosity; however, benevolence is the more general of the two.[23]

Intelligence is not formally defined by the author, but a good deal of the book turns on the merits of knowledge and the duty incumbent on the 'reasonable' man to seek that knowledge which is conducive to righteousness, and to exult in it; for such a man, he writes, "will not delight in a property in which a beast, a brute or an inanimate object will supersede him, but will delight in his pre-eminence in possessing that virtue through which God has set him apart from beasts, brutes and inanimate objects, and this is the virtue of discrimination (*tamyīz*) that he shares with the angels."[24]

A principal virtue, which, according to the author, is a compound of courage, generosity, justice and intelligence, is honesty (*nazāhah*). He who possesses this virtue understands the futility of its contrary, and is courageous enough to be honest, generous enough to be indifferent to what he has missed, and just enough to be pleased with his condition. Covetousness (*ṭamaᶜ*), which is the contrary of this virtue, is made up of the contrary qualities of cowardice, miserliness, injustice and ignorance.[25]

Another major virtue for Ibn Ḥazm is love (*maḥabbah*), defined as "yearning for the beloved and hating to be alienated from him, while desiring to have one's love for him requited."[26] All forms of this virtue are reducible to one; their respective objects differ according to the interest involved or its degree. Thus the love of spouse, ruler, friend, rela-

---

22 *Ibid.*, 30.
23 *Ibid.*, 30.
24 *Ibid.*, 18 *et passim*.
25 *Ibid.*, 49.
26 *Ibid.*, 47.

tive or child simply differs according to the nature of the desired object, of which the lover is equally jealous. The lowest degree of such love is the wish to be well-pleasing and close to the beloved, then to be allowed to enter into converse with him, and, finally, to be bodily united to him.[27]

As to friendship, it consists in being displeased or pleased with what displeases or pleases your friend. Reciprocity is not a necessary condition of this relationship, for one might be a friend or lover of another who does not reciprocate his feelings and good will. The highest form of friendship is that which consists in the willingness to share yourself and your substance with your friend, for no ulterior motive whatever. This type of friendship is extremely rare, but Ibn Ḥazm attests to the existence of two eminent contemporary examples of it in Valencia, but for which his faith in its possibility, as he says, would have been shattered. He does, however, inveigh against the tendency of some to surround themselves with a large assortment of friends or associates. Nothing has a greater semblance to virtue than this vice; its addicts do not understand that genuine friendship requires great patience, sincerity, generosity, fellowship, temperance and mutual assistance. A large retinue of self-seeking associates should not be mistaken for friendship, since many of these associates are no better than brigands or parasites. Genuine friendship involves, in addition, mutual support (*tanāṣur*) either in the service of God, the pursuit of some virtuous activity, or simply out of pure love.[28]

---

[27] *Ibid.*, 47f.
[28] *Ibid.*, 39f.

CHAPTER FOUR

'NOBLE RELIGIOUS TRAITS' (*Makārim al-Sharīʿah*): AL-RĀGHIB AL-IṢFAHĀNĪ (D. CA. 1108)

I. Religious Nobility, Worship (*ʿIbādah*) and Civilization (*ʿImārat al-Arḍ*)

The isolation of the religious component in moral thought led some authors to investigate the grounds of the distinction between the ethical, religious and 'civilizational' element in this thought. A noteworthy example of this tendency is Abu'l-Qāsim al-Ḥusayn al-Rāghib al-Iṣfahānī (d. ca. 1108), who, in addition to a commentary on the Koran, has written what appear to be two complementary versions of religious ethics, *al-Dharīʿah ilā Makārim al-Sharīʿah* (The Means to Noble Religious Traits) and *Tafṣīl al-Nashʾatayn wa-Taḥṣīl al-Saʿādatayn* (Exposition of the Two Births and Acquisition of the Two Felicities).[1]

The foundation of religious nobility, according to al-Iṣfahānī, is the purity of the soul, achieved through education and the practice of the virtues of temperance, forbearance and justice. Its consummation is the acquisition of the virtues of wisdom through instruction, generosity through temperance, courage through forbearance, and the 'rectitude of actions' through justice.[2] Whoever has achieved this condition will have attained the highest degree of nobility, identified in the Koran (49:13) with the greatest piety; he will also become worthy of the office of God's vicegerent (*khilāfah*) on earth, and join the ranks of the divines, martyrs and saints.

This religious nobility differs from religious observance in that the conditions of the latter are clearly defined in the ritual canons, but not those of the former. However, 'religious nobility' cannot be fulfilled unless the religious observances are adhered to; its precepts are to these observances what the essential (*farḍ*) is to the optional (*nafal*) or what justice (*ʿadl*) is to benevolence (*faḍl*). By performing the latter, the agent cannot dispense with performing the former, which is its essential precondition. Both religious nobility and observance differ from social activity or civilization (*ʿimārat al-arḍ*) in that they bear on individual action or obligation, whereas 'civilization' bears on the collective activities of the group, insofar

---

[1] See Ḥājjī Khalīfah, *Kashf al-Ẓunūn*, Istanbul, 1941, 36, 377, 447, and al-Bayhaqī, *Taʾrīkh Ḥukamāʾ al-Islām*, Damascus, 1946, 112f.

[2] See *al-Dharīʿah ilā Makārim al-Sharīʿah*, Cairo, 1299 A.H., 19f.

as they aim at the management of public life and the provision for the livelihood and well-being of this group. Indeed, such administration and provision are not possible for the individual, except in concert with the group. Both the Koran and the Traditions are quoted in support of this necessary social postulate.

Like other ethical writers already discussed, such as al-Ṭūsī and al-Dawwānī, al-Iṣfahānī subordinates these three modes of ethical and religious perfection to the supreme goal of vicegerency (*khilāfah*), explicitly stated on the basis of Koranic passages (7:67,72; 2:28), to be the very *raison d'être* of man's creation. This vicegerency is defined, in Platonic fashion, as "the imitation of God Almighty, according to human capacity,"[3] but is fitted nonetheless into a strictly Islamic framework. The purpose of man's creation by God is worshiping Him, as stated in Koran 51:56, and this worship in turn consists in submitting to Him and complying with His commands and prohibitions. In fact, man is stated to realize his humanity to the extent he conforms to the holy law (*sharīᶜah*) through worship, and to perform his voluntary actions with the intention of seeking to come closer (*taqarrub*) to God. Otherwise his actions are either compulsory, induced by concupiscence, or downright hypocritical.[4]

II. Moral Self-Purification

The correlation between religious and ethical activity is, for al-Iṣfahānī, so organic that religious worship is itself the precondition of moral rectitude. God, he says, did not impose the obligation of worship on mankind for any self-seeking reason, since He is entirely self-sufficient; instead He has imposed this obligation on them in order to remove the impurities and diseases of their souls, whereby they will be able to achieve the eternal life and well-being they have been promised in the life to come. Without sufficient regard to self-consistency, however, the author argues that self-purification is only possible, on the one hand, through conformity to the religious law, and on the other, through the cultivation of those moral and intellectual traits which philosophical moralists have always stressed as the preconditions of moral uprightness. Thus although he accepts, like those moralists, the Platonic trichotomy of the soul, and predicates on it his theory of virtue, his psychology is essentially Avicennian, combining Pla-

---

3 *Ibid.*, 18 and 21. Cf. *Tafṣīl al-Nashᵓatayn wa-Taḥṣīl al-Saᶜādatayn*, Saida, N.D., 29f.; Plato, *Theaetetus*, 176B and al-Kindī, *Rasāᵓil*, Cairo 1950, I, 172, etc.

4 *Tafṣīl al-Nashᵓatayn*, 55 and 59.

tonic and Aristotelian elements.[5] By ordering or regulating (*iṣlāḥ*) the three powers of the soul, its purification, according to him, is readily achieved. The rational power is regulated through education, which enables it to distinguish between truth and falsity in theoretical matters and between right and wrong in practical matters. The concupiscent power is regulated through the practice of generosity and compassion, whereas the irascible (*ḥamīyah*) is regulated through gradual taming (*iṣlāḥ*), leading to the point at which the soul is held in check and courage is achieved. When all the three powers are properly ordered, justice and benevolence (*iḥsān*) arise. In support of this view, the author quotes various Traditions and Koranic verses, which, like verse 49:15, are interpreted to refer to the three principal virtues.[6]

Of the three powers of the soul, the concupiscent is the most recalcitrant, and it is by crushing it that man is able to rise above the bestial level and achieve the 'divine condition'. Al-Iṣfahānī is emphatic, however, chiefly on the basis of various Koranic quotations and Traditions, that despite the many difficulties attendant upon it, the reformation of character is quite possible, repudiating thereby the view of those moralists, who identifying character (*khulq*) with nature (*khalqah*), have denied this possibility altogether.[7] In this process, the practice of virtue which heightens man's disposition to right action plays an important part, just as the practice of vice which heightens the disposition to wrongdoing plays an equally important one.

His classification of the virtues, although conditioned by certain religious elements, follows well-known philosophical lines. Virtues are either theoretical or practical; each of these divisions admits of two subdivisions: human and divine. The first group depends exclusively on human initiative and exercise, the second on a 'divine favor', which determines from birth the moral pre-eminence of the subject, as illustrated by the case of the divinely-assisted prophets.[8]

However, in the detailed analysis of these virtues, the author adopts a different principle of classification, reducing the virtues or 'goods' to five 'divine gifts': otherwordly, psychic, bodily, external and divine (*tawfīqiyyah*). The otherworldly consist of four ingredients: eternal life, infinite knowledge, supreme power and boundless wealth. Otherwordly bliss, however, cannot be attained without the second group of 'psychic' virtues, which consists in turn of four ingredients: knowledge, the perfection

[5] See *al-Dharīʿah*, 12f.
[6] *Ibid.*, 27.
[7] *Ibid.*, 29f.
[8] *Ibid.*, 33.

of reason; piety, the perfection of temperance; courage, the perfection of moral strife; and equity (*inṣāf*), the perfection of justice. These virtues are 'fulfilled' through the bodily virtues of good health, strength, good looks and a long life, as well as the 'external virtues' of wealth, social station, relatives and noble birth. All these virtues finally require, as a precondition for achieving them, the four virtues of divine assistance (*tawfīq*), namely, God's right guidance (*hidāyah*), good counsel (*rushd*), direction (*tasdīd*) and support (*taʾyīd*).[9]

The 'psychic' group, or virtues of the soul, which constitute the core of al-Iṣfahānī's ethical theory, admit of further subdivisions along familiar philosophical lines. Under reason, both theoretical and practical, are subsumed the sub-virtues of sound reflection: good memory, natural keenness (*fiṭnah*), sagacity, good understanding and good retention. Under courage are subsumed generosity and forbearance (*ṣabr*), which gives rise to magnanimity (*shahāmah*) and manliness. Under temperance are subsumed contentment (*qanāᶜah*), and honesty (*amānah*); under justice, mercy (*raḥmah*), patience (*ḥilm*) and pardon.[10]

Al-Iṣfahānī insists on the organic correlation of the five classes of virtue, as well as the interrelations of their subdivisions, which complement and reinforce each other. The 'divine' virtue of 'right guidance', however, plays a predominant role in his moral system. Indeed, he asserts, "no one can achieve any of the virtues without the guidance and mercy of God Almighty, Who is the beginning and end of all good."[11] When this guidance is coupled with the other divine virtues of right direction and support, the agent is blessed with keen understanding and a "careful heart", and he is able to gain the auxiliary goods, a helping teacher or friend, wealth, the assistance of kinsfolk and social station. These external goods ensure that man shall not be forced, by reason of weakness or material need, to stoop to the level of the despicable crowd.[12]

III. The Excellence of Reason

A keynote of al-Iṣfahānī's whole ethical theory, like that of other religious moralists, is the pre-eminence of reason, both as a faculty enabling man to gain knowledge and virtue, and as the essential principle differentiating him from other entities and entitling him to the position of God's vicegerent on earth. Reason is defined on the basis of a well-known Tradition

---

9 *Al-Dharīᶜah*, 35f.
10 *Ibid.*, 42f.
11 *Ibid.*, 44.
12 *Ibid.*, 45f.

as the first substance created and rendered noble by God.[13] Its two subdivisions are natural and acquired. The former is an inborn aptitude which is actualized or perfected by the latter. When fully actualized or 'illuminated' by worldly and otherworldly knowledge, reason gives rise to science (^{c}*ilm*), prudence and wisdom, as well as a long series of subsidiary intellectual virtues, of which the most noteworthy are intelligence, keenness, good understanding, good imagination, insight, eloquence, judgement, divination and inspiration.[14] Its major 'fruits' are the knowledge of God and obedience to Him. This knowledge, according to al-Iṣfahānī, is twofold: (a) general or innate, consisting in the apprehension that man, being created, must have a Creator, and (b) acquired, consisting in the apprehension of God's unity and attributes, as well as the multitude of created animals insofar as they are produced by Him. Acquired knowledge admits in turn of three subdivisions or parts: (a) that which is open to prophets and saints only and is indubitable in character, (b) that which is known with probability and is open to true believers, who, although they may be troubled with doubt, are nevertheless reassured as a result of prolonged reflection, and (c) that which is known by similitude and imitation, and is accordingly never free from doubt.[15]

The interrelations of reason and revelation in the process of acquiring these diverse modes of knowledge are described by al-Iṣfahānī in decisive organic terms. The two are for him complementary: "without revelation (*shar*^{c}), reason will not be rightly guided, and without reason, revelation cannot be made explicit." Reason is the foundation, revelation the edifice, and no edifice can rise except on a sound foundation. The reason for this complementary duality is that by itself reason is unable to gain any but a universal knowledge of reality, such as the goodness of seeking the truth and uttering it and practicing justice, goodness and temperance. The particular application of this knowledge to specific cases, such as abstention from eating pork or drinking wine, is only known through revelation, defined by the author as "the principle regulating sound beliefs and right actions and pointing the way to [man's] welfare in this life and the life to come."[16] It follows that the commissioning of prophets bearing God's message to mankind is indispensable for supplementing or rectifying the partial knowledge of reason. The author recognizes, however, that "just as it is impossible that a dead man should hear unless God has created life, hearing and sight in him, it is equally impossible that he who does

---

13 *Ibid.*, 53.
14 *Ibid.*, 60f. Cf. *N.E.*, VI, 3–11.
15 *Ibid.*, 66f.
16 *Tafṣīl al-Nash*$^{\supset}$*atayn*, 51. Cf. *al-Dharī*^{c}*ah*, 68f.

not apprehend the objects of reason should apprehend the truths of revelation."[17]

IV. Justice and Love

As was customary in philosophical ethical writings, stemming ultimately from Aristotle's *Nicomachean Ethics*, the discussion of justice and love is pursued by al-Iṣfahānī in some detail. First, he observes, justice presupposes equality, and like it belongs to the category of relation. Considered potentially, it denotes a moral trait in man whereby he seeks to achieve equality; when conceived actually, it denotes "that equity which depends on uprightness."[18] However, when applied to God, it denotes the infinite orderliness (*intiẓām*) of His actions.

As a positive trait, justice sometimes means the sum-total of all the virtues and sometimes the highest of them, insofar as man can practice it in himself or in his relations with his fellowmen. The former (Platonic) meaning has been expressed in the Koran in terms of a balance (*mīzān*) and has been described in the Traditions as the principle underlying the subsistence of heaven and earth. It is for that reason that the soul finds offensive the sight of whatever is disorderly or composite in the world.

Another division of justice proposed by the author is into absolute and relative. The former is recognized by reason as universal and necessary, such as the duty to do good to whomever has done you good, and to refrain from wronging whomever has refrained from wronging you. The latter is known by revelation, and is not valid in all places and at all times, such as requiting evil for evil, administering punishment for crime and confiscating the property of the renegade. In an obvious reference to the conflicting views of the Muᶜtazilah and the Ashᶜarites, al-Iṣfahānī observes that some theologians have contended that justice and injustive can only be known through revelation, whereas others have asserted that they can be known through reason prior to revelation (as the Muᶜtazilah—already discussed in Part II—contended). His own view appears to be that both reason and revelation, as we have seen, coalesce in the knowledge of ethical truth.

Genuine justice consists, according to al-Iṣfahānī, in doing the right spontaneously, without a dissimulating, self-seeking search for vainglory, on the one hand, or out of fear, on the other. It is directed either: (a) towards God, through the knowledge of His ordinances, (b) towards one-

---

[17] *Ibid.*, 71.
[18] *Al-Dharīᶜah*, 136. C. *N.E.*, V, 1131^a-12f and V, 1129^a-6.

self, through the subordination of one's other powers to reason, (c) towards one's ancestors, by carrying out their testaments and praying for them, (d) towards one's fellowmen, by rendering to them what is due, and dealing equitably with them in transactions, exchanges or honors, or (e) towards mankind generally, by fostering good counsel and advice, even to rulers and their successors. The chief criteria of justice are three: the divinely revealed Book, the ruler and money.[19]

If justice is regarded as the first major principle of order and harmony in human relations, love, which is even superior to justice, is the second. For, as Aristotle had argued in *N.E.* VIII, 1155^{a}–25, the bond of love (or friendship) dispenses with the need for justice. Al-Iṣfahānī, however, does not mention Aristotle in this connection, but, as he frequently does, proceeds to support this thesis by copious moral maxims, Traditions and quotations from the Koran. It was because of the importance of the bond of love in holding people together that God has laid down the various precepts governing the frequency and occasion of religious congregations, commanding that the faithful should meet five times in the mosque to perform the ritual prayers, once a week in the town to perform the congregational prayer (on Friday), twice in an open space outside the town, and, finally, once in a lifetime with the rest of Muslim nations at Mecca to perform the pilgrimage.[20]

In support of the virtue of love or friendship, the author dwells on the advantages of social fellowship, both material and moral, and the disadvantages of the solitary life. Human association is for him both necessary and desirable, and solitude is to be condemned, except in three cases: that of a ruler engrossed in the management of the affairs of his subjects, that of a philosopher searching for wisdom, and that of a hermit (*mutanassik*), entering into private converse with his Lord. If we abstract from all these conditions, solitude entails, according to al-Iṣfahānī, the very negation of humanity. He does draw, however, a very subtle distinction between two modes of association, religious and intellectual-moral. With respect to the first, it is the duty of the believer to identify himself with the masses in the observances of the religious rituals; with respect to the second, he should dissociate himself completely from them, and concentrate on the private quest of knowledge and virtue. Both modes of association are supported by quotations from the Koran and the Traditions.[21]

The economic-political implications of the principles of human associa-

---

[19] *Ibid.*, 137f. Cf. Miskawayh, *Tahdhīb*, 116f. and 119f. (Zurayk, 103f. and 106f.) and supra.

[20] *Ibid.*, 142f. Cf. Miskawayh, *Tahdhīb*, 141 (Zurayk, 127f.).

[21] *Ibid.*, 145.

tion need not detain us long in this ethical study. There is one fundamental economic concept, however, from which he draws important moral inferences, that of poverty. The fear of poverty is the most potent incentive to industry and hard work, without which the world would have fallen into ruin. The affection of poverty by false Ṣūfīs and ascetics is denounced by al-Iṣfahānī as a frequent excuse for sloth and self-seeking. The Koran and the Traditions commend hard work, as well as mutual assistance in the domains of religious piety and moral conduct. The false Ṣūfī simply helps himself to the good things of life and deprives others from them, without offering anything in return. He becomes thereby a parasite and like all those who shun hard work, he dissociates himself from mankind in general, and joins the ranks of the beast, nay even the dead.[22]

V. Repelling Sorrow and Fear

A considerable part of *al-Dharī^c^ah* is taken up with the analysis of the virtues associated with the three powers of the soul, such as modesty, magnanimity, good faith, humility, good counsel, contentment, piety, forbearance and courage. This analysis abounds in perceptive psychological and practical observations.

The discussion of the virtue of courage leads the author to the discussion of the emotion of fear, which philosophical moralists from the time of al-Kindī had regarded as a radical evil from which man ought to be released through the use of reason. Significantly, however, al-Iṣfahānī is careful to underscore a decisive distinction between the 'otherworldly' fear of God, which the Koran has commended in numerous passages as the essence of piety and submission to God, and the 'worldly' fear of the tribulations and adversities with which human existence is continually troubled. The otherworldly type of fear, it should be noted, became from the time of al-Ḥasan al-Baṣrī (d. 728) the keynote of that religious asceticism which culminated ultimately in Ṣūfism.[23]

'Worldly' fear, on the other hand, is rooted in man's precarious condition in this world and his vulnerability to its calamities. The sorrow generated by this fear is due, according to 'some philosophers' (by whom he clearly means al-Kindī and his successors), either to the loss of what we cherish or the unattainability of what we desire. In this world of generation and corruption, however, permanence is impossible; he who wishes to live in perfect freedom from sorrow is a fool, for he wishes to possess

---

22 *Ibid.*, 149f.

23 See M. Fakhry, *A History of Islamic Philosophy*, 235f. and L. Massignon, *Essai sur les origines*, 168f.

what cannot be possessed and cling to it irrationally forever. It is far better that he should shun the acquisition of those things the loss of which is the occasion of sorrow, and give back with grace those material possessions of which he is, after all, the temporary owner.[24]

As to grief at the prospect of future occurrences, it should be remembered that they are of three types: impossible, necessary or possible. Grief over the first and second does not befit a rational man, since the impossible can never come to be and the necessary can never be altered. As to the possible, it is of two types: that which can be warded off and that which cannot. Grief over the latter, like the possibility of death at an early age, is irrational, and can only add to the sorrow caused by its actual occurrence when it comes to pass. Grief over the former is ingenuous; one should attempt to turn its object away before it actually occurs. If one cannot, one should accept it with resignation, in the full realization that what God has decreed cannot be turned away, as it is stated in the Koran (57:22): "No affliction befalls in the earth or in yourselves, but it is in a Book, before We create it." (trans. Arberry).[25]

Another major cause of grief is the prospect of death. Here too we ought to distinguish between the specific causes of sorrow; one might grieve: (a) at the loss of bodily pleasures, (b) at that of material possessions left behind, (c) out of ignorance of the real nature of what belongs to us, or (d) out of fear at the prospect of punishment for sins perpetrated in this life. Now the antidote of (a) is to understand the real nature of pleasure, as recovery from the diseases of want; the antidote of (b) and (c) is to understand the futility of worldly possessions and seek the genuine possessions reserved for us in the life to come; the antidote of (d) is instant repentance.[26]

More radical is al-Iṣfahānī's admonition that one should not only refrain from fearing death, one should actually cultivate the habit of "loving death and resorting to different devices (*iḥtiyāl*) to take as little notice of death as possible." Here the mystical dimension in al-Iṣfahānī's ethical though comes fully to the fore.

With respect to death, he argues, people are of three types: (1) the wise who understand that life enslaves and death liberates them, and that however long man may linger in this world, he is only on a temporary assignment in it, (2) those who have become so accustomed to worldly existence that they cannot face the prospect of leaving it without regret, (3) those who have been so blinded by sin that they have not only reconciled

---

24 See *al-Dharīᶜah*, 126f. Cf. al-Kindī, *al-Hīlah li-Dafᶜal-Aḥzān*, 31f.

25 See *al-Dharīᶜah*, 127. Cf. al-Kindī, *op.cit.*, 35.

26 *Ibid.*, 127f.

themselves to life in this world, they actually cherish it. The first group will welcome the prospect of death as a form of liberation; the second, once they have left this world and partaken of the marvellous goods of the other world, will welcome it also. The third group are the most pitiable; they cannot leave this world without great agony. However, saints and ascetics have all insisted that death is better for everyone than life: for the virtuous, insofar as it brings him closer to God, and for the wicked since it frees him from the vile temptations and allurements of this world.[27]

---

[27] *Ibid.*, 129.

CHAPTER FIVE

PSYCHOLOGICAL AND ETHICAL INTERRELATIONS: FAKHR AL-DĪN AL-RĀZĪ (D. 1209)

I. Man's Position in the Universe

Fakhr al-Dīn al-Rāzī, one of the eminent encyclopedic authors of the twelfth century, whose contribution to philosophy and theology is considerable,[1] continued the speculation of al-Iṣfahānī and his predecessors on the position of man in the universe as God's vicegerent. His treatise on ethics, entitled *Kitāb al-Nafs wa'l-Rūḥ* (Treatise on Soul and Spirit), opens with a long exposition of the ranks of created entities and man's place in the scale of being, a favorite theme of the Muslim Neo-Platonic philosophers.[2] The first rank is that of the angels, who possess intellect but no physical nature (*ṭabīᶜah*) or desire; the second is that of the lower animals, who possess a physical nature and desire but are devoid of intellect; the third is that of inanimate objects, which are devoid of intellect, physical nature and desire; the fourth is that of mankind, which possesses intellect, physical nature and desire. The Creator, characterized as the Necessary Being by al-Rāzī, belongs in a category apart, being the end towards which all created entities tend. Through the creation of the angels, God has manifested His wisdom and power, whereas through the creation of man He has manifested His generosity and mercy. Man was appointed as His vicegerent on earth, insofar as he possessed the faculty of desire of which the angels were deprived; he served thereby as the link between the divine and physical worlds, although his kinship to the divine world is greater.[3]

The object of human desire, according to al-Rāzī, is the acquisition of knowledge and power to an unlimited degree. This desire, however, is frustrated by the finite nature of man, which makes it impossible for him to achieve power over the material world and knowledge of the divine except in the measure of his own moral and intellectual capacity. A Tradition has epitomized this dual aspect of man's unlimited desire for

---

[1] See M. Fakhry, *A History of Islamic Philosophy*, 319f.

[2] See, for instance, al-Fārābī, *al-Siyāsah al-Madaniyah*, 31f.; Ibn Sīnā, *al-Najāt*, 273, and Miskawayh, *al-Fawz al-Aṣghar*, 150f.

[3] See *K. al-Nafs wa'l-Rūh*, ed. M.S.H. Maᶜṣūmī, Islamabad, 1968, 4f. English translation by Maᶜṣūmī, *Imām Rāzī's ᶜIlm al-Akhlāq*, Islamabad, 1969, 43f. Hereafter Maᶜṣūmī.

knowledge and power as follows: "Two greedy persons (*manhūmān*) will never be satisfied: a seeker for knowledge and a seeker for the world (*al-dunyā*)."[4]

II. The Soul and Its Faculties

Al-Rāzī's first major assertion concerning the soul is that it is something other than the body with which it is associated, and it is exhibited in the consciousness of our ego, as illustrated by such expressions as I return, I hear, I understand. Its unity is then demonstrated along well-known Avicennian lines by reference to the three phenomena of self-consciousness, anger and desire. It is impossible in any of these phenomena that the soul be multiple, or else each of these three powers would tend in an opposite direction and thereby hamper or obstruct the other two. These three powers are in fact three attributes of a single self (or soul) operating with a certain measure of harmony. [5]

Other arguments are given in support of the identity and unity of the soul, such as the single locus of the diverse actions or affections of the individual agent. Animals, including man, are not able to move voluntarily unless the will is actuated by a desire for the good and revulsion from evil, which it apprehends as such. Now the soul is the entity responsible for the perception of the object, whether good or evil, choosing it and moving the body towards it.[6]

The soul is then declared to be other than the body, on both rational and scriptural grounds. The knowledge of the body or its parts is clearly different from that of the soul as given in self-consciousness. For this self-consciousness is independent of the body and remains unchanging, despite the changes which supervene on the body. The Koran supports this thesis: in 3:169 and 71:25, it is asserted that the souls of martyrs survive the death of the body and that of the wicked will be consigned to Hell; in 23:12, 13, 14, the creation of soul (or spirit) is stated to have been preceded by that of body; indeed, spirit is said in 17:85 to belong to the world of command (*amr*) rather than that of creation, to which body belongs.[7] The Traditions confirm this result; a well-known Tradition states that "He who knows himself, knows his Lord." Now it is obvious that the injunction to know the self (or soul) would be meaningless if the soul were identical with body, since the knowledge of the latter is too obvious to need

---

[4] *Ibid.*, 24f. (Maᶜṣūmī, 79f.).
[5] *Ibid.*, 27f. (Maᶜṣūmī, 87f.).
[6] *Ibid.*, 28f. (Maᶜṣūmī, 89f.).
[7] *Ibid.*, 43f. (Maᶜṣūmī, 107f.).

stressing. The Traditions also confirm the survival of the soul after death and this clearly indicates that it is other than the body, which disintegrates at death.[8]

The soul is connected to the body, according to al-Rāzī, through the heart (*qalb*), which is for him the seat of understanding and deliberation. This view is stated to be that of Aristotle and his followers and is supported by numerous Koranic quotations asserting that the heart is the recipient of divine inspiration or admonition, as illustrated by verses 2:97; 7:179; 22:46; and 39:21, as well as a series of prophetic Traditions.[9]

The contrary view that the brain is this seat is ascribed to Galen, who, having divided the soul (following Plato) into concupiscent, irascible and rational, asserts that the heart is the seat of anger, whereas the brain is the seat of thought and deliberation.[10] Al-Rāzī then sets out at some length the arguments of Aristotle's followers against this view of Galen, as well as Galen's counter-arguments against Aristotle. These arguments and counter-arguments appear to derive from Ibn Sīnā's *Canon of Medicine*, although al-Rāzī claims to have derived Galen's arguments from his book on 'Hippocrates and Plato', which "I have studied and from this study derived the gist of my discourse."[11]

The principal faculties of the soul are given in Aristotelian-Avicennian fashion as vegetative, animal and human. Their ramifications are numerous and coincide likewise with the Avicennian table. Without specifying their relationship, however, al-Rāzī introduces in metaphorical vein the Platonic trichotomy of concupiscent, irascible and rational, described as the three 'chiefs' of the 'kingdom' called the soul. The first is located in the liver, the second in the heart and, contrary to what we have already noted, the third in the brain.

The proper management of these different souls is the business of the rational, which is affiliated to the heavenly region and illuminated with the light of divinity.[12]

III. The Critique of Hedonism

The ethical part of *Kitāb al-Nafs wa'l-Rūḥ* begins with the analysis of the different types of pleasure, sensuous and intellectual, and their comparative relation to each other.

---

[8] *Ibid.*, 47f. (Ma^{c}ṣūmī, 112f.).
[9] *Ibid.*, 51f. (Ma^{c}ṣūmī, 119f.).
[10] *Ibid.*, 52 and 60f. (Ma^{c}ṣūmī, 119 and 130f.).
[11] *Ibid.*, 74 (Ma^{c}ṣūmī, 141). Galen is known to have written a treatise dealing with this question from a Platonic-Hippocratic standpoint, entitled *De Placitis Hippocratis et Platonis*. This book is referred to in Jālīnūs, *K. al-Akhlāq li-Jālīnūs*, 26. Cf. *supra*, 63f.
[12] *Ibid.*, 79f. (Ma^{c}ṣūmī, 159f.).

The nature of sensuous pleasure is such that it is shared by both man and beast; it could not therefore constitute the distinctive goal of that activity with which human bliss or perfection is bound up. In fact, a careful scrutiny of pleasure would reveal that it consists essentially in the elimination of pain: the more hungry a man is, the greater is his enjoyment of the pleasure of eating; the longer he is barred from sexual pleasure, the greater is the pain of privation alleviated by copulation; and, finally, the more he is exposed to the pain of heat or cold, the greater is the pleasure of clothing enjoyed by him.[13]

Another criticism is that the gratification of sensuous desire we identify as pleasure is proportionate to the need or desire of the animal; thus a dog will be more pleased with a bone than with a string of pearls, since he needs or desires the one, but not the other. When these needs are satisfied or the desire fulfilled, instead of persisting or increasing, the pleasure actually turns into revulsion; excess of food or sex results not in added pleasure, but rather in pain.

Moreover, the excessive quest for bodily pleasure amounts to a repudiation of humanity; man has not been created in order to occupy himself with the satisfaction of his bodily pleasures, but rather to achieve intellectual apprehension and contemplate the Divine Presence and gaze on the Divine lights. In fact, the real goal of human endeavor is to seek the knowledge of God, obey Him and be united to Him in love. Sensuous pleasures, pursued in excess, can only bar him from achieving these noble goals, and are for that reason reprehensible.[14]

Nor are these pleasures, in this transient world, ever fully realized; they are always mingled with sorrow or attended by remorse or shame, and being unattainable in their fullness, are often the cause of frustration and pain. Human needs and desires are endless, and accordingly their satisfaction is by definition impossible. Christ has said: "The important matters of this world are not accomplished through constant improvement and fulfillment, but rather through abandoning and avoiding them."[15]

One of the means of achieving pleasure is wealth. Its acquisition is sometimes condemned in the Koran, sometimes extolled. However, it is not wealth as such that is commendable or reprehensible, but rather the use to which it is put. If expended in a good cause, such as charity, almsgiving or religious endowment, it is highly commendable. If expended in the satisfaction of bodily pleasures, it is not; in fact, it would serve in that case as an added spur to self-indulgence. Its possession can actually give

---

13 *Ibid.*, 90f. (Maᶜṣūmī, 171f.).
14 *Ibid.*, 99 (Maᶜṣūmī, 181).
15 *Ibid.*, 107 (Maᶜṣūmī, 190.).

rise to other evils, such as turning away from God, avarice, dependence on others and anxiety.[16]

IV. The Quest of Worldly Position (*jāh*) and Related Vices

Like wealth, worldly position is sought sometimes as a means of self-preservation or well-being, sometimes as a means of self-seeking. In the former case, it is clearly permissible, as long as it is sought in moderation. However, the temptation to seek position in undue measure and through illegitimate means, such as falsehood and trickery, is a great one.

The author engages in a psychological analysis of the causes of the love of worldly position. We all love praise whether deserved or not, because it gives us a foretaste of perfection, which is loved for its own sake, and because it reassures us regarding the merit of fine, but imperceptible qualities that we actually possess, but cannot be certain of. Finally, it gives us a sense of power and superiority, either over the author of praise, if he is honest, or over his listeners, whether near or far.[17]

This analysis enables the author to underscore the specific evils of worldly position. Love of worldly position, being a form of power like the love of wealth, answers to a passive urge within the soul, a want from which he who shuns this love is free. Moreover, to achieve worldly domination is to expose oneself to the jealousies and animosities of other aspirants to this domination, and since these aspirants are legion, the seeker of worldly position must surely gird himself to contend against a 'sea of trouble'.

Moreover, the seeker of worldly position is mistaken in his belief that he dominates others, since he has to minister to the needs of others, cajole and humor them, if he is to be repaid by praise or position. In this way he unwittingly reduces himself to the position of a slave to those whom he wishes to dominate. He must also resort to the most far-fetched and devious ways to please them, since the wishes, habits and beliefs of people are so varied and so unpredictable that no one can determine in a fixed manner what he ought to do to achieve this goal. He exposes himself thereby to endless hardships and anxieties and is deflected from occupying himself with worldly and otherworldly pursuits that really matter.[18]

With the love of worldly position also goes the love of praise and the shunning of reproach. Now praise is either well-earned or it is not; in the

---

[16] *Ibid.*, 110f. (Maᶜṣūmī, 202f.). Cf. al-Ghazālī, *Iḥyāᵓ ᶜUlūm al-Dīn*, 5 vols., Cairo, N.D., III, 1762f.
[17] *Ibid.*, 127f. (Maᶜṣūmī, 237f.). Cf. al-Ghazālī, *Iḥyāᵓ*, III, 1847f.
[18] *Ibid.*, 141f. (Maᶜṣūmī, 244f.).

former case, the true object of praise is God Almighty, Who has conferred on its human object the noble traits worthy of commendation; in the latter, it is sheer ignorance. For to delight in the praise of moral traits one does not actually possess is downright stupid. A further defect of praise is that it turns the mind away from God, by causing its object to be puffed up with his own achievements.

If reproach is likewise well-earned, one should be pleased with it, since it serves as an admonition for him to desist from his evil ways. If it is not, one should not resent it, for one might be free from the defect or fault for which he is reproached, but one is certainly not free from defect or fault altogether. Moreover, the approbrium in that latter respect would devolve upon one's critic, for making his accusations falsely. One should in any case be thankful for guarding oneself against evil and falsehood.[19]

Like al-Ghazālī, who is stated explicitly to be his model, al-Rāzī next engages in the discussion of hypocrisy, defined as the securing of a good name by dissimulation, both in religious and mundane matters. Instances of the latter are affectation in outward appearance, dress, speech, external activity or worldly possession. These modes of affectation are reprehensible, because their aim is either to deceive our fellowmen or to deceive God. In the first case, the hypocrite seeks to earn the good opinion of his fellows unjustly; in the second, he mocks God. That is why the Prophet has described hypocrisy in the Traditions as the highest form of polytheism (*shirk*).[20]

A subtle form of hypocrisy consists in feeling pleased at hearing one's virtuous or pious actions praised by others, affecting ascetic demeanor or gestures and rejoicing in being publicly honored or courteously greeted. Since the purpose of pious or virtuous conduct is to shun the things of sense altogether, these outward acts of the hypocrite will simply keep him as far from the spiritual world as possible. Such conduct may, however, be excused if the purpose of the agent is to propagate good deeds through his example, which he wishes to be made public. This motive being praiseworthy, the action is equally praiseworthy, since the test of the goodness or badness of moral actions or ritual observances is ultimately the intention from which it flows. A hypocrite's intention being evil, he will surely forego the reward otherwise due to him for acts of religious or moral rectitude.

Al-Rāzī next engages in the discussion of subtle legalistic points con-

---

[19] *Ibid.*, 149f. (Maᶜṣūmī, 255f.).

[20] *Ibid.*, 165 (Maᶜṣūmī, 273f.). Cf. al-Ghazālī, *Iḥyāᵓ*, III, 1872f. The Tradition is given in the canonical collections and in the *Iḥyāᵓ* as the 'smallest' polytheism. Cf. Wensinck, *Corcordance*.

cerning the type of hypocrisy which nullifies the credit for the action and that which does not. Religious authorities, he informs us, are divided on this question. They distinguish between the kind of hypocrisy which precedes the action and that which emerges in the course of performing it. Al-Rāzī believes the former to be the most grievous, and it certainly nullifies the credit for the action; the latter sometimes does, sometimes does not, depending on the gravity or occasion of the conduct deterring the agent from acting from a perfectly pure motive.[21]

Some have gone so far as to refrain from action altogether, lest they should be accused of hypocrisy, but this is wrong, since the pious or virtuous agent is called upon to do his duty and contend constantly against the Devil who would either discourage him or vitiate his actions by insincerity or self-love.[22]

Many of these subtle moral and religious arguments derive ultimately from al-Ghazālī, and al-Rāzī is often explicit in referring them to this master. However, without denigrating his successor, there is little doubt that al-Ghazālī has stated them with far greater directness and force. The convoluted method of reasoning which was characteristic of al-Rāzī's whole approach to philosophical and theological matters contributes little to the clarification or demonstration of his ethical theses, although it contributes in some degree to demonstrating his erudition.

---

[21] *Ibid.*, 168 (Maᶜṣūmī, 288f.).
[22] *Ibid.*, 174 (Maᶜṣūmī, 311f.). Cf. al-Ghazālī, *Iḥyāᵓ*, III, 1907f.).

CHAPTER SIX

THE SYNTHESIS: AL-GHAZĀLĪ (D. 1111)

I. The Relation of Ethics to the Other Sciences

We have in al-Ghazālī's thought, both speculative and practical, the most articulate synthesis of the fundamental currents in Islamic thought, the philosophical, the religious and the mystical. His ethical theory is contained in his only extant ethical treatise, *Mīzān al-ᶜAmal* (Criterion of Action), and his ethico-religious summa, *Iḥyāᵓ ᶜUlūm al-Dīn* (Revival of the Religious Sciences).[1] In view of the fact that the discussion of ethics in the *Iḥyāᵓ* follows essentially the same lines as the *Mīzān*, to the point of verbal identity in many places, it will be necessary to comment on the relationship between the two books.

There is no question that the *Mīzān* is a more methodical and comprehensive treatise than the corresponding ethical parts of the *Iḥyāᵓ*, entitled "The Book of Training the Soul and Cultivating Moral Traits" and "On the Reality of Grace (*niᶜmah*) and Its Subdivisions."[2] These parts are fitted into the general religious scheme of the *Iḥyāᵓ* and although discursive reasoning is a dominant feature of their style, they start from the premise that "good character is the attribute of the Master of the Apostles," in obvious reference to the Koranic verse which addresses Muḥammad in these terms: "Verily thou art a man of great character" in one of the earliest revelations to him, Koran 68:4. Accordingly, the discussion abounds in Koranic quotations and Traditions, very much in the spirit of the early writings on 'noble character' (*makārim al-akhlāq*), of which, as we have already seen, the book of the Ḥanbalite writer, Ibn Abi'l-Dunyā is a notable example.[3]

However, the discussion of ethics in the *Iḥyāᵓ* sounds in part as an earlier draft of the more extensive accounts in the *Mīzān*, in part as a summary. It is significant, however, that this latter work is not mentioned in the *Iḥyāᵓ* at all, whereas the former appears to be referred to in a number of passages in the *Mīzān*.[4] Accordingly, the *Mīzān* should be regarded

---

[1] Al-Ghazālī composed two summaries of the *Iḥyāᵓ*, one in Arabic, *Kitāb al-Arbaᶜīn fī Uṣūl al-Dīn* (Cairo, 1963), and one in Persian, *Kīmiyā-yi Saᶜādat* (Tehran, 1954). As its title suggests the latter has an ethical interest.

[2] See *Iḥyā ᶜUlūm al-Dīn*, II, 1426–1549 and *Iḥyāᵓ*, IV, 2234–2262.

[3] See *supra*, 151f.

[4] References to various *quarters* (sing. *rubᶜ*) of the *Iḥyāᵓ* are given in *Mīzān al-ᶜAmal*, Cairo, 1342 A.H., 42, 124 and 127.

as the principal ethical treatise of al-Ghazālī, and our analysis will be based on it, except for occasional corroborating references in the *Iḥyā*ʾ.

Written somewhat late in al-Ghazālī's life, the *Mīzān* forms part of a trilogy, which includes *Miʿyār al-ʿIlm* (Standard of Knowledge), *Tahāfut al-Falāsifah* (Incoherence of the Philosophers) and the present treatise. Al-Ghazālī himself has recognized the correlation of these three works and the organic unity binding them together,[5] and although the second of these works is the most illustrious, its intent is essentially logical, whereas the *Mīzān* embodies the substance of a positive moral theory of a high order.

Al-Ghazālī places his reader at the center of the ethical problem from the very first lines. Happiness, being the objective (*maṭlūb*) sought by the ancients and the moderns can only be attained if knowledge (*ʿilm*) is joined to action (*ʿamal*). The former requires a standard (*miʿyār*), distinguishing it from other activities; the latter a criterion (*mīzān*), which will determine in a lucid and succinct manner, rising above passive imitation (*taqlīd*) and aiming at demonstrative certainty, "that [type of] action conducing to happiness and distinguishing it from that which conduces to wretchedness."[6]

By happiness we should understand, according to al-Ghazālī, that otherworldly condition of unadulterated pleasure, unbounded riches, undiminished perfection and unsurpassed glory enduring for all time. No one who believes in the existence of such a condition could possibly refrain from striving hard to attain it. However, some have been diverted from its pursuit, by reason either of their denial of any but the intellectual pleasures, as some 'metaphysical' philosophers and Ṣūfīs have actually done, or their repudiation of survival after death, as the atheists and hedonists have done. Against all these groups al-Ghazālī urges a variation on Pascal's wager and an exhortation to take stock of human fallibility.[7]

However, whether we deny the reality of otherworldly happiness or not, it is noteworthy that the philosophers, the Ṣūfīs and the masses at large are in agreement that happiness, as such, consists of two components: knowledge (*ʿilm*) and action (*ʿamal*). Action in this context

---

[5] See *Miʿyār al-ʿIlm*, Cairo, 1961, 348; *Tahāfut al-Falāsifah*, ed. M. Bouyges, Beirut, 1927, 17; and *Mīzān al-ʿAmal*, 2, 49 *et passim*. The writing of the *Iḥyā*ʾ was started after 1098; the *Tahāfut* was completed in 1095; the *Miʿyār* definitely preceded that date and was probably followed by the *Mīzān*. Cf. M.A. Sherif, *Ghazālī's Theory of Virtue*, 4f.

[6] *Mīzān*, 2.

[7] See Mīzān, 7f. By the 'metaphysical philosophers' al-Ghazālī appears to mean the Arab Neo-Platonists, who, like Ibn Sīnā, described man's ultimate felicity in purely intellectual terms. See *supra*, 82, 87, 91f.

denotes "the harnessing of the passions of the soul, the controling of anger and the curbing of those propensities so as to ensure that they will submit to reason."[8] Therein consists man's genuine happiness and emancipation from the bondage of the passions.

As for knowledge, al-Ghazālī insists from the start on the decisive distinction between 'imitation' (*taqlīd*) and 'demonstration'. The former is denounced by him as a form of blindness and the earnest searcher is exhorted not to be content with it, but to rise above it to the plane of 'demonstrative knowledge.'[9] He recognizes, however, the difficulties attendant upon acquiring this knowledge and argues that, considering the ignorance and torpor of the majority of mankind, the ordinary man should occupy himself with action and confine himself to that measure of knowledge essential to right action only.

The determination of that measure of knowledge leads al-Ghazālī to make a full tabulation of the theoretical and practical sciences. The theoretical sciences, as given by him, include the sum-total of the 'philosophical sciences', which formed the core of the Greek-Arab syllabus in the tenth and the eleventh centuries, and of which al-Fārābī's *Iḥṣāʾ al-ʿUlūm* is a good instance. The subject-matter of these sciences includes the knowledge of God, His angels, apostles, the physical Creation and its many ramifications, both heavenly and terrestrial; but to underscore the religious tenor of his tabulation, al-Ghazālī insists that the knowledge of created entities is not to be sought on its own account, but "insofar as they are related to God's power" and reveal His Lordship.[10] He insists likewise that the linguistic and 'ancillary' sciences, which vary from time to time and from place to place, cannot contribute anything to the everlasting 'perfection' of the soul which the moralist must seek, and should accordingly be excluded from the list of profitable sciences.

The practical sciences, on the other hand, include, according to him: (a) ethics, defined as the knowledge of the soul, its properties and moral traits, (b) household economy, and (c) politics, or the 'management' of the affairs of the land (*al-balad*). The religious science of jurisprudence (*fiqh*) is not irrelevant to (b) and (c), insofar as it deals with the principles of transaction, marriage, penalty and taxation.[11]

Al-Ghazālī is emphatic that ethics is the paramount practical science, for he who cannot manage or direct his soul will be ill-equipped to manage

---

[8] *Ibid.*, 12.

[9] *Mīzān*, 8f. and 17f. Cf. *al-Munqidh min al-Ḍalāl*, ed. F. Jabre, Beirut 1959, 10f.

[10] *Ibid.*, 41f. and 123f. Cf. *Iḥyāʾ*, I, 29f. and 38f. and *al-Munqidh*, 20f., especially 23.

[11] *Ibid.*, 42 and 123f.

the affairs of others. He is equally emphatic that, as Miskawayh, the Brethren of Purity and other moralists have insisted, the ethical enquiry should begin with the knowledge of the soul, its powers and properties. This knowledge is the precondition of cleansing the soul, as the Koran itself asserts,[12] and is the prelude to the knowledge of God, which the Traditions and 'certain revealed scriptures' have expressed in this well-known Tradition: "He who knows himself best, knows his Lord best."[13]

II. The Powers and Virtues of the Soul

Al-Ghazālī's analysis of the powers of the soul follows well-known Aristotelian-Avicennian lines. To the 'animal soul' belong the powers of motion, desire and perception; to 'the human', those of knowing and acting, or the theoretical and practical powers. The practical power (*al-ᶜāmilah*) is a faculty or principle "moving the body of man to perform certain particular actions involving reflection and deliberation, as directed by the knowing or theoretical power."[14] To the extent the 'corporeal powers' are vanquished by the practical, virtuous traits arise in the soul; to the extent, contrariwise, it is vanquished by these powers, vicious traits arise.

Without denying the 'relative' efficacy of the theoretical or cognitive powers of the soul, al-Ghazālī argues in this and other treatises that the ultimate source of knowledge is God, Who imparts it to us through diverse means; our sole duty consists in keeping our soul in constant readiness to receive the divine illumination, by cleansing it and keeping it pure and unadulterated. For the obstruction is never God's, but rather man's; that is why the Prophet has said: "Your Lord has [reserved for you] in your lifetime certain breezes; expose yourselves to them", and "Whoever comes closer to me by one span, I will come closer to him by one yard, and whoever comes to me walking, I will come to him running."[15] The degrees of this proximity to God are innumerable and upon these degrees depend the stations of philosophers, saints and prophets, the highest degree being that of the prophet to whom are revealed all the realities, without strife or acquisition, but through "divine illumination" (*kashf ilāhī*) only. Al-Ghazālī warns, however, against the temptation of those extravagant Ṣūfīs who, like al-Bisṭāmī and al-Ḥallāj, have contended that beyond the stage of proximity (*qurb*) there is a stage of union (*itti-*

---

12 Koran 91:9–10. See *Mīzān*, 10. Cf. Miskawayh, *Tahdhīb*, 1.
13 *Ibid.*, 18.
14 *Ibid.*, 20.
15 *Ibid.*, 24.

ḥād) or immanence (*ḥulūl*). The highest point that the soul can attain is proximity to, not union with God.[16]

The analogy between the moralist's and the Ṣūfī's call to purify the soul and cleanse it leads al-Ghazālī to examine the differences between the two. They are in accord with respect to action but differ with respect to knowledge. The Ṣūfīs argue that the laborious search for this knowledge is unnecessary; all that is needed is withdrawal from the world and turning with undivided attention towards God Almighty.[17] Once the soul is fully cleansed, it will be in a state of readiness to receive, in the manner of prophets and saints, the revelation meted out to them by divine mercy. The 'theorists' (*al-nuẓẓar*), as he calls them, on the other hand, question the practicality of the Ṣūfī way and point to the many hazards and distractions to which the soul is exposed unless it has been previously guarded against error or illustion, through training in logic, the 'standard of knowledge.'[18]

That either path is fully adequate to the attainment of happiness, the ultimate good of human endeavor, al-Ghazālī does not deny; their respective profitability differs from person to person, and from place to place. To proceed methodically, however, we should start by considering the principal powers of the soul, the rational, the irascible and the concupiscent. When these powers have been rightly ordered (*uṣliḥat*) in the desired manner and to the desired degree, and the powers of anger and appetite subordinated to the rational, justice arises. This justice is the foundation on which the heaven and the earth have been established and the path of religious piety and praiseworthy moral rectitude. In support of this thesis he cites numerous Traditions and Koranic verses purporting to commend good character, which is synonymous, according to him, with the 'management' of the three powers of the soul. He even extracts from verse 49:15 a Koranic basis for this thesis. This verse reads in Arberry's translation:

> The believers are those who believe in God and His Messenger, then have not doubted, and have struggled with their possessions and their selves in the way of God; those—they are the truthful ones.

Belief and the denial of doubt in the first part of the verse refers, according to him, to certain knowledge or true wisdom; the struggle with possessions refers to the virtues of temperance and liberality, which are associated with the 'management' of the concupiscent power, and the struggle with

---

[16] *Ibid.*, 23. Cf. *Mishkāt al-Anwār*, ed. A. ᶜAfīfī, Cairo, 1964, 57 and M. Fakhry, *History of Islamic Philosophy*, 250.
[17] *Ibid.*, 34.
[18] *Ibid.*, 36.

their selves refers to the virtues of courage and fortitude, which correspond to the 'management' of the irascible power (*ḥamīyah*).[19]

There are, however, three stages in the process of struggling against passion (*hawā*): (a) Man may be vanquished by it, so that it becomes his object of worship or God, as the Koran has put it in verse 25:43. This is the condition of the majority of mankind; (b) he may be in constant warfare with it, alternately losing or gaining the struggle. This is the condition of the highest grade of mankind, other than prophets and saints; finally (c), he may overcome his passion and subdue it completely. This is the condition of great success and the 'present heaven' (*al-naᶜīm al-ḥāḍir*), of true liberty and emancipation from passion.[20]

However, this last condition is full of pitfalls. Many an arrogant or selfish scholar or believer feels that he has achieved this condition, whereas in fact he is misguided by Satan. The 'counsel of reason' and that of passion can only be distinguished from each other if we follow the rules of genuine knowledge laid down in logic (*miᶜyār al-ᶜilm*). In general, however, we should note that reason prescribes the most advantageous course of action, even if it is attended by hardship (*kulfah*), whereas passion prescribes rest and the quitting of strife. Whenever you are faced with two courses of action, you ought to choose the course which you dislike, rather than the one you like, but to grasp this truth is not possible without a 'divine light' or 'heavenly support'. However, whenever you are in doubt, you should turn to God for guidance.[21]

Nevertheless, al-Ghazālī lays down a series of practical rules for harnessing the evil propensities of the soul through a process of 'training and struggle' (*riyāḍah wa-mujāladah*), which is a keynote of the 'mystical way' which he regards as inseparable from the moral life. This procss should aim at cleansing the soul by recourse to diverse practical steps, beginning with inculcating in it through constant repetition those traits which render the habit of right action perfectly manageable. Thus to achieve the traits of liberality or humility, one should persist in performing, at near intervals, acts of liberality or humility.

An effective device in combating the soul's propensity to evil is to adopt the therapeutic methods of physicians who apply to the symptoms of a given disease the contrary principles or antidotes, so as to counterbalance them and thereby restore the equilibrium of the humors which we identify with health. Thus if the soul is inclined to inordinate passion, cowardice or avarice, it should be trained to affect actions of temperance, liberality

[19] *Ibid.*, 44.
[20] *Ibid.*, 48.
[21] *Ibid.*, 150.

or courage until the 'equilibrium' of virtue is achieved. Like other Muslim moralists, however, al-Ghazālī believed human nature to be originally in a neutral state of equilibrium, which bad company or education corrupts. He supports his view by quoting the well-known Tradition which states that "every child is born in a state of nature (*fiṭrah*); his parents cause him to become a Jew, a Christian or a Magian."[22]

Pursuing the analogy of medicine further, al-Ghazālī prescribes in addition to the method of therapy that of hygiene. The former method is intended to eradicate the vices, the latter to inculcate the virtues in the soul. These virtues and vices are easily accessible, according to al-Ghazālī, insofar as they are fully laid out in religious writings (*sharᶜ*) and collections of prophetic wisdom (*ādāb*).[23] However, in tabulating the virtues, he follows the beaten path of the philosophers. The four principal virtues are wisdom, courage, temperance and justice. Each of these virtues is a mean between two extremes, the mean being determined by 'practical wisdom', defined as a "condition or virtue of the rational soul, enabling it to manage (*tasūs*) the irascible and concupiscent powers and to determine their movements according to the right measure of expansion or contraction."[24] It is in fact the power which determines the rightness and wrongness of actions.

The difficulty of determining the mean which Aristotle had underscored is equally stressed by al-Ghazālī, who compares it to the 'straight path' (*al-ṣirāṭ al-mustaqīm*) mentioned in the Koran and asserted to be thinner than a hair and sharper than the edge of a sword. It follows, according to him, that man should constantly turn to God for guidance, since without His guidance and mercy no one can be guarded against the hazards of vice in this life.[25] However, he is emphatic that it is through the conjunction of reason and revelation (*al-ᶜaql wa'l-sharᶜ*) that the moral perfection of 'moderation' is achieved; it is the function of reason in the first instance to reveal to us the purpose underlying the creation of the subordinate powers of passion and anger, which, once they are harnessed by practical wisdom, virtue and moderation, will arise in the soul.[26]

His tabulation of the subdivisions of the principal virtues does not always accord with that of the philosophical moralists already discussed, and the source of these subdivisions in Greek-Arabic ethics cannot be determined. On the whole, his table, patterned on his predecessors like

---

[22] *Ibid.*, 60. Cf. *Iḥyāᵓ*, II, 1448 and *al-Munqidh*, 11.

[23] *Ibid.*, 63. In *al-Munqidh*, however, he argues that the ethical knowledge of the philosophers was taken from the writings of the Ṣūfīs. See *al-Munqidh*, 24.

[24] *Ibid.*, 65. Cf. *Nicomachean Ethics*, II, 1107ᵃ-1-5 and VI, 1140ᵇ-5f.

[25] *Mīzān*, 67.

[26] *Ibid.*, 68.

Miskawayh and Ibn Sīnā, appears to be partly an exercise in ethical ingenuity and partly an adaptation of al-Rāghib al-Iṣfahānī's classification, already discussed. Al-Ghazālī, it is said, greatly admired *al-Dharīʿah* written by that author. Thus the subdivisions of wisdom are given as:

(a) Sagacity (*ḥusn al-tadbīr*)
(b) Sound judgement (*jūdat al-dhihn*)
(c) Perspicuity (*thaqābat al-raʾy*)
(d) Right opinion (*ṣawāb al-ẓann*).[27]

Those of courage are given as:

(a) Generosity (*karam*)
(b) Self-assurance (*najdah*)
(c) Magnanimity (*kibar al-nafs*)
(d) Endurance (*iḥtimāl*)
(e) Patience (*ḥilm*)
(f) Steadfastness (*thabāt*)
(g) Nobility (*nubl*)
(h) Manlincss (*shahāmah*)
(i) Composure (*waqār*)

The subdivisions of temperance are:

(a) Modesty (*ḥayāʾ*)
(b) Shyness (*khajal*)
(c) Forgiveness (*musāmaḥah*)
(d) Fortitude (*ṣabr*)
(e) Liberality (*sakhāʾ*)
(f) Sound calculation (*ḥusn al-taqdīr*)
(g) Amiability (*inbisāṭ*)
(h) Good humor (*damāthah*)
(i) Self-control (*intiẓām*)
(j) Contentedness (*qanāʿah*)
(k) Equanimity (*hudūʾ*)
(l) Piety (*waraʿ*)
(m) Cheerfulness (*ṭalāqah*)
(n) Mutual aid (*musāʿadah*)
(o) Indignation (*tasakhkhuṭ*)
(p) Wit (*ẓarf*).[28]

In discussing the virtue of justice, he distinguishes between three dif-

---

[27] *Ibid.*, 71. Cf. *Iḥyāʾ*, IV, 1437, where two other subdivisions are added: discrimination in subtle matters and secret wiles of the soul. For a concordance of al-Ghazālī, Miskawayh and Ibn Sīnā, see M.A. Sherif, *Ghazālī's Theory of Virtue*, 178–180.

[28] *Mīzān*, 72f. Cf. *Iḥyā*, IV, 1437.

ferent varieties of this virtue: (a) political justice, which is concerned with the orderly relation of the different parts of the city to each other, (b) moral justice, concerned with the orderly relation of the parts of the soul to each other, and (c) economic justice, concerned with the rules of equity in business transactions.

These kinds, as well as the equation of justice with the 'whole of virtue', correspond roughly to the Aristotelian scheme, as laid down in *Nicomachean Ethics*, V, chapters 1,2,6 and 7. Al-Ghazālī, who, as we have seen, regarded this virtue as the foundation upon which the heavens and the earth have been established, does not give any subdivision or 'species' of this virtue, unlike Miskawayh and his school.[29]

III. Types of Good or Happiness

As we have already seen, al-Ghazālī, like Aristotle, identifies happiness with the chief good of man, but unlike him, he gives as its two primary divisions otherworldy and this-worldly. He is emphatic, however, that the first is the genuine variety; the worldly variety is spoken of as happiness purely metaphorically. His preoccupation with otherworldly happiness, however, does not divert his attention from other subordinate modes of happiness or good; he asserts instead that whatever conduces to the ultimate good is good too. Indeed, he goes so far as to assert that otherworldly happiness itself cannot be achieved without certain subordinate goods which are to it what the means is to the end. These goods include: (a) the four principal virtues, which have already been discussed and are in fact identical with the 'fundamentals of religion',[30] (b) the bodily virtues of health, strength, good looks and a long life, (c) the external virtues of wealth, kin, social position and noble birth, and, finally, (d) the 'divine virtues of guidance (*hidāyah*), good counsel (*rushd*), direction (*tasdīd*) and support (*ta'yīd*). Some of those modes of happiness, such as the virtues of the soul, are essential to otherworldly happiness, others to the virtues above them in the scale, in varying degrees. Hence wealth is an indispensable means to piety and charity, whereas children and relatives are valuable aids both in adversity and prosperity.[31]

Divine guidance (*hidāyah*) occupies a special position in al-Ghazālī's scheme of the virtues; it is for him the foundation stone of all good, as the Koran and Traditions assert in numerous passages, such as Koran 20:50, which speaks of God as giving "to everything its created nature and then

---

29 See *supra*, 112.

30 *Mīzān*, 84f. and 90f. Cf. *Iḥyā*, III, 2234f. and al-Iṣfahānī, *al-Dharīah*, 35f.

31 *Ibid.*, 85f. Cf. *Iḥyā'*, III, 2248f. Cf. al-Iṣfahānī, *al-Dharī'ah*, 35f. and *supra*, 179.

guiding it'', and the Tradition which states that ''no one will enter Paradise without God's mercy'', meaning His guidance. Its effects are three: (a) to enable man to distinguish between good and evil, either through the light of reason which God has imparted to all mankind, or through the instruction of the prophets, (b) to enable him to rise by degrees to the acquisition of the highest knowledge, or increase his stock of good works, and, finally, (c) to serve as the light which emanates from the world of prophecy and spiritual pre-eminence (*wilāyah*), whereby man has access to realities which reason alone cannot discover by itself. This is what the Koran (2:120) has called ''God's own guidance'' or the 'absolute guidance'', and is called life and light in Koran 6:122.[32]

By good counsel, says al-Ghazālī, we mean ''that divine providence which assists man in turning towards his chosen goals, by strengthening his resolve to do what conduces to his righteousness and deters him from what conduces to his destruction''.[33] This counsel is inward, as the Koran asserts (21:51) ''We have indeed imparted to Ibrahim his good counsel (*rushd*) previously and were fully conversant therewith.''

Right direction, on the other hand, consists in man's directing his will and movements towards the desired goal, so as to attain it in the shortest time possible. It differs from good counsel in that the latter is limited to exhortation and advise, whereas right direction involves active assistance and reinforcement.

As to divine support (*taʾyīd*), described in the Koran as the 'assistance of the Holy Spirit,'[34] it is the act of empowering man, by granting him inner insight and outer physical capacity, to carry out the designs of his will. Indeed, man is incapable of any good without keen understanding, close attention, a sagacious heart, a concerned teacher, adequate wealth and a devoted clan (*ʿashīrah*) guarding him from aggression, all of which are gifts conferred on him by God.[35]

The relation of pleasure to happiness is discussed in the course of discussing the different types of good. Such goods may be divided into: (a) the useful, either always or on occasion, (b) the desirable, either in itself or for the sake of something else, or (c) the pleasant. (b) and (c) are not unrelated, since pleasure is defined as the attaining of the object of desire, and desire is defined as the soul's inclination to lay hold or possess the object of its yearning (*shawq*).[36]

---

[32] *Ibid.*, 89f. Cf. *Iḥyāʾ*, III, 2248f.
[33] *Ibid.*, 86.
[34] The Koran 2:87,253; 5:110; 16:102.
[35] *Mīzān*, 90. Cf. *Iḥyāʾ*, III, 2250.
[36] *Ibid.*, 92.

The divisions of pleasure are given as: (a) intellectual, such as the pleasures of learning or wisdom, (b) biological, common to man and the other animals, such as eating, drinking and sex, and (c) social or political, such as the lust for conquest or social position. The noblest of these pleasures and the most exclusively human is the first, which endures forever and is rewarded by everlasting bliss in the life-to-come. The mark of its nobility is that its possession requires no custodians and that it increases with use. It is profitable under all circumstances and at all times, unlike earthly possessions, which are often the occasion of sin, require constant vigilance and diminish with use.[37]

All together, al-Ghazālī lists, on the basis of a quotation from the writings of the fourth Caliph ᶜAlī, eight varieties of pleasure: that of eating, drinking, sex, attire, habitation, smell, hearing and sight. Two of these are particularly nefarious from an ethical and religious point of view, the pleasure of the belly and that of sex; they are followed in descending order by the pleasures of social station (*jāh*), accumulation of wealth, rivalry and competition.[38] The brunt of his critique of hedonism, however, is directed against the first two. The desire for food is the root of all the vices, since by increasing desire, excessive nourishment (*imtilāᵓ al-baṭn*) increases the power for lust (*al-hawā*), and lust is the principal aid of Satan. Although taking food in quantities sufficient for survival is permissible, any excess is not only reprehensible, but is downright harmful. It has been prohibited by the Koran and the Traditions almost as emphatically as the drinking of wine, which is "one of the greatest devices of the Devil in destroying reason (...) and exciting the passions and beastly powers [of the soul]."[39]

The *Iḥyāᵓ*, with its special stress on the ascetic and mystical virtues, dwells at some length on the virtues of hunger and the wickedness of satiety (*shabaᶜ*). The argument is reinforced by copious quotations from the Traditions, the Old Testament and the sayings of philosophers and mystics. He lists ten 'advantages' of hunger and five methods of combating the lust of the belly, which he regards as the root of all other forms of lust, including that of sex. Here too he is concerned to warn against the evils of excess. Sex practiced in moderation is essential for the preservation of the species, the release of surplus secretions which can harm the body, as well as guarding one through lawful union against the occasions of temptation.[40] When it reaches the inordinate length of erotic passion (*ᶜishq*),

---

37 *Mīzān*, 93.
38 *Iḥyāᵓ*, II, 1484. Cf. *Mīzān*, 94f.
39 *Mīzān*, 97. Cf. *Iḥyāᵓ*, II, 1485f.
40 *Mīzān*, 97f. Cf. *Iḥyāᵓ*, II, 1521.

however, it brings man to a condition lower than that of the brute, by reducing him to a level of slavery and humiliation worse than that of these brutes. For, as al-Rāzī had argued, brutes are content to satisfy their lust from any source whatever, whereas the lover will not be gratified until he is united to the one object of his passion.[41]

The most effective way of combating sexual lust is not to yield from the start to the 'concupiscence of the eye' and that of the mind. For once lust has taken hold, it is extremely difficult to eradicate. However, despite the vehemence of his language and the intensity of his diatribe, al-Ghazālī does not prescribe or even commend the ideal of celibacy, but following the traditional Islamic norm exhorts the young, including the Ṣūfī novice (*murīd*), to abide by the rules of abstinence and self-control, reinforced by prolonged fasting or hunger, until such rules prove of no avail. Thereupon, the novice is advised to marry.[42]

IV. The Quest of God

The cornerstone of al-Ghazālī's ethics is the mystical exhortation to the soul to engage in a relentless search for God. His otherworldly and theocentric ideal takes, in the first instance, the form of denouncing: (a) the folly of pining at the loss or unattainability of earthly possessions, (b) the sorrow occasioned by worldly afflictions, and (c) the presumpion of invulnerability to the divine decree. In the second instance, it takes the form of inveighing against the fear of death born of man's false conception of his condition in this world and the inevitability of death. The truly reasonable man will dwell constantly on the thought of death, resign himself to misfortune, quit oppression, jealousy and solicitude for worldly possessions, and cultivate the habits of contentment and repentance, preparing himself thereby to meet his Lord with unmixed joy. For, as the Prophet has said, "he who loves to meet God, God lovest to meet, and he who hates to meet God, God hates to meet too."[43]

The true seeker after God then will not be disturbed by loss or misfortune and will have no thought for anything other than proximity (*qurb*) to Him. However, the number of genuine seekers is very small, while the pretenders are legion. There are, nevertheless, two methods of distinguishing the genuine seekers from the false. First, to insure that all their voluntary actions are determined by the prescriptions or the prohibitions of the religious law (*sharᶜ*), for it is impossible for the seeker to embark on

---

41 *Mīzān*, 97f. Cf. *Iḥyāʾ*, II, 1521, and *supra*, 73.
42 *Iḥyāʾ*, II, 1523.
43 *Mīzān*, 154f.

his journey before cultivating all the moral and religious virtues discussed in this book (i.e. the *Mīzān*) as well as the supplementary duties (*nawāfil*), which constitute the essence of genuine piety. Those who recommend their neglect are ultimately motivated by sloth or capriciousness. In relation to the 'divine path' (*sabīl al-lāh*), religious and moral obligations are nothing but preliminary steps leading to the final stage of divine encounter. So long as he is in this world, man is a slave to passion and should therefore be constantly on his guard against the insinuations of the Devil by performing these obligations in full.[44]

The second method is to insure that God is constantly present (*ḥāḍir*) in the seeker's heart. By this presence we should understand genuine contrition, adoration and submission, born of the awareness of the beauty and majesty of God. Its mark is never-ending preoccupation with the thought of God, so that even if he is forced to be temporarily distracted from this thought, he will not, like the passionate lover, allow his mind to stray from its object for long.

There are altogether three conditions without which the 'divine march' cannot be achieved: extreme concern (*ḥirṣ*), full resolve (*irādah*) and constant search (*ṭalab*). The essence of concern is the apprehension of the beauty of the object, necessitating yearning and passion (*ᶜishq*); the essence of apprehending is concentration on the beauty of this object, to the exclusion of every other. As the company of the beloved lasts, the passion will increase in intensity, in proportion as hitherto unsuspected traits of beauty are revealed to sight. That is why the divine beauty and majesty may at first appear dim to the novice, but as his gaze is strengthened, he will discover therein fresh aspects of beauty which will heighten his passion and bring him 'closer' to God.

By this 'closeness' or proximity, we should not understand, as the corporealists and anthropomorphists (*mushabbihah*) do, geographical or local contiguity, but rather spiritual affinity, analogous to that of the disciple to his master, causing him to ascend continually to the perfection of this master. This ascent may appear at first difficult, or even impossible, but if the novice proceeds gradually, he will experience no undue hardship, but will be able to rise by degrees to the highest level. From the stage of men of learning, he will be able to rise to that of saints, then to that of prophets and, finally, to that of angels. Having attained that final stage, the "God-seekers will be wholly divested of human characteristics and will turn into angels in human form."[45]

The vulgar in their ignorance have been misled into comparing the

---

[44] *Mīzān*, 156f.
[45] *Ibid.*, 160.

'proximity' to God to that of approaching the 'house' He occupies in heaven, as He sits upon a throne under a green parasol, or to being gratified at the receipt of 'gifts of worship' offered to Him by His servants, just as gifts are offered to the king by his subjects. For God in His perfection transcends all those royal attributes of anger, gratification or rejoicing at the subservience of His subjects or their servility. These terms and their equivalents are indeed predicated of him in scripture, but only in an allegorical sense, so that those who understand will understand them and those who repudiate them will repudiate, each according to the measure of his capacity.[46]

---

[46] *Ibid.*, 161.

APPENDIX A

THE CONTEMPLATIVE IDEAL IN ISLAMIC PHILOSOPHY: ARISTOTLE AND AVICENNA

I

By the contemplative, or philosophical ideal, as W. Jaeger has called it,[1] I mean the threefold contention: (a) that intellectual activity is the highest activity (in some normative sense of highest), (b) that it is a self-rewarding and self-sufficient activity, and (c) that it is the activity of which God either partakes (as all forms of rational theism presuppose), or the one which constitutes His very essence (as Aristotle, Anaxagora, Hegel and others have asserted). A clear implication of (a) and (c) is that to the extent man aspires to partake of this activity, he partakes of the divine life, or achieves a condition of self-divinization which some forms of mysticism and idealism have set up as their ultimate ethical or spiritual objective.

It is well known how Plato in the *Theaetetus* (176[B])[2] has advanced the deal of ὁμοίωσις τῷ θεῷ as man's loftiest goal in his heavenward flight, but throughout most of his life Plato's thought had remained "so close to life", as Jaeger has put it, that he could ill afford to allow the practical, and especially the political life, to be absorbed by the contemplative, at least up to the time of writing the *Republic*. It was probably late in life that Plato moved away from the Socratic ideal of a life of virtue illuminated by the knowledge of the good, as is attested by his identification of the good with the Pythagorean one in his lectures "On the Good".[3]

The same vacillation between the theoretical and practical ideals that had marked the development of Plato's thought characterized that of Aristotle as well; from the *Protrepticus*, through the *Eudemean Ethics*, and on to the *Nicomachean*, we witness a gradual rarefaction or refinement of the theoretical ideal in a more pronounced fashion than Plato.[4] The ultimate severing of the bond between the practical and theoretical ideals that had conditioned the 'Platonic' phase of his thought is finally effected in the

---

[1] See W. Jaeger, *Aristotle. Fundamentals of the History of his Development*, Oxford, 1948, 426 et passim.

[2] Cf. *Laws*, IV, 716c.

[3] See Aristoxenus' report, as quoted by Jaeger, *op.cit.*, 434, note 3.

[4] See *op.cit.*, 435, where Jaeger says of Aristotle: "In a certain sense he is an even purer representative of the theoretic life than Plato." Cf. also, 393f., and 80f. and 239f., for Aristotle's ethical development.

Nicomachean Ethics, and appears at any rate to be the logical consequence of Aristotle's identification in the *Metaphysics* of God with Noūs. This metaphysical development in Aristotle's thought was the decisive signal of the emancipation of his thought from Plato and of his ability to boldly cut the knot tying the ethical and the theoretical.

It is my purpose in this appendix to highlight some aspects of Aristotle's ethical intellectualism[5] and some of the problems it raises, on the one hand, and the manner in which Arabic Peripetatic philosophers, represented by Ibn Sīnā (Avicenna, d. 1037), tried to solve them, on the other. A by-product of my analysis, I hope, will be the added sharpening of the antithesis between what must be regarded as two generically different ideals: the theoretical and the practical.

My text is the well-known passage in the *Nicomachean Ethics*, X,7,1177a 12f, in which Aristotle states that the highest activity κατὰ τὴν κρατίστην (ἀρετὴν) of which man partakes is the activity of reason, which "more than anything else in man" is man (ὁ κατὰ τὸν νοῦν βίος εἴπερ τοῦτο μάλιστα ἄνθρωπος) (*N.E.* 1178a 6–7).[6] This activity is then characterized (*N.E.* X, 1177b 19f) as: (a) superior in worth (σπουδῇ), (b) being its own end (οὐδενὸς ἐφίεσθαι τέλους), (c) pleasant in itself (d) self-sufficient, (e) leisurely, (f) unwearisome (ἄτρυτον), and (g) divine. The last characteristic is introduced conditionally into the discussion, but follows logically from the equation in *Metaphysics* L, 1072b 17f. of the activity of thought with the best in itself (καθ' αὑτὸ ἄριστον), life eternal and complete blessedness, which are then identified with God (τοῦτο γὰρ ὅ θεὸς) in a mode of direct transposition.

This metaphysical characterization of God would have had no direct bearing on the contemplative ideal of life, but for the fact that man, like God, is declared to *be* reason (*N.E.* X, 1178a 8), with the inevitable qualification that he is nevertheless imperfect reason, compared with God Who is "always in that state in which we sometimes are" (*Met.*, X, 1072b 24). We are called upon by what one might call the imperative of divine excellence to partake of the divine perfection, which is really the perfection of thought. In this respect the cycle appears to be fully closed.

However, in other respects, it leaves undetermined the precise object of the human activity of contemplation. The object of divine thought we know from *Met.* X, 1074b 34 to be God himself, again identified with "the most excellent of things" (αὑτὸν ἄρα νοεῖ, εἴπερ ἐστί τὸ κράτιστον). The

---

[5] To avoid engaging in well-known exegetical controversies, I will confine my remarks, with few qualifications, to the *Nic. Ethics*, which is generally regarded as Aristotle's most characteristic ethical writing. Cf. e.g. Jaeger, *op.cit.*, 229.

[6] Cf. *N.E.* IX, 1166a 17 and 23.

object of human contemplation, we are briefly informed in *N.E.* X, 1177a 15, is "things noble and divine" (καὶ ἔννοιαν ἔχειν περὶ καλῶν καὶ θείων),[7] whereas the logical consequence of the identification of divine and human activity with reason would have required that it should also be God himself. Aristotle stops short of this conclusion from what appears to be an instinctive aversion to mysticism, and he is satisfied to assert instead that it is "certain noble and divine things", rather than God Himself.[8]

II

In the Arabic Neo-Platonic tradition which stems ultimately from Plotinus and Proclus, but is thoroughly conditioned by Aristotelian elements, the object of the contemplative activity is specified with far greater precision, and the inevitable mystical implications of the original Aristotelian thesis are fearlessly drawn. For the purposes of this appendix, I will take the great Arabic Neo-Platonist Ibn Sīnā (d. 1037) as a representative of this current in Islamic thought, although other equally important figures, such as Ibn Bājjah (d. 1138) and Ibn Rushd (d. 1198) will be referred to.

The cornerstone of Ibn Sīnā's metaphysics is a complex emanationist scheme, at the top of which stands the One of Plotinus, identified with the Unmoved Mover of Aristotle and designated by Ibn Sīnā as the Necessary Being. What emanates from this Necessary Being is: (a) a series of separate intelligences, (b) a series of 'celestial' souls, and (c) a series of heavenly bodies. The function of each one of the intelligences is to impart to the corresponding heavenly body the *universal*, circular motion in which, as part of the cosmic system of concentric heavenly spheres, it is involved; the function of the celestial souls is to impart to these spheres the *particular* and voluntary motions which belong to them. All together there are ten spheres, starting with the outermost sphere and ending with the sublunary world, and there are ten corresponding intelligences (or intellects), each of which, like Aristotle's separate intelligences, is unmoved and immaterial, and yet is able to impart motion to its sphere through the power of its attraction, like the 'object of desire' (ὀρεκτὸν), as Aristotle expresses it in *Met.* X, 1072a 25.[9]

---

[7] Cf. also *N.E.* VI, 1141a 20 and 1141b 3, where this object is described as τῶν τιμιωτάτων τῇ φύσει.

[8] In the *Eudemean Ethics*, VIII, 1249b 20, 38, the good of man is declared to be τὸν θεὸν θεραπεύειν καὶ θεωρεῖν. Cf. Jaeger, *op.cit.*, 240–43. The 'noble and divine things' of the *N.E.* can only be: the stars, the intelligences, or the eternal first principles of knowledge.

[9] See Ibn Sīnā, *al-Najat*, 277; and *K. al-Shifa*ᵓ (*Ilāhiyāt*), 410. Cf. M. Fakhry, *A History of Islamic Philosophy*, 156f.

Of these intelligences, the most important is unquestionably the last, called the active intellect by Ibn Sīnā and the Arab Neo-Platonists generally. In the elaborate emanationist scheme which they developed, and which appears to have no specific Greek predecessor, this active intellect performs three fundamental functions. First, as a cosmic principle, it imparts, as already mentioned, motion and development to the sublunary world of generation and corruption, which lies under its direct jurisdiction. Second, as an ontological principle, it endows the terrestrial entities with their 'substantial forms' once they are 'disposed' through the action of their elemental compounds and the influence of the heavenly bodies. Finally, as an epistemological principle, it imparts to the human intellect once it has likewise been 'disposed', through study or instruction, the intelligible forms which constitute the very stuff of knowledge. It is in that latter respect, as Ibn Sīnā has it and as St. Thomas Aquinas was to comment in *Summa Theol.* I, q. 84, a. 4 (Resp.), the 'storehouse' in which all the intelligibles are eternally placed.[10]

The whole process of human cognition thus becomes a gradual progression or ascent from the lowest condition of potentiality to the highest condition of actuality , or the apprehension of those intelligibles stored away in the active intellect. The name that Ibn Sīnā and his successors gave to this progression is not union with, or even vision of, but rather conjunction or contact (*ittiṣāl*) with the active intellect.[11] When the human soul has attained this condition, writes Ibn Sīnā, it realizes its 'proper perfection', which is to "become identified with the intelligible world in which the form of the whole, its rational order and the good overflowing from it are inscribed."[12] To express this point more graphically, the soul becomes through conjunction with the active intellect a replica of the intelligible world—a mirror in which the beauty and order of that world are reflected. This was obviously Ibn Sīnā's way of glorifying the contemplative ideal of which the philosopher alone can fully partake.

---

10 St. Thomas contrasts Plato's and Avicenna's views of cognition as follows:

Avicenna, setting this opinion (i.e. Aristotle's) aside, held that the intelligible species of all sensible things, instead of subsisting in themselves without matter, pre-exist immaterially in some separate intellects (. . .) From the Agent Intellect, according to him, intelligible species flow into our souls, and sensible species into corporeal matter. And so Avicenna agrees with Plato in this, that the intelligible species of our intellect are derived from certain separate forms, but these Plato held to subsist in themselves, while Avicenna placed them in the Agent Intellect. See *Summa Theol.* I, q. 84, a. 4 (Resp.).

On the metaphor of a storehouse or closet, Arabic *khaznah*, see especially *Avicenna's De Anima*, 242f.

11 See Ibn Sīnā, *Aḥwāl al-Nafs*, 130, and *al-Najāt*, 293. Cf. M. Fakhry, "Three Varieties of Mysticism in Islam," in: *Int. Journal for Phil. of Religion*, II (1971), 198–207.

12 *Aḥwāl al-Nafs*, 130.

What the actual content of the cognitive experience in question is, according to Ibn Sīnā, can only be surmized. In what appears to be an attempt to enumerate the basic components of this experience, Ibn Sīnā gives the following tentative list:

(a) The first principles of demonstrative knowledge, expounded by Aristotle in *Metaphysica* IV and in *Analytica Posteriora* I.

(b) The final causes of universal (i.e. heavenly) motions, to the exclusion of the particular and infinite motions of generabilia and corruptibilia which can never be fully circumscribed, by reason of their infinity.

(c) The form of the Whole and the interrelationships of its parts and the order binding them together.

(d) Providence and the mode of its operation throughout the whole universe.

(e) God, His existence, unity and the manner in which He can be known.

(f) The order governing the created world and the relation of its components to God.

III

There are obvious analogies of this view with that of Plotinus, whose views on this question are not free from ambiguity. He speaks in the *Enneads* of vision (ὄψις, θέα), union (ἕνωσις), ecstasy (ἔκστασις), and contact (συνάπτω, ἐπαφή, θίξις) and argues that this contact is achieved through likeness (ὁμοιότητι) or kinship (τῷ συγγενεῖ).[13] The proximate object of union or contact for him is Nous, whereas the ultimate object is the One, so that the conclusion is unavoidable that union with Nous is an intermediate stage in the soul's journey to its original Source and Author.[14]

"When the soul has good fortune with Him (i.e. the only One) and He comes to it, or rather when His presence becomes manifest, when it turns away from the things present to it and prepares itself, making itself as beautiful as possible, and comes to likeness with Him (. . .) then it sees Him suddenly appearing in itself (for there is nothing between, nor are they still two, but both are one." (*Enn.* VI, 7, 34, Armstrong). "So if one sees that one's self has become this (i.e. union with self), one has it as a likeness of the Divine, and if one goes on from it, as image to original,

---

[13] *Enneads*, VI, 9, 9–10.

[14] *Enneads*, VI, 1, 11; 3, 17; VI, 7, 34–36; 9, 11. Cf. J.M. Rist, *Plotinus: The Road to Reality*, Cambridge, 1967, 220f.

one reaches the end of one's journey (. . .) (He) rises through virtue to Nous and through wisdom to the Divine (. . .) an escape in solitude to the solitary (φυγὴ μόνον πρὸς μόνον).'' (*Enn.*, VI, 9, 11, Armstrong).

Despite the terminological vacillation and ambiguity, Plotinus has definitely moved away from the Aristotelian concept of the philosopher's abstract relation to the Supreme Being, in the direction of active or substantial union. The ultimate object of this union is for him no other than the One or God.[15] The distance which separates Plotinus from Aristotle on this point is great. Aristotle, as we have already noted, stopped short of the logical conclusion that the ultimate object of finite reason is that of infinite reason itself, i.e. the Divine Being himself. The transcendence of his Unmoved Mover is such that not only does he wish to spare him the indignity of idle curiosity (for, as he asks rhetorically in *Met.* XII, 1074b 25: ''Are there not some things about which it is incredible that it should think?'', adding with still greater emphasis: ''There are even some things which it is better not to see than to see'' (line 32). He even wishes to spare the Unmoved Mover the cumbersome business of everyday commerce with the world, including man. The Unmoved Mover, as is abundantly clear from the *Metaphysics*, takes no thought of man altogether, and man out of a desire to return the divine compliment, so to speak, retaliates in kind. Only in one passage does there appear to be a departure from this line of thought. In *Met.* XII, 1072a 26, Aristotle appears to *imply* that God is both the ''primary object of desire'' (τὸ πρῶτον ὀρεκτόν) and the primary object of thought (τὸ πρῶτον νοητὸν) and commentators, like Alexander and Zabarella, who identified God with the active reason of *De Anima*, III, 430a 17, naturally exploited this identification. But, as Ross has put it, ''Aristotle makes no actual mention of God in this passage of *De Anima*, and though the pure never-ceasing activity of thought here described is in some respects like that ascribed to God in the *Metaphysics*, Aristotle probably did not identify the two.''[16] In *Eudemean Ethics*, VIII, 1248a 23 and 1239b 20, Aristotle states that the good of man consists in serving and contemplating God (τὸν θεὸν θεραπεύειν καὶ θεωρεῖν), but that position was abadoned in the *Nicomachean Ethics*.[17]

---

[15] As Rist has put it in *Plotinus*, p. 221: ''Plotinus very frequently uses such language (i.e. that of vision or contemplation) (. . .) But faithful to Plato though he may wish to be, Plotinus cannot remain satisfied with this language. The aim of the mystic is not *seeing*, but *being*. It is not vision, but union which is the goal and end of life.'' Cf. also Rist, *Eros and Psyche*, Toronto, 1964, 87f.

[16] D. Ross, *Aristotle*, London, 1949, 153.

[17] Cf. Jaeger, *op.cit.*, 240–43.

IV

It will appear more clearly now what the precise relationship of the Avicenna concept of 'conjunction' with the active intellect is to the Plotinian concept of union with the One, on the one hand, and the Aristotelian concept of contemplating "noble and divine things", on the other.

The object of Avicenna's conjunction is the active intellect, an emanation ten times removed from God. The essence of this conjunction is 'vision', rather than union in the strict sense. Only in one place does Avicenna appear to abandon the language of conjunction (*ittiṣāl*) and to replace it by that of union (*ittiḥād*), and that in a mystical treatise *On Love*. Here he writes that the ultimate goal of the rational soul is "to love the absolute good instinctively (...) and the highest degree of approximation to it is to receive its manifestation truly; I mean, in the most perfect way possible, and this is what the Ṣūfīs call union."[18]

In another place, *al-Ishārāt*, he dwells on the "stations of (mystical) knowers" with some insistence, but here he appears to be simply struggling to reconcile the visionary or contemplative ideal, inherited from Aristotle, with the 'unitary', inherited from Plotinus, without much success.[19] His own sympathies are distinctly on the side of vision or contemplation. To understand the causes of his failure, it is necessary to recall that the genuine protagonists of mystical union in Islam were the extravagant Ṣūfīs (whose mysticism was conditioned to some extent by Hindu elements), such as the two great pantheists al-Bisṭāmī (d. 874) and al-Hallāj (d. 922),[20] and between those practical mystics and the Muslim 'Peripatetics', of whom Ibn Sīnā is the most illustrious, there was no love lost. Both Ibn Bājjah (d. 1138) and his great successor Ibn Rushd (d. 1198) inveigh vehemently against those mystics who have exceeded the 'limits of nature' in their claim to be united or identified with God. For Ibn Rushd, in particular, the line should be sharply drawn at the outermost limits of man's intellectual capacity, but not beyond it. Man, who is the intermediate link between the temporal world of nature and the eternal world of the

---

18 *R. al-ᶜIshq*, in: M.A.R. Mehren, *Traités Mystique d'Avicenne*, Leiden, 1899, 22.

19 See *al-Ishārāt wa'l-Tanbīhāt*, III, Ibn Sīnā speaks here of the 'stations of knowers' and argues that the "purified knowers (...) are able to attain the world of holiness and blessedness and to become inscribed with the highest perfection" (*Ibid.*, III, 96). He admits the existence of 'stations' that discourse cannot attain. "Whoever wishes to know about it should train himself gradually to become one of the 'people of vision' (*al-mushāhadah*) rather than 'oral converse' (*al-mushāfahah*); and one of those who have arrived (*al-wāṣilūn*), rather than those who simply heard the report." *Ibid.*, 99–100.

20 See R.C. Zaehner, *Muslim and Hindu Mysticism*, London, 1960, 110f. et passim. Cf. my article, "Three Varieties", *op.cit.*, 205f.

separate intelligences, can only enter into relationship with the lowest of these intelligences, i.e. the active intellect, but this relationship remains for him, as it was for Aristotle, exclusively intellectual. It is, he writes in his treatise on conjunction, "no other than apprehending actually something entirely immaterial in a manner analogous to sensation."[21] This something is then declared to be the active intellect, as it is apprehended by the "material intellect" of man."[22] This apprehension is what he means by conjunction; in it man partakes of the highest mode of operation proper to the active intellect and the separate intelligences generally, i.e. self-apprehension. Through this self-apprehension (which is clearly analogous to Aristotle's Unmoved Mover's mode of apprehending itself), the perfection proper to the mind is achieved, and human nature is thoroughly fulfilled.[23] The object of this apprehension is not God, but rather a subordinate, semi-divine agency which lies on the periphery of the world of generation and corruption.

As I have argued elsewhere,[24] we have in this theory of conjunction or contact the most dramatic expression in Islamic thought of a humanism which tended to bypass in a very subtle fashion the theocentric and otherworldly ideal of Islam, by locating the center of his spiritual and intellectual life in an extra-mundane entity vastly removed from God, and in which all mankind, and especially the privileged class of philosophers, is called upon to partake.

V

In a Greek philosopher like Aristotle, this humanism would not have raised any serious problems, but the persistence of Muslim Neo-Platonists and Peripatetics in defending it in such unequivocal terms is truly surprising. St. Thomas, whom I have already quoted, was able to accept the epistemological implications of the theory of the active intellect, which he considered as a faculty of the human soul,[25] without sacrificing the fundamentally Biblical and Semitic conception of God's everpresence to man and his unceasing interest in him, and without leaving God out of the reach of human intelligence, as the later Aristotle and his Arab commentators actually did. God is for him the ultimate source of that illumination we designate as intellectual knowledge.[26] He is likewise the goal towards

---

[21] *R. al-Ittiṣāl*, Appendix to *Talkhīṣ K. al-Nafs*, ed. ᶜUthmān Amīn, Cairo, 1950, 123.

[22] See *Talkhīs ma baᶜd al-Ṭabīᶜah*, Cairo, 1950, 145, and *R. al-Ittiṣāl*, 123f.

[23] See *R. al-Ittiṣāl*, 121 and *Averrois Cordubensis Commentarium Magnum in Aristotelis De Anima Libris*, ed. F.S. Crawford, Cambridge, Mass., 1953, 495f.

[24] See my article "Three Varieties of Mysticism," 202.

[25] *S. Theol.* I, q. 79, a. 4.

[26] *Ibid.*, q. 84, a. 5. Cf. *Cont. Gent.* III, 53.

which man's whole nature tends, as its first principle and final goal. And although he agrees with both Aristotle and Avicenna that man's ultimate happiness consists in the contemplation of truth,[27] he disagrees with them that the object of this contemplation can be anything other than God, the absolute Truth. Thus he writes in *Summa Contra Gentiles*, III: "Everything tends to a divine likeness as its own end. Therefore a thing's last end is that whereby it is most of all like God. Now the intellectual creature is especially likened to God in that it is intellectual (. . .) (and) it is more like God in understanding actually than in understanding potentially and habitually (. . . .) Furthermore, in understanding actually, the intellectual creature is especially like God in understanding God, for by understanding Himself God understands all things." Again: "Man's natural desire in knowledge tends to a definite end. This can be none other than the highest thing knowable, which is God."[28]

St. Thomas Aquinas satisfies in this subtle way the profoundly intellectual aspirations of the mind to contemplate truth, as laid down by Aristotle, and its spiritual aspirations to be assimilated to God, as adumbrated by Plato, and to achieve that happiness or beatitude which is its ultimate goal. Remarkably enough all this is done without sacrificing the contemplative ideal or belittling it in the least.

---

[27] See *In Ethic. Arist. Expositio., Lect.* XI, 2110: "Sic ergo patet quod ille qui vocat speculationi veritates, est maxime felix, quantum homo in hac vita felix esse potest".

[28] *Cont. Gent.* III, 25. Cf. also 37.

APPENDIX B

The following excerpt from Ibn Sina's *Risāla fi'l-Nafs* (Epistle on the Soul, from *Aḥwāl al-Nafs*, pp. 130–135) gives a succint account of the soul's 'perfection' and its capacity for 'duplicating' the intelligible world. It appears to be intended as a summary of his earlier views, and may be taken as representative of his later and maturer thought on the question of 'conjunction' (*ittiṣāl*).

The perfection proper to the rational soul is to become an intelligible world in which the form of the Whole (universe), the intelligible order proper to that Whole and the good permeating it are inscribed, starting with the First Principle of the Whole and passing on to the superior substances that are purely spiritual and of which it (i.e. the universal soul) is the principle, then on to those spiritual substances that have a certain relation to (physical) body, then to those bodies of higher forms and powers,[1] and so on, until it has encompassed the form of all being. Thereupon, it is transformed into an intelligible world corresponding to the existing one entirely, and engaged in contemplating absolute truth,[2] absolute goodness and absolute beauty. It becomes united to it, imprinted with its archetype and form, circumscribed by it and transformed into its substance.

let us now compare this perfection to the other perfections sought by the other powers (of the soul), and we will find that it is of such excellence that it would be wrong to say that it is better or fuller than they, since it has no proportion to them in any manner, whether in point of virtue, fullness, multiplicity or any other form of enjoyment that the different modes of perception, which we have already mentioned, generate.[3]

As for duration, how can one compare the eternal to the changeable and corruptible mode of duration? As for the intensity of conjunction (*al-wuṣūl*),[4] how can one compare that whose conjunction is mere surface-contact to that which permeates the substance of its recipient, so as to become almost identified with it, without any discontinuity. For the act of thinking, the thinker and the object of thought are one or nearly one.

That the knower, however, is more perfect is obvious; that he has a

---

[1] That is, the heavenly bodies.

[2] The text appears to be corrupt here; it reads *al-ḥusn* for what I assume to be *al-ḥaqq*.

[3] The reference is to the inferior modes of perception (*idrāk*), such as external sensation, imagination or memory, discussed earlier by the author.

[4] Or arrival. This term derives from the same root as *ittiṣāl*, conjunction.

greater capacity for perception (*idrāk*) will appear at the barest investigation. For he has a greater number of perceptible objects and a greater diligence in understanding the object, stripping it of those accretions which do not enter into its essence, except accidentally, and investigating its inner and outer nature. How indeed can this mode of apprehension be compared to that?[5] And how can sensuous, bestial or irascible pleasure be compared to this felicity and pleasure? However, while we are still in this world, incarcerated in our bodies and wallowing in vice, we are unable to partake of that pleasure whenever we are allowed to partake of a measure thereof, as we have already mentioned in our preliminary remarks. That is why we do not go out to seek it or yearn for it, unless we are fated to throw away the yoke of passion and anger, as well as their sister-feelings, and to catch a glimpse of that pleasure. It will perhaps be possible for us then to form a faint and dim image thereof, especially if problems have been resolved and the valued objects of our search have been clarified. Our enjoyment of that (experience) is similar to the sensuous enjoyment of delicious, savory objects or of their smells at a distance.

Moreover, when we are separated from our bodies, our soul—if it has been aroused while still in the body to an awareness of its perfection, which had been the object of its quest, even though it had not attained it despite its yearning for it (. . .)—will experience at its loss a measure of pain equivalent to the pleasure which would necessarily result (from its acquisition), as we have stated, and shown its lofty position. Therein would consist the misery and punishment which neither the fire's dissolution of the limbs of the body or its transformation, nor the destruction of the humors by excessive cold, could equal (. . .).

Were the intellectual power of the soul to attain that degree of perfection which would enable it, once it has left the body, to achieve the self-realization it is destined to achieve, our case would be similar to that of a person drugged who was given to taste the most savory object and to partake of the most delectable condition, but was unable to feel any of it. As soon as the drug's effect had worn off, however, he was able to partake of that marvelous pleasure at once. That pleasure is not of the same type as sensuous and bestial pleasures in any sense, but is analogous to that good condition which belongs to the immaterial and living substances, and accordingly is superior to and nobler than any other pleasure (. . .).

As for the extent of apprehending intelligible forms that a man's soul should attain, to be able to pass beyond that level of misery,[6] and in

[5] The contrast is between the rational and sensuous modes of apprehension or perception (*idrāk*).

[6] The wretched condition of those who either fall short of the human perfection mentioned above, or obstinately cling to false beliefs.

transcending or exceeding it to hope for happiness—that is not a matter I can expound upon except in tentative terms.

Thus I believe (*aẓunn*) that it consists in a man's soul of: (a) apprehending the immaterial principles truly, and assenting to them with conviction, insofar as they are known to him demonstratively, (b) apprehending the final causes of those matters occuring in the sphere of universal motion,[7] but not in that of particular motions which are infinite, (c) comprehending the form of the Whole and the relation of its parts to one another, and the order flowing from the First Principle down to the farthest entities falling under its jurisdiction, (d) conceiving Providence, its order and modality, (e) ascertaining what type of being belongs to that Entity (*al-dhāt*) which is antecedent to the Whole, what unity pertains to it, and how it cognizes without any form of multiplicity or change, and (f) realizing how other existing entities are arranged in relation to it.

Thereupon, as the seer increases in prespicuity, his capacity for happiness will increase proportionately. It is as though man will not be freed from attachment to this (lower) world and its cares unless his relation to that (higher) world has been firmly established, and he has acquired a yearning for what exists yonder and a passion strong enough to prevent him from looking back at what he has left behind.

---

[7] That is, the spheres of the heavenly bodies or stars.

APPENDIX B′

I give below a translation of a chapter entitled 'On Providence, Showing the Way in Which Evil Enters Into the Divine Decree'. The Arabic text is given verbatim in both *Kitāb al-Najāt*, ed. Majid Fakhry, Beirut, 1985, pp. 320-326, and *Kitāb al-Shifā*ʾ (*Al-Ilahiyyat*), ed. Fr. Anawātī and Saʿīd Zāyid, Cairo, 1960, pp. 414-424. I have indicated the minor variations in these two parallel texts in the footnotes.

It behooves us, having reached this point, to engage in the discussion of providence. It has doubtless become clear to you from what we have already expounded that it is not possible for the higher causes to do what they do, in matters of providence[1] for our sake; or to be generally concerned for anything, be impelled by any motive or be moved by any preference. You could not possibly deny the wonderful effects manifested in the generation of the world, the parts of the heavenly bodies and the parts of plants and animals, which could not arise fortuitously, but require a certain governance (*tadbīr*). You should know, then, that providence consists in that the First knows the order of goodness pertaining to existence, and how He is Himself the cause of goodness and perfection, as far as possible, and how He is well pleased with it in the aforementioned manner; whereupon, He apprehends the order of goodness to the highest degree possible and so emanates in the fullest way that conduces to order, as far as possible. This then is the meaning of providence.

You should also know that evil has many senses. We call evil deficiency, such as ignorance, weakness and deformity; and we call evil that which resembles pain and grief accompanying therein the apprehension of the cause, and not simply the loss, of something. For the cause which is contrary to the good, bars the good, and necessitates its privation, may be such that the injured object does not apprehend it; as in the case of a cloud which overshadows, and thus bars the shining of the sun upon that which requires the sun for its full growth. If this requirer possesses apprehension,[2] he would apprehend that he did not benefit (from the sun's light), but does not apprehend that in so far as the cloud prevented it, but rather in so far as he possessed sight. And he is not affected adversely by that, injured or deficient, in so far as he possesses sight, but

[1] Missing in *al-Shifā*ʾ, 414.

[2] I read *darrākan*, as in *al-Shifā*ʾ, 415.

in so far as he is something else.[3] Sometimes (the cause) is concomitant and is apprehended by him who apprehends the privation of good health, as in the case of one who suffers the loss of contact in an organ due to a lacerating heat. For, in so far as he apprehends the loss of contact through a power in that organ, he apprehends the harmful effect of heat also; so that the two modes of apprehension would coalesce therein:

a. apprehending in a manner similar to our apprehending non-existing things, as already mentioned, and
b. apprehending in a manner similar to our apprehending existing things, as already mentioned, too.

Now, this existentially apprehended object is not evil in itself, but rather in relation to that thing. As to its want of perfection or good health, that is not evil in relation to it only, so that it could be imagined to have an existence whereby it is not evil; since its very being in it is only[4] evil and the mode of its being is evil, too. Thus blindness can only exist in the eye, and in so far as it exists in the eye, can only be evil; there is no other respect in which it is not evil. However, heat, for instance, if it is deemed evil in relation[5] to one who is injured by it, has another aspect whereby it is not evil. Evil *per se* consists in privation, but not every privation; but only the privation of those fixed perfections pertaining to its kind and nature and necessitated by the very nature of that thing. Evil *per accidens*, however, is that which bars or withholds perfection from that which deserves it. There is no good that results from an absolute evil, except in name; it is not therefore an actual evil. (Were it to exist actually, it would correspond to universal evil.) For everything which exists in a state of utmost perfection and does not contain an element of potentiality, involves no evil; evil attaches only to that which by its very nature has an element of potentiality, and that by virtue of matter.

Now, evil attaches to matter, either due to a first condition supervening on it, or to some adventitious condition following upon it. An example of the condition, which has in itself attached to matter in the first place, is the fact that there has supervened upon a certain matter upon its origination some extrinsic causes of evil, and thus a certain habit has become ingrained in it. That habit will then resist its proper disposition for that perfection which it was fated to receive an evil parallel to it; such as the matter from which a man or a horse is formed, when such adventitious causes have supervened upon it so as to render it viler in humour or harder in substance. Thus it did not receive the proper design,

[3] That is, by virtue of his own nature.
[4] Added in *al-Shifā͗*, 416.
[5] Added in *al-Shifā͗*, 416.

fashioning or straightening, and so the shape was deformed and the perfection of humour and constitution required did not arise, not because the agent did not permit it, but rather because the patient did not receive it. As to the adventitious condition from outside, it could be one of two things:

a. either one which prevents, impedes or expels the agent of perfection, or
b. a constant opposite which destroys the perfection.

An instance of the former is the presence of many clouds and their accumulation, or the shadows cast by high mountains, preventing thereby the sun from acting upon the fruits and thus achieving their perfection; an instance of the latter is the frost's preventing some plants from attaining their perfection at the right time, and losing thereby their proper disposition and what follows upon it.

Now all the causes of evil occur only in what exists in the sublunary world, but the totality of what exists in the sublunary world is trivial by comparison to the whole realm of being, as you have learnt. Moreover, evil affects individuals only and at certain times, whereas the species are well preserved; and real evil does not touch most individuals, except for a particular kind of evil.

You should know also that the evil which is synonymous with privation is either evil with respect to something necessary, or useful and close to the necessary; or is not evil in that respect, but evil with respect to that condition which is possible in the fewest cases. Were it to exist, it would only be evil with respect to what is an accessory perfection ensuing upon secondary perfections and is not a concomitant of the nature of the possible in which it inheres. (This variety is other than the one we are considering and it is the one which we have excluded.) Moreover, it is not evil with respect to the species, but rather with respect to a factor superadded to what is necessary for the species; such as ignorance of philosophy, geometry or such like. For, that is not evil in so far as we are humans, but evil with respect to the perfection deemed best if possessed by all; you will learn about it later. However, it becomes really evil if required by some individual person or individual soul; and it is only required by the individual, not in so far as he is a person or a soul, but rather in so far as he becomes convinced of the beauty of that (knowledge), desires it and becomes well disposed to receive it, as we will explain to you in the sequel. However, prior to that, it is not one of those (perfections), to which the nature of the species inclines necessarily, in the same way that it inclines towards the secondary perfections ensuing upon the primary perfections; if it did not, it would be a privation required by nature.

Evil in individual entities, therefore, is rare; nevertheless, the existence of this evil in things is a necessity ensuing upon the need for the good. For, had these elements not been such as to oppose each other and be affected by the predominant agent, it would not have been possible for those noble species to arise therefrom; and had not fire, from among these elements, been such that, were the collisions which occur in the course of the necessary cosmic permutations to lead to contact with the garment of an honest man and to cause it to burn necessarily, fire would not have been a source of general utility.

It follows necessarily that the good that is possible in these will be good only following the occurence of the like of that evil through it and with it. Moreover, His diffusion of the good does not require that the predominant good should be left out on account of a rare evil, so that leaving it out would be worse than that evil; because the privation of that whose existence is possible in the nature of matter, if there are two privations, is worse than one privation. That is why a reasonable person prefers to be burned by fire, provided he can escape from it alive, to dying without pain. For if he were to forgo this kind of good, that would be an evil greater than the evil resulting from its production. It would also be necessary for that reason, which comprehends the mode of necessary governance pertaining to the order of the good, to understand the entitlement of this type of things to exist in a manner which justifies whatever evil occurs with it necessarily. Therefore, it is necessary for its existence to emanate.

If someone were to say, "Yet, it would have been possible for the First Governor to produce a pure good free from evil," we would answer, "That would not have been possible with respect to this type of being, although it would have been possible with respect to absolute being." However, if some kind of absolute being were exempt (of evil), it would not be this kind. For that is what has actually emanated from the First Governor and exists in intellectual, psychic and heavenly matters;[6] whereas that other kind has remained a possibility and its production could not be abandoned due to the fact that the evil which might become intermingled with it (while its principle did not exist originally and was left out so that this evil may not exist), would indeed have been a greater evil than its existence. Its existence was, therefore, the lesser of two evils.

Moreover, it would have been necessary for the beneficient causes which precede these causes conducing evil *per accidens*, not to exist, since the existence of the former entails the existence of the latter. Thus the greatest disturbance of the universal order of goodness would have

[6] That is, in the higher or celestial sphere.

arisen. Yet, if we did not attend to that and directed our attention to the divisions of the possible, in point of existence, into the kinds of entities which differ in their respective conditions, then being exempt from evil would have arisen. Yet, if a type of being which can only exist in this manner, such that its non-being is a greater evil than its being remained, then its existence must emanate, in so far as from it will emanate the being which is more appropriate, in the manner already mentioned.

We say anew that evil is used in many senses:

1. We call evil blameworthy actions; and
2. we call evil their moral principles; and
3. we call evil the pains and sorrows and the like; and
4. we call evil, finally, the failure of anything to attain its perfection or its loss of what belongs to it.

Now, pain and sorrows, although their connotations are existential and they are not privations, appear in fact to belong to the category of privation and deficiency. The evil which is predicated of actions, too, is relative either to him who loses his perfection, if this evil touches him, such as injustice, or to a certain perfection stipulated in religious[7] legislation, such as adultery. The same is true of morals, which are evil due to the emanation of these (actions) from them, and they accompany the soul's loss of those perfections which ought to belong to it. In fact, we find no action which is said to be evil but is a perfection in relation[8] to its agent; it is merely an evil in relation to the cause which receives it; or in relation to another agent who impedes its action upon that matter, upon which it has a greater right to act. Injustice, for instance, derives from a faculty which seeks conquest: that is the irascible, conquest being its perfection; and for that purpose it was created, in so far as it is irascible; I mean that it was created so as to be directed towards conquest, seeking it and rejoicing in it. This action, then, is a good in relation to it; if it fails to achieve it, that would be an evil as far as it is concerned. (Conquest) is indeed an evil in relation to the oppressed or to the rational faculty, whose perfection consists in mastering that faculty and dominating it; should it fail to achieve that goal, that would be evil with respect to it.

The same is also true of the cause which produces pains and sorrows, such as fire when it burns. For burning is the perfection of fire, but it is an evil in relation to one who has been robbed of good health thereby, due to the loss he has incurred. As to the evil whose cause is some imperfection or deficiency inherent in its natural constitution, and not

---

[7] As in *al-Shifāʾ*, 419.
[8] As in *al-Shifāʾ*, 419. The *Najāt* reading is garbled.

because an agent has caused it, but rather because the agent has failed to cause it—that in reality is not an evil in relation to anything.

As to those evils which accompany certain things which are good, they arise from two causes:

1. a cause pertaining to matter, which is susceptible of both form and privation; and
2. a cause pertaining to the agent. For,
   a. since it is necessary that material entities derive from it; and
   b. since it is impossible that matter should have that mode of being which plays the role of matter, unless it is susceptible of form and privation; and
   c. since it is impossible that it should not then be susceptible of opposites; and
   d. since, finally, it is impossible that active forces should have the capacity for actions which are contrary to other actions that have already come into being, while they do not perform their proper action, it follows that it is impossible that something should be created the purpose thereof being that intended by fire, and yet it does not burn.

Moreover, if the whole[9] could only be fulfilled if there is in it that which heats and that which is heated, it follows that the useful purpose served by the presence of these two will entail certain injuries resulting from burning and being burned, such as the fire burning a limb of an ascetic person. However, the most frequent case is the occurence of the good intended by nature, and the permanent case, too. In fact, the most frequent case is that most individual members of the species are guarded against burning; but as regards the permanent, it happens that many species cannot be preserved permanently without the existence of the like of the fire, provided that it burns. It is only in a minority of cases that injuries actually result from fires as sometimes result from them; and the same is true of the rest of the causes resembling that. Thus it would not have been desirable to abandon the frequent and permanent advantages for the sake of infrequent evil purposes; and that is why the goods resulting from those things were willed by a Primary Will in the manner which makes it appropriate to say that God, may He be exalted, wills things and wills at the same time the evil which is *per accidens*; since He knew that it was bound to occur necessarily and therfore took no account of it. The good, then, is required necessarily *per se*, whereas evil is required *per accidens*, yet all is predetermined.

[9] That is, the universe.

Similarly, with respect to matter, it was known that it is incapable of certain things and that perfections do not attain it in certain things; yet that which is achieved in it is incomparably greater than what is not achieved. If this is the case, then it would not have been part of divine wisdom to abandon the fixed, permanent and frequent goods for the sake of evils pertaining to individual things which are not permanent. We rather say that things, in the imagination, are either:

1. such that, were they to be imagined as existing, their existence cannot possibly be anything but evil absolutely; or
2. conversely, are things whose existence is good and cannot possibly be evil or deficient; or
3. things in which goodness preponderates, if they happen to exist, (it being impossible for them to be otherwise by their very nature); or
4. things in which evil preponderates; or
5. finally, things in which those two conditions are equivalent.

As to what has no evil within it, it does exist in nature; but that, which is totally evil or predominantly or equivalently evil, does not exist at all. However, as to that in which the good preponderates, it is fitting for it to exist, so long as the predominant part in it is good.

If it is said, "Why then was not evil excluded from it originally, so that it could be totally good?", we would say, "Then they would not have been those same existing things. For, we have already said that their being is such that it is impossible for them to be such that no evil attaches to them. Were they, however, made to be such that no evil arises from them, then their being would not be the same being that belongs to them now, but rather the being of other existing things which are other and actually exist in fact; I mean, such that no evil attaches to it." An instance of this is that, if the being of fire were to burn, and the being of that which burns were to burn the garment of a poor man if it chances to touch it (since the being of the poor man's garment is to be susceptible of being burned); and if, moreover, the being of the variety of motions pertaining to things were of this type that contact would accompany it, and the being of contact between the agent and the patient such that action and passion will accompany it, it would follow that if the latter conditions did not exist, the former would not exist either.

Thus, throughout the whole, the active and passive powers, the heavenly and earthly, the physical and the psychic, have been arranged in such a way as to conduce to the universal order, as well as the impossibility that, being what they are, they will not conduce to evils. It follows, then, from the conditions of the world, in relation to one another, that there might arise in a certain soul the form of bad belief, infidelity or some other evil in a certain soul or body, in such a way that, were it to be such, the universal order would not subsist. Therefore, no account was taken of the evil consequences which are bound to arise necessarily, and it was said, "I have created these for the Fire and I do not care; and I have created those for Paradise and I do not care."[10] It was also said, "Everyone is led to follow the path he was created for."

If someone were to say, "Evil is not rare or infrequent, but rather most frequent," (we would respond), "That is not the case; evil is, rather, plentiful, but is not most frequent. There is a difference between the plentiful and the most frequent; for there are many things which are plentiful, but not most frequent, such as diseases which are plentiful but not most frequent." Now, if you ponder this kind of evil, which we are referring to, you will find that it is less common than the good which corresponds to it and could exist in its own matter, let alone in its relation to other everlasting goods. Sure enough, the evils which consist in the deficiencies of secondary perfections are very frequent but they do not belong to the category of evils we are talking about. These evils, such as ignorance of geometry and want of great beauty and the like, are not of the type that affects the primary perfections, or the perfections ensuing upon them, of which the utility is apparent. These evils are not due to the action of a certain agent, but rather due to the agent's failure to act, because the patient is not disposed or does not move towards the reception (of its action). These evils are merely privations of certain goods, by way of the superabundance or excess of matter.[11]

---

[10] A *qudsī* Tradition (*Ḥadīth*) in which God speaks in the first person.
[11] Missing in *al-Shifāʾ*, 422.

APPENDIX C

THE MYSTICAL IDEAL, OR THE QUEST OF GOD: AL-GHAZĀLĪ[1]

> "You should know that those who tread the path of God are few, although the pretenders are legion. We shall inform you of two signs that you should always keep before your mind, and by which you should judge both yourself and others."

I

The first sign is that all your voluntary actions shall be governed by the criterion of the religious law (*al-shar*ᶜ) and be fully dependent upon its determinations, with respect to initiating actions or desisting from them, going forward or stopping short. For it is impossible to follow this path unless one has acquired all the noble traits of the religious law, and this in turn is not feasible without the cultivation of character, in the manner we have previously described.[2] This cannot be achieved unless one refrains from a host of permissible actions; how then can it be done by one who has not refrained from prohibited ones? Nor can it be attained unless one constantly practices supererogatory actions; how then can he who neglects necessary obligations attain it? The religious law, in laying down certain obligations upon mankind, has in fact limited itself to those obligations or prohibitions of which the masses of the vulgar are capable, to the extent that their observance does not result in the destruction of the world. For he who follows the path of God must turn away from the world to such an extent that were his example followed by the whole of mankind, the world would fall into ruin. How then can it be attained by simply observing the necessary obligations and duties, to the total neglect of supererogatory ones? That is why God has said: "The servant shall continue to come close to Me, through supererogatory actions, until I deign to love him. Once I have loved him, I shall be his hearing and sight, whereby he is able to hear through Me and see through Me."[3]

---

[1] This passage is a translation of the concluding chapter of al-Ghazālī's *Criterion of Action*, entitled "Showing the Sign of the First Mansion of the Travelers towards God Almighty." See *Mīzān al-ᶜAmal*, 155–65.

[2] *Mīzān al-ᶜAmal* is an ethical treatise, devoted predominantly to the cultivation of character. See *supra*, 193f.

[3] An alleged *qudsī* tradition, revealed directly to Muḥammad by God.

In short, the neglect of ritual obligations and the practice of prohibited actions can only result from incurable sloth or overpowering passion. And how can he who is reckoned the slave of sloth or passion ever follow the path of God? Should you nonetheless say that the follower of the path of God is one who is engaged in struggling against sloth or passion, whereas he who has already overcome them has arrived, and is no longer a traveler, it will be replied that this statement is the essence of arrogance and the misconception of the nature of the path, as well as the intended goal. Indeed, were he to shed all his base qualities, his relation to the intended goal would be similar to that of one who intends to go on a pilgrimage. However, being besieged by creditors, he first settles his accounts with them and cuts them off. The base bodily qualities which dominate mankind are similar to those creditors who have taken him by the cuff, or to wild beasts in search of prey. If he eliminates or repels them, he would be repelling worldly cares, and then he can prepare himself to start upon the path of God. Indeed, his case would be similar to that of a vain *divorcée* who aspires to marrying the Caliph, and having completed the post-marital period (*ᶜiddah*) barring this marriage, she supposes that all the obstacles have been smoothed over,[4] whereas all that has happened is her readiness, by reason of the elimination of the impediment. What remains is the condescension of the Caliph and his gracious assent. That indeed is a divine favor; not everyone who purifies himself will reach the Friday congregation, nor will the woman who has completed her period be granted everything she wishes.

If you ask: Will the follower of the path ever reach a point whereby he will be released of certain ritual obligations, so that he will not be morally injured by the performance of certain prohibited actions, as has been said of some Ṣūfī masters who tolerated these matters—you should understand that this is the height of arrogance, and that the authoritative doctors have asserted that if you see a man walking on water, while he engaged in performing deeds contrary to the religious law, you should know that he is a devil, and this, indeed, is the truth. The reason for this is that the law is straight and liberal, so that whatever need arises or necessity presses has been allowed for by the law. Hence whoever oversteps the limit of such tolerance does not act from necessity, but rather from caprice or passion. Man, so long as he lives in this world, cannot guard against the subjection of passion, or its restored mastery over him after it had been subjugated; therefore, he should always be on his guard against it. For it is inconceivable that one should be called upon to violate the religious law by anything

[4] In Islamic law, a divorced or widowed woman is not allowed to remarry before a statutory period (*ᶜiddah*) following the death of her husband or her separation from him.

other than the desire for luxury and ease, or some type of lust and sloth. All this shows that one is a prey to those base traits ensuing upon it. He who cleanses his soul and allows it to feed upon the genuine sciences will be fortified in his perseverance in worship; prayer would become to him like the apple of his eye, and nightly solitude the sweetest thing to him, as he communes with his Lord. This sign is indispensable in the early stages, and endures to the end, although the stages in the journey towards God Almighty are infinite. Death simply interrupts this journey, so that everyone will be left, upon death, at the point which he reached during his earthly career. For man dies in the condition he has attained in this life.

II

The second sign is that his heart be present unto God in a necessary and unaffected way, in whatever state he may be in. This presence, which should be a source of great delight, consists in contrition, entreaty and submission, at the thought of what has been manifested to him of God's majesty and magnificence. He should not quit any of these various stages and conditions, even while occupied with the urgent needs of his body, such as eating, performing his natural functions, washing his clothes and such like. Indeed, his condition in all these matters should be like that of a lover who has stayed up all night and wearied long in the expectation of his beloved. Upon his arrival, he rejoices greatly, but is forced by the need to perform a natural function to leave him in order to go to the water-closet. However, although compelled to leave him bodily, his heart will be present with him in such a way that, were he spoken to while in that state, he will not hear anything, because of his obsession with the thought of his beloved. For nothing he might do then can turn him away from his beloved, even if so compelled.

The seeker ought to behave that way in all his worldly pursuits; in fact, he ought to have no other pursuit, save the necessary cares of his body, while his heart remains thoroughly engrossed in the thought of God Almighty, with the utmost adoration and humility. If the lust for intercourse is not unlikely to be roused in one who has been gripped by it, and has been attracted by the beauty of a human form created from a dirty and foul sperm and bound to turn before long into a vile cadaver, although he carries his excrement within him, how can that be impossible in regard to apprehending the infinite majesty and beauty of God?

On the whole, following this path cannot be achieved without intense concern, full resolve and great solicitude. The basis of concern and solicitude is the apprehension of the beauty of the object sought, necessitating yearning and love, whereas the basis of apprehending the beauty of that object is contemplation, or the focussing of the faculty of sight upon it, to the exclusion of all other visible objects. Likewise, to the extent there appears to you part of God's majesty, your yearning and concern will be aroused, and in that proportion will be your endeavour and response. Moreover, love might increase by reason of constant fellowship, especially if in the process beautiful ethical traits, originally concealed, are revealed, so that love might be intensified.

Moreover, what appears of the beauty of God's countenance and majesty may at first seem dim due to the dimness of the newly-iniated novice's apprehension; however, as his desire and yearning are heightened, he will continue to persevere in contemplating that beauty, and, by reason thereof, he will discover certain qualities which will enhance his love at every point. As the lover desires proximity to his beloved, thus does the novice desire proximity to God Almighty. This proximity, however, is not proximity in point of place, or in point of surface contact of the bodies involved, or of the perfection of the beauty of form, to the extent it has become a visible object, whose form is present in the faculty of sight. This proximity is instead the proximity of perfection, but not in place; representations thereof will only give a remote imagining of these matters. However, comparing it to the love of the student for his teacher, as he seeks proximity to him in point of perfection, is a more accurate representation; since he seeks to come closer to him through the movement of learning, and he will constantly draw a little nearer, his ultimate goal being the latter's rank. In some cases, this will be possible, whereas in other cases it may not. Progress in rank, by virtue of which he is distant, is nevertheless possible, whereby he comes comparatively closer. Although attainment of the goal is here impossible, movement from the lowest point in the direction of the highest is certainly possible. It may be that the representation formed by the student is a definite rank, so that he does not love the rank of his teacher, but yearns to ascend step by step, without aspiring to the highest degree at once. As soon as he attains that rank, he will aspire to the one above.

This is how those who are unlearned should emulate the learned, who are the heirs of the prophets. For the learned seek to emulate the saints, and the prophets to emulate the angels, so that they will eventually be divested of human qualities altogether and turn into angels in human form. In fact, angels themselves have many ranks, the highest in rank being always the object of the love of the lower and the target of his contemplation. The privileged angels are those who are not separated from the True First by any intermediary, and theirs is the purest beauty and the most perfect splendor, compared to the perfect and splendid beings beneath them. Similarly, every perfection or beauty, compared to the beauty of the Divine Presence, is an object of contempt.

This is how you should actually conceive of proximity to God Almighty, instead of conceiving of Him as occupying a particular residence in Paradise and you moving accordingly closer to the entrance of that residence. For then your proximity would be one of place, which the Lord of Lords far transcends. Nor [to seek proximity to him] by offering Him the gift of worship, that He might be well-pleased and rejoice at its reception, and accordingly be well-disposed towards you. This, indeed, is how subjects seek the proximity of their kings, earning thereby their good pleasure and fulfilling their goals. This is frequently called approximation, but God far transcends the condition which justifies applying to kings pleasure and displeasure, rejoicing at being served, exultation at the submission and subservience of their subjects, or joy at compliance with their orders. To believe any of this is a mode of ignorance.

If you say, nonetheless, that most of the vulgar believe this to be the case, then consider how far from the condition of knowledge is he who wishes to buy ambergris from a dyer's shop. How can you aspire to a lofty position when you gauge truth by its holders? You might as well gauge truth by wild asses.[5] For there is little difference between the vulgar who have not practiced the life of learning and those romping assess fleeing a lion. Do you not see how they have adhered to the belief that God sits on a throne under a green parasol, let alone their other anthropomorphic beliefs?

Most people are in fact anthropomorphists, but anthropomorphism (*tashbīh*) is of varying degrees. Some refer to human analogies, in point of form, attributing to God hands, eyes, the ability to go down or move in space. Others attribute to Him fury, good pleasure, anger or rejoicing, whereas God Almighty is free from all these qualities. These terms have been applied in a special manner and in an allegorical way in scripture. Accordingly, they are properly understood by those who understand them, but denied by those who do not. Were all people equal in understanding, there would be no sense in the Tradition: "Many a legal scholar brings his learning to one who is more learned, and many a legal scholar is not a legal scholar (*faqīh*) at all."

---

[5] This is a reference to a well-known saying of the Caliph ᶜAlī (d. 661), which reads in full: "Do not attempt to know the truth by its holders. Once you know the truth, you will know its genuine holders." Quoted by al-Ghazālī also in *al-Munqidh min al-Ḍalāl*, 25.

BIBLIOGRAPHY

Works used in this book are given in this bibliography. However, some other relevant sources are also listed.

A. Primary Sources

ʿAbd al-Jabbār, al-Qāḍī, *Al-Mughnī fī Abwāb al-Tawḥīd wa'l-ʿAdl*, various editors. Cairo, 1962–.

——. *Sharḥ al-Uṣūl al-Khamsah*, ed. ʿAbd al-Karīm ʿUthmān. Cairo, 1965.

Al-ʿĀmirī, Abu'l-Ḥasan, *Al-Amad ʿala'l-Abad*, ed. E.K. Rowson. Beirut, 1979. New edition with Engl. translation and commentary by E.K. Rowson. New Haven, Conn., 1988.

——. *Kitāb al-Saʿādah wa'l-Isʿād*, ed. M. Minovi. Wiesbaden, 1957–58.

Aristotle, *Kitāb al-Akhlāq*, ed. ʿA.R. Badawī. Kuwait, 1979.

Al-Ashʿarī, Abu'l-Ḥasan, *Al-Ibānah ʿan Uṣūl al-Diyāna*. Hyderabad, 1321 A.H.

——. *Maqālāt al-Islāmiyyīn*, ed. H. Ritter. Istanbul, 1929–30.

Al-Baghdādī, ʿAbd al-Qāhir, *Al-Farq bayn al-Firaq*. Beirut, 1973.

——. *Uṣūl al-Dīn*. Istanbul, 1928.

Al-Bāqillānī, Abū Bakr, *Kitāb al-Tamhīd*, ed. R.J. McCarthy. Beirut, 1957.

Al-Baṣrī, al-Ḥasan, *Risālat al-Ḥasan al-Baṣrī ilā* ʿAbd al-Malik ibn Marwān *[fī'l-qadar]*, ed. H. Ritter, in: *Der Islam*, XXI (1933), 67–83.

Al-Bayḍāwī, Muḥammad, *Anwār al-Tanzīl*. Leipzig, 1846.

Al-Bukhārī, Muḥammad, *Al-Jāmiʿ al-Ṣaḥīḥ*, ed. L. Krehl and Th.W. Juynboll. Leiden, 1862–1908.

——. *Ṣaḥīḥ al-Bukhārī*. Cairo, 1973.

Al-Dawwānī, Jalāl al-Dīn, *Akhlāq-i Jalālī* (*Lawāmiʿ al-Ishrāq fī Makārim al-Akhlāq*). Calcutta, 1911. Engl. translation by W.F. Thompson, *Practical Philosophy of the Muhammadan People*. London, 1839.

Al-Fārābī, Abū Naṣr, *Fuṣūl al-Madanī*, ed. D.M. Dunlop. Cambridge 1961.

——. *Fuṣūl Muntazaʿah*, ed. F. Najjār. Beirut, 1971.

——. *Iḥṣāʾ al-ʿUlūm*, ed. ʿU. Amīn. Cairo, 1931–48.

——. *Al-Jamʿ bayna Raʾyay al-Ḥakīmayn*, ed. A. Nader. Beirut, 1960.

——. *Kitāb Ārāʾ Ahl al-Madīnah al-Fāḍilah*, ed. A. Nader. Beirut, 1959. New edition with Engl. translation and commentary by Richard Walzer. Oxford, 1985.

——. *Al-Siyāsah al-Madaniyyah*, ed. F. Najjār. Beirut, 1964.

——. *Taḥṣīl al-Saʿādah*. Hyderabad, 1345 A.H. New edition by Jaʿfar Āl Yāsīn. Beirut, 1981.

——. *Al-Tanbīh ʿalā Sabīl al-Saʿādah*, Hyderabad, 1377 A.H. New edition by Jaʿfar Āl Yāsīn. Beirut, 1985.

Al-Ghazālī, Abū Ḥāmid, *Iḥyāʾ ʿUlūm al-Dīn*. Cairo, n.d.

——. *Mishkāt al-Anwār*, ed. A. Afīfī. Cairo, 1964.

——. *Mīzān al-ʿAmal*. Cairo, 1342 A.H.

——. *Al-Munqidh min al-Ḍalāl*, ed. F. Jabre. Beirut, 1959.

Ibn Abī Uṣaybiʿah, Abu'l-ʿAbbās, *ʿUyūn al-Anbāʾ fī Ṭabaqāt al-Aṭibbāʾ*, ed. Nizār Riḍā. Beirut, 1965.

Ibn Abi'l-Dunyā, *Kitāb Makārim al-Akhlāq*, ed. James A. Bellamy. Wiesbaden, 1973.

Ibn ʿAdī, Yaḥyā, *Tahdhīb al-Akhlāq*, ed. J.F. ʿAwaḍ. Cairo, 1913. New editions by Naji al-Takriti (Beirut and Paris, 1978) and by Jād Ḥātim (Beirut, 1986).

Ibn Anas, Mālik, *Al-Muwaṭṭaʾ*. Cairo, 1951.

Ibn Bājjah, Abū Bakr, *Al-Rasāʾil al-Ilāhiyyah*, ed. M. Fakhry. Beirut, 1968.

Ibn Fātik, al-Mubashshir, *Mukhtār al-Ḥikam wa-Maḥāsin al-Kalim*, ed. ʿA.R. Badawī. Madrid, 1958.

Ibn Ḥanbal, Aḥmad, *Al-Musnad*. Cairo, 1313/1895.
——. *Al-Fatḥ al-Rabbānī*. Cairo 1955.
Ibn Ḥazm, Abū ʿAlī, *Kitāb al-Akhlāq wa'l-Siyar*, ed. with French translation by N. Tomiche. Beirut, 1961. New edition by Eva Riad. Uppsala, 1980. Spanish translation by M. Asín Palacios, *Los Caracteres y la Conducta*. Madrid, 1916.
Ibn al-Nadīm, Muḥammad, *Kitāb al-Fihrist*, ed. G. Flügel. Leipzig, 1871–72. Also Cairo edition, n.d.
Ibn Rushd (Averroes), Abu'l-Walīd, *Commentary on Plato's Republic*, ed. and Engl. translation by E.I.J. Rosenthal. Cambridge, 1956. Also *Averroes on Plato's "Republic"*, trans. R. Lerner. Ithaca and London, 1974.
——. *Faṣl al-Maqāl*, ed. A. Nader. Beirut, 1961.
——. *Risālat al-Ittiṣāl*, Appendix to *Talkhīṣ Kitāb al-Nafs*, ed. A.F. al-Aḥwānī. Cairo, 1950.
——. *Talkhīṣ Kitāb al-Nafs*, ed. A.F. al-Aḥwānī. Cairo, 1950.
Ibn Sīnā, al-Ḥusayn, *Aḥwāl al-Nafs*, ed. A.F. al-Aḥwānī. Cairo, 1952.
——. *Avicenna's De Anima*, ed. F. Rahman. London, 1959.
——. *Al-Ishārāt wa'l-Tanbīhāt*, ed. S. Dunyā. Cairo, 1960.
——. *Kitāb al-Shifāʾ (al-Ilāhiyyāt)*, ed. G. Anawātī, S. Zāyid et alia. Cairo, 1960.
——. *Al-Najāt*, 2nd ed. Cairo, 1938. New edition by Majid Fakhry. Beirut, 1985.
——. *Risālah fī ʿIlm al-Akhlāq*, in: *Tisʿ Rasāʾil*. Constantiniyah, 1298 A.H.
Ikhwān al-Ṣafāʾ, *Rasāʾil Ikhwān al-Ṣafāʾ*. Beirut, 1957.
Al-Iṣfahānī, al-Rāghib Abu'l-Qāsim, *Kitāb al-Dharīʿah ilā Makārim al-Sharīʿah*. Cairo, 1299 A.H. New edition by Abu'l-Yazīd al-ʿAjamī. Cairo, 1985.
——. *Tafṣīl al Nashʾatayn wa Taḥṣīl al-Saʿādatayn*. Saida, n.d.
Jālīnūs (Galen), Kitāb al-Akhlāq li-Jālīnūs, ed. P. Kraus, in: *Bulletin of the Faculty of Arts* (Egyptian University), V, 1 (1937), 1–51. Also edited by ʿAbdarraḥmān Badawī, *Dirāsāt wa-Nuṣūṣ fīʾl-Falsafa wa'l-ʿUlūm ʿind al-ʿArab*, Beirut, 1981, 190–211. Study by F. Klein-Franke, 'The Arabic Version of Galen's Perī Ethōn,' in: *Jerusalem Studies in Arabic and Islam* I (1979), 125–50. Engl. translation by J.N. Mattock, in: *Islamic Philosophy and Classical Tradition*. Columbia, South Carolina, 1973, 235–60.
Al-Juwaynī, Abu'l-Maʿālī, *Kitāb al-Irshād ilā Qawāṭiʿ al-Adilla fī Uṣūl al-Iʿtiqād*, ed. J.D. Luciani. Paris, 1938.
Al-Khayyāṭ, al-Ḥusayn, *Kitāb al-Intiṣār*, ed. A. Nader. Beirut, 1957.
Al-Kindī, Abū Yūsuf Yaʿqūb, *Risālah al-Ḥīlah li-Dafʿ al-Aḥzān*, ed. H. Ritter and R. Walzer, 'Uno scritto morale inedito di al-Kindī,' in: *Atti della Reale Accademia Nazionale dei Lincei*, VI, 8. Rome, 1938. See also S. van Riet, 'Joie et bonheur dans le traité d'al-Kindi sur l'art de combattre la tristesse, in: *Revue Philophique de Louvain*, 61 (1963), 13–23.
——. *[Al-] Rasāʾil al-Falsafiyyah*, ed. M. ʿA.H. Abū Rīdā. Cairo, 1950–53.
Al-Māturīdī, Abū Manṣūr, *Kitāb al-Tawḥīd*, ed. F. Kholeif. Beirut, 1970.
Al-Māwardī, ʿAlī ibn Muḥammad, *Adab al-Dunyā wa'l-Dīn*. Cairo, 1955.
Miskawayh, Aḥmad, *Al-Fawz al-Aṣghar*. Beirut, 1319 A.H.
——. *Fī Māhiyat al-ʿAdl*, ed. and Engl. translation by M.S. Khan. Leiden, 1964.
——. *Al-Ḥawāmil wa'l-Shawāmil*, ed. A. Amīn. Cairo, 1951.
——. *Al-Ḥikmah al-Khālidah* (Jāwīdān Khirad), ed. A.R. Badawī. Cairo, 1952.
——. *Kitāb al-Saʿādah*. Cairo, 1928.
——. *Tahdhīb al-Akhlāq*, ed. C.K. Zurayk. Beirut, 1966. Engl. translation by C.K. Zurayk, *The Refinement of Character*. Beirut, 1968.
Muslim, b. al-Ḥajjāj, *Ṣaḥīḥ*, ed. M.F. ʿAbd al-Bāqī. Cairo, 1374–75/1955–56.
Al-Rāzī, Abū Bakr, *Rasāʾil Falsafiyyah*, ed. P. Kraus. Cairo, 1939.
Al-Rāzī, Fakhr al-Dīn, *Kitāb al-Nafs wa'l-Rūḥ*, ed. M.Ṣ.H. Maʿṣūmī. Islamabad, 1968.
——. *ʿIlm al-Akhlāq*. Engl. translation by M.Ṣ.H. Maʿṣūmī. Islamabad, 1969.
Al-Sarrāj, Abū Naṣr, *Al-Lumaʾ*, eds. ʿA.Ḥ. Maḥmūd and Ṭ. ʿA.B. Surūr. Cairo and Baghdad, 1960.
Al-Shahrastānī, ʿAbd al-Karīm, *Al-Milal wa'l-Niḥal*, ed. A.A. al-Wakīl. Cairo, 1968.
——. *Nihāyat al-Iqdām*, ed. A. Guillaume. London, 1934.
Al-Ṭabarī, Muḥammad ibn Jarīr, *Jāmiʿ al-Bayān*, 2nd edition. Cairo, 1373/1954.

Al-Ṭabarsī, *Majma*ᶜ *al-Bayān*. Beirut, 1961.
Al-Tirmidhī, M. b. ᶜĪsā, *Ṣaḥīḥ*. Cairo, 1292.
Al-Ṭūsī, Naṣīr al-Dīn, *Akhlāq-i Nāṣirī*. Teheran, 1344 A.H. Engl. translation by G.M. Wickens, *The Nasirean Ethics*. London, 1964.

B. Western Sources & Translations

Arberry, A.J., *The Koran Interpreted*, New York, 1970.
——. 'The Nicomachean Ethics in Arabic,' in: *Bulletin of the School of Oriental and African Studies* (London), XVII (1955), 1-9.
——. 'Some Plato in an Arabic Epitome,' in: *Islamic Quarterly*, II (1955), 86-99.
——. *The Spiritual Physick*. London, 1950 (Engl. translation of Abū Bakr al-Rāzī's *al-Ṭibb al-Rūḥānī*).
Arkoun, M., *Contribution à l'étude de l'humanisme arabe au IVe/Xe siècle: Miskawayh (320/325-421) = (932/936-1030), philosophe et historien*. Paris, 1970.
——. 'Deux épîtres de Miskawayh,' in: *Bulletin d'Études Orientales* (Institut Français de Damas), XVII (1961-62), 7-74.
——. *Essais sur la pensée islamique*, 2nd edition. Paris, 1984.
——. 'Notes et documents, Miskawayh, de l'intellect et de l'intelligible,' in: *Arabica*, VI (1964), 180-87.
——. 'Textes inédits de Miskawayh,' in: *Annales Islamalogiques* (Institut Français d'Archeologie Orientale du Caire), V (1963), 181-205.
Bellamy, J.A., 'The Makārim al-Akhlāq by Ibn Abi'l-Dunyā,' in: *The Muslim World*, LIII (1963), 106-19.
Berman, L.V., 'A Note on the Added Seventh Book of the *Nicomachean Ethics* in Arabic,' in: *Journal of the American Oriental Society*, 82 (1962), 555.
——. 'Excerpts from the Lost Arabic Original of Ibn Rushd's *Middle Commentary on the Nicomachean Ethics*,' in: *Oriens*, XX (1967), 31-59.
——. (ed.) *The Hebrew Versions of Book Four of Averroes' Middle Commentary on the Nicomachean Ethics*. Critical edition with introduction. Jerusalem, 1981.
Daiber, H., *Das theologisch-philosophische System des Mu*ᶜ*ammar Ibn* ᶜ*Abbād as-Sulamī (gest. 830 n. Chr.)*. Beirut-Wiesbaden, 1975.
De Boer, T.J., 'Ethics and Morality (Muslim),' in: *Encyclopaedia of Religion and Ethics*, V, 501-13.
Donaldson, D.M., *Studies in Muslim Ethics*. London, 1953.
Dunlop, D.M., *Aphorisms of the Statesman*. Cambridge, 1961.
——. 'The Arabic Tradition of the Summa Alexandrinorum,' in: *Archives d'histoire doctrinale et littéraire au moyen âge*, 49 (1983), 253-63.
——. 'The Nicomachean Ethics in Arabic, Books I-VI,' in: *Oriens*, XV (1962), 18-34.
——. 'Observations on the Medieval Arabic Version of Aristotle's Nicomachean Ethics,' in: *Atti dei Convegni* (Fondazione Alessandro Volta, Accademia Nazionale dei Lincei) 13, Rome, 1971, 229-49.
Fakhry, M., *A History of Islamic Philosophy*. New York and London, 2nd edition, 1983.
——. 'Al-Kindī wa-Suqrāṭ,' in: *al-Abḥāth*, 16 (1963), 23-34.
——. 'The Platonism of Miskawayh and its Implications for his Ethics,' in: *Studia Islamica*, XLII (1975), 39-57.
——. 'Three Varieties of Mysticism in Islam,' in: *Int. Journal for Phil. of Religion*, II (1971), 198-207.
Hourani, G.F., *Islamic Rationalism: The Ethics of* ᶜ*Abd al-Jabbār*, London, 1971.
——. *Reason and Tradition in Islamic Ethics*. Cambridge, 1985.
——. 'Two Theories of Value in Medieval Islam,' in: *The Muslim World*, L (1960), 269-78. Also in *Reason and Tradition in Islamic Ethics*. Cambridge, 1985.
Ibn Rushd (Averroes), Abu'l-Walīd, *In Moralia Nicomachia Expositione* (In Aristotelis Libri Moralem totam ... cum Averrois Cordubenisi ...). Venice, 1562. Reprint, Minerva GmbH, Frankfurt am Main, 1966.

Izutzu, T. *Ethico-Religious Concepts in the Qurᵓan*. Montreal, 1966.
Jadaane, F., *L'influence du stoïcisme sur la pensée musulmane*. Beirut, 1968.
Jaeger, W., *Aristotle. Fundamentals of the History of His Development*. Oxford, 1948.
Khadduri, M., *The Islamic Conception of Justice*. Baltimore and London, 1984.
Lerner, R. See Ibn Rushd.
Lyons, M.C., 'A Greek Ethical Treatise,' in: *Oriens*, XIII–XIV (1960–61), 35–57.
Massignon, L., *Essai sur les origines du lexique technique de la mystique musulmane*. Paris, 1922.
Mohaghegh, M., 'Notes on the "Spiritual Physic" of al-Razi,' in: *Studia Islamica*, XXVI (1967), 5–20.
Pines, S., 'Un texte inconnu d'Aristote en version arabe,' in: *Archives d'histoire doctrinale et littéraire du moyen âge* (Paris), 1955, 5–43. Addenda et corrigenda, *idem*, 1959, 295–99. Also in: Pines, S., *Studies in Arabic Versions of Greek Texts and in Medieval Science*. Jerusalem and Leiden, 1986, 157–200.
Rosenthal, E.I.J., *Political Thought in Mediaeval Islam*, Cambridge, 1958.
Rosenthal, F., 'On the knowledge of Plato's Philosophy in the Islamic World,' in: *Islamic Culture*, XIV (1940), 387–422.
Sherif, M.A., *Ghazālī's Theory of Virtue*. Albany, N.Y., 1974.
Sweetman, J.W., *Islam and Christian Theology*. London, 1945–67. (Part I, Vol. I embodies a translation of Miskawayh's *al-Fawz al-Aṣghar*.)
Thompson, W.F. See al-Dawwānī.
Von Grunebaum, G.E., 'Concept and Function of Reason in Islamic Ethics,' in: *Oriens*, XV (1962), 1–17.
Walzer, R., *Greek into Arabic. Essays on Islamic Philosophy*. Oxford, 1962.
——. 'Porphyry and the Arabic Tradition,' in: H. Dörrie, *Porphyre: 8 exposés suivis de discussions* (Entretiens sur l'antiquité classique, xii). Vandoeuvres-Genève, 1966, 275–299.
Walzer, R. and P. Kraus, *Galeni Compendium Timaei Platonis*. London, 1951.
Wensinck, A.J., *A Handbook of Early Muhammadan Tradition*. Leiden, 1927.
——. *Concordance et indices de la tradition musulmane*. Leiden, 1936 and 1962.
——. *The Muslim Creed*. Cambridge, 1932.
Wickens, G.M. See al-Ṭūsī.
Zurayk, C.K. See Miskawayh.

Addenda

Butterworth, Charles, *Philosophy, Ethics and Virtuous Rule. A Study of Averroes' Commentary on Plato's "Republic"*, American University of Cairo Press, Cairo, 1986.
Fouchécour, Ch.-H. de, *Les notions morales dans la littérature persane du 3e/9e au 7e/13e siècle*, Paris, 1986.
Al-Ghazālī, Abū Ḥāmid, *The Alchemy of Happiness*, trans. Claud Field, London, 1980.
Inati, Shams, *An Examination of Ibn Sina's Solution for the Problem of Evil*, University Microfilms International, 1984.
Kraemer, Joel L., *Humanism in the Renaissance of Islam*, Leiden, 1986.
Rosenthal, Franz, *The Muslim Concept of Freedom*, Leiden, 1960.
Al-Sijistānī, Abū Sulaymān, *Muntakhab Ṣiwān al-Ḥikmah*, ed. A.R. Badawi, Teheran, 1974.
Zainaty, George, *La morale d'Avempace*, Paris, 1979.

INDEX OF PROPER NAMES

ISLAMIC PHILOSOPHY, THEOLOGY AND SCIENCE

TEXTS AND STUDIES

ISSN 0169-8729

1. IBN RUSHD. *Metaphysics.* A Translation with Introduction of Ibn Rushd's Commentary on Aristotle's Metaphysics, Book Lām, by Ch. Genequand. Reprint 1986. ISBN 90 04 08093 7
2. DAIBER, H. *Wāṣil ibn ʿAṭāʾ als Prediger und Theologe.* Ein neuer Text aus dem 8. Jahrhundert n. Chr. Herausgegeben mit Übersetzung und Kommentar. 1988. ISBN 90 04 08369 3
3. BELLO, I.A. *The Medieval Islamic Controversy Between Philosophy and Orthodoxy.* Ijmāʿ and Taʾwīl in the Conflict Between al-Ghazālī and Ibn Rushd. 1989. ISBN 90 04 08092 9
4. GUTAS, D. *Avicenna and the Aristotelian Tradition.* Introduction to reading Avicenna's Philosophical Works. 1988. ISBN 90 04 08500 9
5. AL-ḲĀSIM B. IBRĀHĪM. *Kitāb al-Dalīl al-Kabīr.* Edited with Translation, Introduction and Notes by B. Abrahamov. 1990. ISBN 90 04 08985 3
6. MARÓTH, M. *Ibn Sīnā und die peripatetische "Aussagenlogik".* Übersetzung aus dem Ungarischen von Johanna Till. 1989. ISBN 90 04 08487 8
7. BLACK, D.L. *Logic and Aristotle's* Rhetoric *and* Poetics *in Medieval Arabic Philosophy.* 1990. ISBN 90 04 09286 2
8. FAKHRY, M. *Ethical Theories in Islam.* Second expanded edition 1994. ISBN 90 04 09300 1
9. KEMAL, S. *The Poetics of Alfarabi and Avicenna.* 1991. ISBN 90 04 09371 0
10. ALON, I. *Socrates in Medieval Arabic Literature.* 1991. ISBN 90 04 09349 4
11. BOS, G. *Qusṭā ibn Lūqā's Medical Regime for the Pilgrims to Mecca.* The Risāla fī tadbīr safar al-ḥajj. 1992. ISBN 90 04 09541 1
12. KOHLBERG, E. *A Medieval Muslim Scholar at Work.* Ibn Ṭāwūs and his Library. 1992. ISBN 90 04 09549 7
13. DAIBER, H. *Naturwissenschaft bei den Arabern im 10. Jahrhundert n. Chr.* Briefe des Abū l-Faḍl Ibn al-ʿAmīd (gest. 360/970) an ʿAḍudaddaula. Herausgegeben mit Einleitung, kommentierter Übersetzung und Glossar. 1993. ISBN 90 04 09755 4
14. DHANANI, A. *The Physical Theory of Kalām.* Atoms, Space, and Void in Basrian Muʿtazilī Cosmology. 1994. ISBN 90 04 09831 3
15. ABŪ MAʿŠAR. *The Abbreviation of the Introduction to Astrology.* Together with the Medieval Latin Translation of Adelard of Bath. Edited and Translated by Ch. Burnett, K. Yamamoto and M. Yano. 1994. ISBN 90 04 09997 2

16. SĀBŪR IBN SAHL. *Dispensatorium Parvum (al-Aqrābādhīn al-ṣaghīr).* Analysed, Edited and Annotated by O. Kahl. 1994. ISBN 90 04 10004 0
17. MARÓTH, M. *Die Araber und die antike Wissenschaftstheorie.* Übersetzung aus dem Ungarischen von Johanna Till und Gábor Kerekes. 1994. ISBN 90 04 10008 3
18. IBN ABĪ AL-DUNYĀ. *Morality in the Guise of Dreams.* A Critical Edition of *Kitāb al-Manām*, with Introduction, by Leah Kinberg. 1994. ISBN 90 04 09818 6
19. VON KÜGELGEN, A. *Averroes und die arabische Moderne.* Ansätze zu einer Neubegründung des Rationalismus im Islam. 1994. ISBN 90 04 09955 7
20. LAMEER, J. *Al-Fārābī and Aristotelian Syllogistics.* Greek Theory and Islamic Practice. 1994. ISBN 90 04 09884 4